HELL'S NOT FAR OFF

JOSH HOWARD

HELL'S NOT FAR OFF

BRUCE CRAWFORD AND THE APPALACHIAN LEFT

WEST VIRGINIA UNIVERSITY PRESS / MORGANTOWN

ISBN 978-1-959000-10-5 (paperback) / 978-1-959000-11-2 (ebook)

Library of Congress Cataloging-in-Publication Data
Names: Howard, Josh (Public historian), author.
Title: Hell's not far off : Bruce Crawford and the Appalachian left / Josh Howard.
Description: First edition. | Morgantown : West Virginia University Press, 2024. |
    Includes bibliographical references and index.
Identifiers: LCCN 2023043225 | ISBN 9781959000105 (paperback) | ISBN
    9781959000112 (ebook)
Subjects: LCSH: Crawford, Bruce, 1893–1993. | Journalists—Virginia—Wise
    County—Biography. | Political activists—Appalachian Region—Biography.
    | Environmentalists—Appalachian Region—Biography. | Employee
    rights—Appalachian Region. | Appalachian Region—Social conditions—
    20th century. | Appalachian Region—Economic conditions—20th century.
    | LCGFT: Biographies.
Classification: LCC PN4874.C775 H69 2024 | DDC 071.55/743092[B]—dc23/
    eng/20231023
LC record available at https://lccn.loc.gov/2023043225

Book and cover design by Than Saffel / WVU Press
Cover image: *View of west approach portal* (Kentucky Route 840 Bridge, spanning
Cumberland River, Loyall, Harlan County, KY), HAER no. KY-14-4, Historic American
Engineering Record Collection, Library of Congress Prints and Photographs Division.

To the Tufted Titmouse and the American Kestrel

CONTENTS

ACKNOWLEDGMENTS

The seeds of this book began in a different world, one without a pandemic and with the lives of many loved ones. Appreciation for their support and love will never be properly conveyed as they are no longer with us. Others deserve credit for encouraging me to take the leap—and the time—to assemble thoughts into words. Proper credit must be attributed, and I hope my gratitude is conveyed here and in the following pages.

I am grateful to West Virginia University Press for taking a chance on me and letting these ideas flow. Thank you as well to the Library of Virginia and the Virginia Chronicle project for digitizing *Crawford's Weekly*. What a wonderful resource for current and future scholars and for anyone who wishes to read more of Crawford's writings. Thank you to Janay Tate for taking the time to speak with me in Norton about your family's and your own history. May there be a future where local journalism returns in force to Norton, Wise County, and the rest of southwest Virginia.

The support of incredible, brilliant archivists working at libraries, archives, and other repositories throughout the country was instrumental in my bringing this work to completion. Angela Harvey of the University of Virginia's College at Wise, Stewart Plein and Jessica Eichlin of the West Virginia and Regional History Collection at West Virginia University, and innumerable staff of the Albert and Shirley Small Special Collections Library at the University of Virginia welcomed me to their facilities and provided top-tier archival support.

The COVID-19 pandemic interrupted and forever altered our lives while this project was at a critical research juncture. In response, even more archivists and librarians provided excellent research support beyond their job descriptions that must be acknowledged. Thank you to those who responded to phone calls and emails, and those who scanned documents and mailed flash drives both during and before the pandemic. Kari Salisbury of Appalachian State University, Chris Cialdella and Lisa Schoblasky of the Newberry Library, many staff at the West Virginia State Archives, and Eri Mizukane of the University of Pennsylvania Libraries—thank you all. There are undoubtedly dozens of other librarians and archivists who completed the often-thankless archival labor whose names I will never know. Your work is deeply appreciated.

And of course, family support means everything. Thank you to my mother, Tracey; to Frank for being an unmoving rock; to Matt for being a sounding board for any topic; and to the rest of my family who have listened to me prattle on about my work. Many beloved family members were lost during the years this project developed: Alice and Spud Howard, Josephine and Jessie Morris, and Maxie and Jack Monroe. I will continue to miss you all forever.

And finally, thank you to my partner, Elizabeth Catte. This project would not have happened without your support, both as a partner and editor, and you alone know what has driven me. You are good and deserve good things. May every year forward together be better than the last.

INTRODUCTION

On April 16, 1935, Bruce Crawford made an announcement: "I have quit publishing Crawford's Weekly. It was too radical for its bourgeois customers and not radical enough for me. Like capitalism, it was full of contradictions. Hence it could not go on." He continued,

> So I have let go! I have, for a consideration amounting to a salvage, turned over to my competitor "all that was mortal" of Crawford's Weekly—its machinery, advertising contracts, and nearly-expired subscription list—and let the rest of Crawford's Weekly "put on incorruptibility"—as in the Biblical sense, only that which no longer exists can! If and when a fascist regimentation comes (and what could a weekly paper drawing support from fascist elements do to prevent its coming?), I shall not have any bourgeois appurtenances that can be laid hold of to cramp my style. I have joined the great unemployed. If I get into trouble and my head cracked, neither customers nor creditors can deplore my activities or accuse me of being recreant to obligations! If I get shot in the leg again, or go to jail, there won't be that damned feeling of apology to the respectable. Now, as a liberal graduating into radicalism, with the more tangible roots to bourgeois life severed, I hope to know a new and meaningful freedom, whatever the hardships.[1]

Emily Tapscott Clark, a respected southern writer and Crawford contemporary, described Crawford's Weekly as "a diminutive and enlightened paper published in a Virginia village."[2] The neighboring Smyth County News wrote upon Crawford's newspaper scene departure, "Among those who will miss the weekly the most are Bruce Crawford's fellow editors. His paper was easily the most quoted weekly in the State and his blasts periodically involved him in a joust of typewriters with one or another of his fellow newsmen, to the edification and entertainment of the reading public."[3] And the *Country Editor and World Press News* wrote of the paper that "it maddens or gladdens wherever read. . . . The charm of *Crawford's Weekly* is to be found in the human element of its editorials, rather than in the ideas expressed. 'I guess you'll have to send me that paper again,' said a former subscriber, who had been 'maddened.' 'I just can't get along without it; but do keep your feet on the ground.'"[4]

Who was Bruce Crawford, the man hammering out enlightened, edified, and entertaining editorials from the Appalachian landscape in Wise County, Virginia? First and foremost, Crawford was and should be remembered as an ancestor of all leftists and intellectuals in Appalachia. Present-day Appalachia's fights were his, and his fights are still ours. When violent white supremacists threatened his community, when corrupt coal companies denied miners pay, and when corporations drove his hometown deeper into poverty, there Crawford stood, fought, and wrote, his typewriter and printing press clacking away for decades. He spoke truth to power when it was demanded of him and often when it was not. Too often, he was the lone voice of the many have-nots when so many others spoke for the haves.

How should Bruce Crawford's legacy be acknowledged and preserved? Does he fit within a canon despite writing no books? Does he merit inclusion in a historiography despite never being trained as a historian? Was he a notable leftist activist despite never leading an organization outside of his small hometown? And should he be remembered as an important political thinker despite never holding elected office? Better described as a public intellectual than anything else, Crawford fit within each of these characterizations. His contributions to each must be considered both in the name of righteousness and for the sake of helping us better see the Appalachian intellectual landscape. At the very least, Bruce Crawford's life provides a glimpse into the mind of a southwest Virginian who thought deeply at a time when most of America believed southwest Virginians did not think at all.

Bruce Crawford's writings crossed my desk no less than four different times before he finally caught my attention. Reading through hundreds of articles written by Bruce Crawford with a twenty-first-century eye makes clear the parallels between his time and my own. For instance, climate change is and will likely be the defining crisis of the twenty-first century, in terms of both extreme weather and the political schisms caused by science denialists. Capitalism is destroying the global environment, sometimes quite deliberately, and time is running out for any corrective measures. In 1934 Crawford published an editorial about a conversation he had with a "Hill Billy" neighbor who dropped by the office for a chat. The Dust Bowl crisis was in the process of destroying western farmland and clearly the two worried that recent heatwaves were part of a long-term trend:

> Our friend from the hills said: "I have read your writing about the need for reforestation and the danger of more droughts in certain parts of our country. And, you know, I believe more than ever in the prophecy that the world will be destroyed by fire the next time, instead of water. Not by sudden conflagration. . . . Not at all. It will be a gradual drying up of soil, because the forests will be neglected by thoughtless generations and there will be less and less moisture.
>
> Those dust storms are reminders—they're warnings from Nature that she can't be trifled with by folks who think they are civilized but are just about as civilized, really, as a boy with a match in a hayloft. I'm afraid that after the situation gets so far along, there will be no way of reforesting quickly enough to prevent deserts. The people will begin to move away, some early if they have nothing saved up, others will stay for night life as long as they have money to hire slaves to fan them . . . and many will die off because they won't have enough git-up to leave."
>
> Maybe our visitor has it sized up correctly. Who knows? We have been uneasy this sweltering week. Every time our sleeves drip perspiration and our fanny sticks to the editorial chair as if it had an application of printer's padding cement, we feel like saying, with our prophet from the timbers, "Hell's not far off." [5]

Virginia's environmental and energy discourse in the late 2010s was dominated by the—still ongoing—fight against pipelines. As of 2023 brave Appalachian protestors bind themselves to heavy equipment in a desperate attempt to save mountains, streams, wildlife, and their homes. They do what courts and legislators do not, having been betrayed by elected officials. The Commonwealth seems to view beautiful mountain landscapes as little more than sparsely populated mountains across which natural gas must traverse to get to market. The irony running through the modern environmentalism fight is that those same elected officials crow loudly about Virginia's outdoor tourism potential and the growth of green energy industries.

Writing in 1926, Bruce Crawford made similar points about his Wise County home. Wise County was known as a coal mining region, but Crawford envisioned a future where coal and tourism coexisted. It was openly known by 1925 that the federal government would likely build a national park in the Great Smokies and the Blue Ridge mountains, so southwest Virginia ran the risk of being excluded from the growing tourism industry. "Mine coal we must, but let's do something else besides," wrote Crawford. "Let's preserve our wonderful natural scenery, exploit our caves and waterfalls, and make of our coal mines objects for sight-seers."[6] Crawford believed that people would visit Wise County to visit both natural wonders like High Knob and Natural Tunnel and industrial sites like coal mines. Coal might keep the lights on and houses warmed, but it could also line community pockets with cash from visitors. There was no reason to sacrifice the land.

Wealthy corporate donors dominate American politics, especially since the *Citizen's United v. Federal Election Commission* ruling in 2010, and both major parties tend to pursue "centrist" or "unity" candidates who can pull in the most donors and perceived support, Donald Trump notwithstanding. Both parties, in a global view, are center-right, pro-capitalism, pro-business organizations. The windows may be dressed a different color and the rhetoric radically different, but if push came to shove, both sides would bail out Wall Street sooner than forgive student debt.

In an analysis of the 1924 presidential election, Crawford reminds us, the modern reader, that big money donors and centrists are hardly new. In his view, Democrats, Republicans, and Big Business conspired to nominate "safe men" to both party tickets. Party differences were minor details compared to the importance of sustaining capitalism and placating the masses. "Dick, Harry, and Thomas may vote for either candidate they want to, so long as they imagine they are 'having a voice' in the government," so Crawford viewed American democracy for the masses. This younger version of Crawford even went so far to question democracy itself, asserting, "There is really no use in going to the polls . . . what difference will it make who is elected." Such an opinion was somewhat radical for 1924 Wise County but would not be out of place in 2023.[7]

And finally, America's current labor crisis pushed further into oblivion by gig economies, job losses sparked by mechanization, and stagnant wages would have been familiar to Crawford as well. Twenty-first-century thinkers include solutions from the Left and Right—investment in public education, public jobs guarantees, tax cuts for wealthy businesses, and universal basic income—but these are unlikely to pass legislatures with enough funding to make a meaningful difference.

Crawford too thought of what similar developments meant for workers, especially coal miners, though he envisioned a far more hopeful future than most. Machines should not be feared, for they will "lighten our work and shorten our work hours." Crawford was firmly of the school of thought that mechanization would allow people to pursue their dreams "as teachers, actors, artists, musicians, writers, clowns, and jazzers-up." [8]

Dozens of such examples leap from Bruce Crawford's writings throughout his four-decade writing and editing career. At first glance, Crawford wrote about major problems that twenty-first-century America is still failing to solve—environmental destruction, Big Energy, divisive two-party politics, and declining labor rights. How can a nation not have solved such basic ills of capitalism in the intervening near century? And how can one not be utterly disheartened by this fact?

Instead of wallowing in such a despairing thought, hope can be found in the past. In our current moment, the speed of news alongside amnestic hot takes suggests that our lived experience is unique, that the rich and powerful are fully unassailable, and that the rest of us can only pray to a broken political system. Bruce Crawford tells us that we are not alone. His problems were ours and ours are his, and he had some solutions that maybe we too should try. In his own time, many people did not take Crawford seriously—and those who did treated him as a radical—yet he successfully changed Appalachia, Virginia, West Virginia, and even the federal government a little bit. For a radical newspaperman in rural southwest Virginia, that is an incredible achievement. Given the current state of things both within Appalachia and nationally, it's important that we take Crawford's ideas seriously now. We might need them for ourselves.

Bruce Crawford founded *Crawford's Weekly*, his personal newspaper based out of Norton, for two reasons—to satisfy his own ego and to create a public space for radical mountain politics. From an early age, Crawford viewed himself as a professional equal, or soon-to-be equal, of writer-intellectuals like John Fox Jr. and Louis Jaffe. Most of Crawford's newspaper experience as a young man came from the *Coalfield Progress*, which was too flimsy a springboard for his ambition in his view. The *Coalfield Progress*, and for that matter all other local newspapers, cozied up to coal operators and typically censored writing critical of corporate coal. A new, personal platform would satisfy both Crawford's ego and desire to scream about injustice. By the end of the 1920s, Crawford proved his inflated self-esteem was not misplaced. Critics around the country recognized *Crawford's Weekly* as one of the best editorial pages in the nation.[9] Members of the Black press recognized Crawford as a rare white editor willing to stand against lynching. The Baltimore *Afro-American*, for instance, encouraged "organizations and leaders" throughout the country to "express appreciation" of Bruce Crawford, especially since Crawford's stance garnered him a loss of income via canceled subscriptions and pulled advertisers.[10] High-profile writers like Theodore Dreiser, John Dos Passos, and Sherwood Anderson referenced Crawford as their friend and peer.

Newspaper editorship in the early twentieth century was an explicitly partisan activity. By 1920 about half of all newspapers operated independently of party machines, though many independent editors clearly supported one party or organization over the rest.[11] In Virginia, Democratic Party and Democrat-supporting newspapers dominated the newspaper scene. The *Lynchburg News*, published by U.S. Senator Carter Glass, was Democratic; Norfolk's two largest papers—the *Ledger-Dispatch* and *Virginian-Pilot*—were both Independent Democrat; and the *Richmond Times-Dispatch* was Democratic. Crawford's biggest rival, the *Coalfield Progress*, was also a Democratic publication. That so many newspapers were officially Democratic should come as no surprise given the Democratic Party's dominance with supermajorities in the state's General Assembly and an unbroken chain of Democratic governors spanning 1886 to 1970. The party regularly rewarded Democratic newspapers with access and advertising revenue. In other words, it paid to be a Democratic newspaper in 1920s Virginia.

Crawford developed his own philosophy of journalism, one crafted through practice and a growing disdain for capitalism and political parties. A Crawford philosophy of journalism, as explained to Theodore Dreiser in 1935, could be generally defined as oriented locally and reflective of the "struggles, aspirations, achievements, births, and deaths of its people." The metaphor regularly used by Crawford was that of a tree. A good newspaper absorbed information from the locality like a tree absorbed nutrients from the soil and received air, sun, and water from nature. Editors could differ from their community's values on important issues but must be careful not to strike at their own roots. Otherwise, their job evaporates in the form of canceled subscriptions. Also like a tree, journalism was not to be flashy. Editors garner satisfaction in steady, sustainable reporting and a loving community even with a "lousy bank balance."[12]

No matter what Crawford wrote to Dreiser about journalism, he desperately yearned to advance far beyond what Norton journalism could provide. He wanted to be a writer—a *real* writer—of fiction, poetry, nonfiction, long-form journalism, and social criticism. Editing a small, rural weekly paid the bills, but a writer was a public intellectual, revered both locally and afar for their social commentary and literary guile. He never achieved this goal. Something deep in his personal values, whether from his father's influence, empathy with the working man, or political predilections, drove Crawford down a sometimes-destructive path. While other public intellectuals carefully selected hills to die on, Crawford climbed every mountain guns blazing.[13] This approach created a lot of Crawford enemies—the Klan, coal companies, Republicans, most Democrats, and other Wise County writers. To some, he was an elitist gadfly, while to others he was a working-class Communist. Frank Monroe Beverly, a poet from Dickenson County, summed it up, claiming that Crawford "evidently thinks we are deformed cranks and monstrosities." In reality, Crawford refused to publish some of Beverly's work, but so it goes with small newspapers. It was no wonder then that Crawford eventually looked beyond Norton for his fame.[14]

"Meliorist"—one who believes that people can fundamentally improve the world by their actions—was the self-inflating descriptor Crawford chose for himself.[15] This was true in relation to many topics like lynching, politics, and anti-capitalism, but Crawford possessed significant shortcomings when writing about race and gender. He occasionally used racial slurs in his writing even when advocating for racial equality. For instance, he scorned uneducated African Americans for not bettering themselves (in his view) and was incapable of recognizing the racist structural inequalities of his world.

Crawford similarly possessed conflicting views on women. "It is not a good thing for a town to be run by men alone," wrote Crawford in 1922, supporting a campaign for women to serve on town council. *Crawford's Weekly* editorials supported the right of women to serve on juries, the hiring of women in traditionally male-dominated industries, and the normalization of birth control. However, his support for women's rights typically came from a patriarchal worldview. He suggested that women be allowed on town council but only if the council were split into two gender-segregated subcommittees; councilmen would handle "business and the more material interests of the town" while councilwomen would "keep an eye on the community's higher interests," meaning beautification, morality, and protecting children. Readers were further reassured that such a town council would be little burden on the female councilors' homemaking. Council met just one night a month, and nothing prevented a female councilor from bringing her husband along as support.[16]

Crawford understood, perhaps above all else, the long-lasting impacts caused by the structural inequalities of capitalism. In his words, "all men are not equal" under American capitalism. "Pass by a cemetery and see if all are equal," he wrote, observing that "high monuments, low monuments, and no monuments all greet you. . . . Read history and the great are placed on record, while the less great and those with no records are unheard of and unsung."[17] Like unnamed individuals in Crawford's article, he too has been unequal in death.

Historians have paid little to no attention to Crawford or other southwest

Virginia socialists. Jerry Bruce Thomas, the preeminent expert on West Virginia during the New Deal, is the lone exception, but Thomas focused on Crawford's three-year career working for the Federal Writers' Project. Similarly, Appalachian socialist newspapers are hardly a footnote in the historical literature. Comparing work on newspapers to that on labor organizing, especially in early twentieth century coalfields, further reveals the utter lack of credence given to the power of editors in shaping local narratives.[18] Crawford's friends and colleagues, such as Theodore Dreiser, Sherwood Anderson, Louis Jaffe, and John Dos Passos, each have been subjects of numerous books and articles. Some, like Dreiser, have had as many books written about them as they themselves generated in their entire career. No equality in death for Bruce Crawford then, it seems.

To understand the importance of Bruce Crawford's thoughts, writings, and political actions, one must view his life in four parts. Crawford essentially reinvented his career three times, so tackling each in sequence offers the method to understand his life. The first chapter, "A Young Newspaper Editor," explores Crawford's growth from his origins as a small-town journalist who, on occasion, tackled difficult subjects. Crawford grew his newspaper, *Crawford's Weekly*, through the 1920s from an upstart weekly to one of the most prominent in the region. The newspaper, while covering regular news, also mounted a series of campaigns on social causes important to Crawford, including combating Appalachian stereotypes, eliminating the Ku Klux Klan, promoting anti-lynching legislation, criticizing polls taxes and prisons, and demonizing coal barons and capitalism. However, Crawford was not without fault and often published articles with regressive views on race that cannot go unchallenged, most notably his embrace of Anglo-Saxonism, a white supremacist viewpoint growing in popularity among Virginian academics during the 1920s.

The second chapter, "Getting Shot in Harlan County," details Crawford's career from 1929 until he officially shuttered *Crawford's Weekly* in 1935. The year 1929 was chosen because Crawford rapidly became more active in academic and intellectual circles that year, especially in relation to academia and to labor activism. Academic writing introduced Crawford to an intelligentsia network he would have never met in Norton, while labor activism got him shot by a cop. Crawford covered the Harlan miner strikes in 1931 nominally as a journalist, though he harbored full support for the miners. An unprovoked police officer attacked Crawford, shooting him in the leg, thus making him a minor celebrity within pro-union, socialist, and Communist circles. From this incident forward, Crawford's activist energies expanded as he moved even further to the left politically.

The third chapter, "A Critic Fails at Politics," details the downfall of *Crawford's Weekly* and the Crawford family's permanent departure from Norton, Virginia. It begins with the New Deal, more specifically Crawford's brief embrace, then ultimate denunciation of the Roosevelt's administration's federal programs. Crawford parlayed his New Deal criticism into a run for Congress in 1934 as an Independent, promising a better socialist alternative to either the New Deal or Republican return to 1920s policy. In the absence of electoral success, Crawford suddenly closed his newspaper and briefly flirted with a career at a socialist organizer before taking a new job as a newspaper editor in Bluefield, West Virginia. He and Kate seemed likely to make Bluefield their new home for good, but a New Deal opportunity arose that brought them into West Virginia state politics.

The fourth chapter, "The Editor as Public Historian," follows Crawford's second career as editor of the West Virginia branch of the Federal Writers' Project from late 1938 to early 1942, a short time on the job that deeply impacted West Virginia state politics and the writing of state history. In writing the official state history book, Crawford's team inserted labor history into the narrative, including stories like those of Mother Jones, the Hawk's Nest Tunnel disaster, and the Battle of Blair Mountain, forcing future state historians to reckon with West Virginian labor history, a topic that most at the time sought to bury. Crawford also went toe-to-toe with West Virginia governor Homer Holt, a conservative and anti–New Deal Democrat, decisively outsmarted him and, in doing so, accelerated the dismantling of West Virginia's conservative, anti-Communist wing of the Democratic Party.

The fifth chapter, "An Inability to Adapt," addresses Crawford's relationship with political consulting, social commentary, and his postretirement career. This chapter also covers the largest time frame, spanning from the early 1940s until the end of his public career in the 1970s. Crawford accepted an appointment within the West Virginia government in the early 1940s and became a loyal party bureaucrat for a few years. But within five years, he reinvented himself yet again, this time as a political advertising consultant for the West Virginia Democratic Party. Throughout the end stage of his career, Crawford returned to writing newspaper editorials, primarily for the *Roanoke Times*, though these writings truly picked up after his retirement in the mid-1960s. Crawford's postretirement editorials reveal a troubled ex-socialist frustrated with what he saw as lacking social progress for poor Appalachians, though he tended to blame the poor often for their own woes. Such writings demonstrated his decline as savvy thinker but also offer an avenue for reflection upon the utter failings of the American Left to institute any meaningful change. Perhaps most importantly, it allows for a conclusion far from hagiography, instead searching for Crawford's answers to our modern problems.

CHAPTER 1

A YOUNG NEWSPAPER EDITOR

BEGINNINGS

Robert Bruce Crawford was born on December 5, 1893, in Dooley, a small coal mining community in Wise County just outside of Norton, Virginia, the oldest of four children raised by Nannie and Douglas Crawford.[1] Douglas Crawford's work, or more accurately, his search of work as a general laborer, moved the family all over, including Wise County, rural Oklahoma, and back to Douglas's childhood home in Fayette County, West Virginia. The Crawford family returned to Wise County near Norton by at least 1910 when Douglas Crawford took a steady carpentry job and opened a small general store. Living as a teenager in the booming Virginia coal fields, Bruce Crawford attended high school while also working to repair mine cars, install pump lines, and as a builder in Dante to help support his family and save money for college.

Wise County in the 1910s experienced an unprecedented population growth, one of the highest rates in the state. What was a rural community of a few thousand two generations earlier was radically changed by a single industry—coal. Dozens of companies formed during the 1880s to exploit the region's vast coal deposits. Over the next few decades, company labor demands brought thousands of new people into Wise County, including poor whites displaced from farms, African Americans, and immigrants from Southern and Central Europe. The county's population more than doubled from 1900 to 1920; Norton's quintupled over the same period. It must have been a dynamic, active time for young Bruce Crawford, especially from the vantage point of an active family-run general store.

In 1912, fresh out of high school, Bruce Crawford was hired as coeditor of the *Daily Progress*, later renamed the *Coalfield Progress* in 1924. A half-dozen newspapers were in print in Norton during the 1910s, and the *Daily Progress* was the one that survived long-term.[2] Details about Crawford's *Daily Progress* tenure are poorly documented—just a handful of issues survive—but there is evidence the young Crawford possessed lofty ambitions. He wrote a letter in 1914 to John Fox Jr., a significant celebrity author in southwest Virginia for his bestselling 1908 novel, *The Trail of the Lonesome Pine*. Crawford enclosed a short story and asked Fox for his "candid opinion" on his writing abilities. Fox responded briefly, beginning his response with "I don't think this story is solvable—because there isn't enough to it."[3] Confidence bruised but not busted, Crawford left Norton that same year to enroll at West Virginia University to earn a degree in journalism or English.[4] However, he permanently left Morgantown about a year after his arrival and never explained his decision. Having only enrolled for a single semester, he did not graduate and would never earn a college degree.

By Crawford's account he then "rambled through the South, afoot and afloat and had many arrange [*sic*] experiences." This description was only partially true. He first created a new job for himself in Norton by starting a newspaper. The *Reporter* was a short-lived weekly, with its first issue dated November 1915; in 1916 it merged with the *Miners' Enterprise*, an unrelated newspaper printed in Coeburn. *Miners' Enterprise* itself was an independent offshoot of the Republican-aligned *Miners' Journal*, created when Rufus G. Caudill, the editor of the *Enterprise*, splintered away citing political differences. The new Crawford-Caudill publication, creatively named the *Norton Reporter and Miners' Enterprise*, was edited by Crawford as politically independent paper for a little over a year. Crawford's sidelined his editorial career by enlisting in the U.S. Army to serve in World War I, but the newspaper continued including a brief publication run after the war.[5] Circulation peaked at about 1,280 weekly, which was respectable given Wise County's population of about forty-six thousand in 1920. Few issues of these early Crawford newspapers survive, but those that do suggest he primarily covered local news from a nonpartisan political perspective. Advertisements in the newspaper were locally oriented and included nearly all of Norton's biggest stores, such as Cohen's Department Store, the Ladies Shoppe, Sterling Hardware Company, Emmerson Mann Drug Company, and First National Bank, as well as a few other businesses from smaller nearby towns. Never were there any advertisements for explicitly political causes beyond regular campaign advertisements.[6]

The return from war marked a change in Crawford's ambition as he formed his own newspaper—*Crawford's Weekly*. After an honorable discharge, Crawford grew dissatisfied with his old reporting job, so he quit in July 1919 to save money and plan a new project. He launched *Crawford's Weekly* less than two years later as a weekly newspaper with an explicitly radical bent. *Crawford's Weekly* had a weekly circulation of fifteen hundred by the end of 1920, which was more than any of his former newspaper employers and impressive considering Norton's population of just three thousand.[7] For the rest of the 1920s and beyond, Crawford's exclusive career focus was the weekly paper bearing his namesake.

Returning home from war also brought marriage. Crawford and Ethel Kate Lay, a local schoolteacher who went by Kate, got married and moved in together during 1922. Little documentation of their relationship or of Kate's family was made public. She was the daughter of a Coeburn storeowner with six siblings, many of whom were college educated and lived throughout Virginia, West Virginia, and Pennsylvania. Both Bruce and Kate generally kept personal and professional life separate to an astonishing degree, even though they worked together on *Crawford's Weekly* often. Kate Crawford served as the secretary-treasurer of Crawford Printing Company from 1923 until its dissolution in 1935, but she remained unseen except for in the business office. Children were never in their plans either. Most likely, Crawford kept his family out of his paper for practical reasons. He received plenty of death threats in his career from fascists, racists, coal company owners, private coal company guards, and a devil's row of unnamed foes. The less he said of Kate, his siblings, and his parents, the better for their safety.

Crawford's radical politics and editorial skills likely came from his father, who passed away in January 1933.[8] In an era when Bruce Crawford's peers attended elite state schools like the University of Virginia, he relied on his own practical training received in the Crawford household. Douglas Crawford's radical politics became apparent during the 1890s in Oklahoma Territory. Having become a great admirer of Mother Jones in West Virginia, the elder Crawford protested and organized against labor conditions facing himself and other employees of the Rock Island Railroad, the primary employer in the area. Initially, railroad construction proceeded as expected, but a domino effect of problems began once the U.S. Department of Interior got involved. The 1893–94 Enid and Pond Creek Railroad War was a complex affair of land acquisition, speculation, railroad politics, and Cherokee Nation sovereignty. In short, the Department of the Interior exacerbated problems between the government, railroad company, and the Cherokee Nation.[9] As often happened in such conflicts, workers were powerlessly stuck between the major actors in the war over new capital.

Douglas Crawford's participation was first as creator of the *Trainwrecker*, a weekly newspaper critical of both railroad company and government, and later as a radical, anti-company protestor. From the perspective of Douglas Crawford and his allies, wealthy railroad companies created a system of isolated company towns to control and exploit workers while the U.S. government refused to even acknowledge, much less correct, the problem. Compounding matters was the brazenness of railroad company contempt for worker-residents, as the Rock Island Railroad instructed its conductors to ignore local speed limit laws when passing through some towns. Appeals to Congress fell on deaf ears as powerful railroad lobbies easily maintained control over their elected men.[10] Frustration mounting and peaceful options exhausted, Douglas Crawford and his fellow workers resorted to direct action. In an interview given exactly ninety years later, Bruce Crawford reflected on his father's Oklahoma activism and editorship. Clearly, young Bruce learned quite a bit from his father in Oklahoma, so much so that it inspired him to take up editor-activism.

> Now my dad knew about the Trojan Horse, the Boston Tea Party, Coxey's Army of unemployed, and the railroad strike at Martinsburg, West Virginia. In that strike, federal troops quelled the whole town that was in sympathy with the strikers. So now Dad talked somebody into starting a weekly paper called The Train Wrecker. They whipped up sentiment for a dramatic move which, they hoped, would cause Congress to compel the railroad to stop its trains there.
>
> One night before a freight was to rumble through, the citizens turned out to a man and disjointed both rails. Then they lifted the track and twisted it over like a corkscrew. . . . The engineer, Dad said, mistook the fanned-out ties for a windmill on the track, opened his throttle to heave it off. . . . The train ran aground. Nobody was hurt. The town cheered. By special act Congress gave them a station.
>
> Long afterwards when Dad would relate this tale, I imagined how someday I'd start a paper of my own. Only it would wreck, not trains, but myths and shams and public wrongs.[11]

Bruce Crawford, full of new ideas gained during his World War I experience, returned home to start a new newspaper and publish biting essays of his own design. Foreshadowing what would become an expansive Appalachian writing tradition, the first topic to catch Crawford's attention was the stereotype that all people from his home region were poor, dumb, and backwards. Crawford's essay "The Mountain White" first appeared in the special October 1920 industrial edition of *Crawford's Weekly* as a mocking rebuttal to the jokes and jabs he received while in the military, especially from his fellow Virginians. "The average East Virginian still has the idea that the typical Southwest Virginian is a bold, bad guy, long on the use of moonshine liquor and quick on the trigger," he wrote, noting their ignorance of the "governors, prominent educators, preachers, doctors of medicine, noted lawyers, engineers, and a few writers of growing reputations" who called southwest Virginia their home.[12]

"The Mountain White" was an especially important Crawford essay in terms of its style. When he was at his peak, Crawford embraced comedy, derision, and open mockery. His loathing of elites was impossible to miss, as was his disdain for ignorance or bigotry. Of the so-called Mountain White, so far as Crawford was concerned they only existed in Hatfield-McCoy feud myths. In his typical fashion, he drove his point home through a comedic, invented vignette that is worth quoting in full:

A Mountain White, according to leading authorities, is a creature of pure Anglo-Saxon blood, who lives in a log cabin where newspapers never circulate and where Bibles and prayers are unknown, way, way up in the Appalachian mountains. Lest the intelligent reader consider this odd specimen a mere chimera, it should be stated at the outset that there are 3,000,000 of these people. As the total population of the infected area hardly exceeds this number, it should not be hard for the investigator to view them singly or in pairs, clans, or tribes, if only he will take the trouble to run up to Wise County, Virginia, or to Scott, Dickenson, Russell, or in fact any of the mountain counties of Virginia. Is it not on record that there are hundreds of people in the town of Appalachia alone who have never seen a New Testament or heard a prayer? Are there not 10,000 people in Dickenson County who have never heard of Jesus?

Recently a well-informed traveler dropped off the train at a little station down in Lee County for the purpose of admiring the scenery and viewing the natives. As he alighted nervously he heard a strangely familiar sound which he at once mistook for a still in full blast—or do the blasted things make any noise now? It was a Ford out here in these hills! A man in overalls and old straw hat sat at the throttle and barked: "Jonesville!" The educated stranger commandeered the car and began to pump the chauffeur for picturesque bits about himself and family, for the young man was plainly a

Mountain White—had to be, for there are nothing else out here in the sticks, barring an occasional cultured traveler.

But the driver's English was amazingly good, and his mind keen. The college bred gentleman begged an explanation of this strange thing.

"Where did you make the acquaintance of books, magazines, and ideas?" he implored of the Mountain White.

"I was born in a mountain home not many miles from here," he good-naturedly elucidated. "I was graduated from the high school at Jonesville, attended Emory and Henry four years, and did my Ph.D. work at Johns Hopkins."

The civilized adventurer did not recover completely from the shock until he reached Clintwood, Virginia. "Are you related to Joy Sutherland, magazine writer and newspaperman?" he chortled jocularly to his host of the same name. Mine host was genial, albeit a Mountain White, and he drawled (all Virginians drawl), "He is a distant relative—a distant relative. He is away in Richmond just now. He is my son." In this little city buried away among the wretched ten thousand people over whom good-hearted philanthropists are weeping there were discovered a native mountain white principal of a Norfolk high school and an ex-high school teacher from Richmond. Thereupon our traveler fled. He was last seen heading for the Kentucky mountains where we hope he will find people just as white and just as mountainous as he found in these parts.

Up in New York an estimable young man recently sued for and recovered $3,500 from the Russel Sage Foundation for printing his picture and labeling it "Toughest Kid in Hell's Kitchen," years ago, when he was not old enough to protect himself, in one of their books on "Vices of Boyhood."

All of which leads us to suggest the famous Mountain White, there "ain't no sich animal," or if there is, he is no less white nor any more so than Henry Clay Beattie or Left Louis or Gyp the Blood. Due credit and lots of space will be given the wild-eyed reformer who will bring to our attention a man, woman, or child belonging to a well defined, peculiar and distinct race measuring up to all the specifications that go with the type so well advertised "out in the world" as the Mountain White.

Again, and in the supposed vernacular, we tell the world "there ain't no sich animal." [13]

"The Mountain White" demonstrated Crawford's creativity in proving a simple point—southwest Virginia was not a haven for feuding backwoodsmen but was instead populated by an ambitious, educated populace. Newspapers in this era commonly attempted to attract outside investors with bland economic statistics, but Crawford showed that biting criticism could accomplish the same.

Crawford also published news from far outside of southwest Virginia to better connect his Appalachian community to the wider American world. Major league baseball scores and boxing results from the northeast appeared regularly in *Crawford's Weekly*. He also published advertisements for golf equipment companies, including information on how to join the recently constructed Lonesome Pine Country Club in nearby Big Stone Gap. Showing both his popularity and his readerships' sense of humor, Crawford once joked that his newspaper would get so successful that he would someday retire to the Florida coast. In response, readers mailed several boxes of oranges and grapefruits to the *Crawford's Weekly* office urging him to go sooner rather than later. Bruce Crawford's community was hardly an illiterate land, but writers from the previous generation, namely Mary Noailles Murfree via *In the Tennessee Mountains* (1884) and George Cary Eggleston through *Camp Venture* (1903), had firmly entrenched the idea of primitive Appalachia in the minds of well-read America. This was the stereotype Crawford had to challenge his entire career in defense both of his home and of his aspirational identity as an intellectual-activist.[14]

Challenging stereotype through "The Mountain White" was one of dozens of examples where Crawford's writings identified and condemned injustice throughout his long career, especially during the 1920s. Crawford's 1920s editorials focused on what were, to him, obvious positions that should be held by all working-class people—the Ku Klux Klan must be stamped out, lynching was a despicable practice, poll taxes violated constitutional rights, and coal companies oppressed coal miners. By the end of the 1920s, *Crawford's Weekly* published more philosophical arguments on Communism, capitalism, and labor rights, and by the mid-1930s, Crawford would take on powerful politicians directly. But his first years of publication demonstrate a young editor hungry for direct, immediate change ready to put his and his family's life on the line for the greater good.

THE KLAN

Crawford's Weekly, in its earliest years, risked its existence to target the Ku Klux Klan in a long editorial campaign. In Crawford's view, the Klan was a bigoted, violent menace that risked undoing decades of southwest Virginian progress. Part of this progress was the slow march toward integration and better understanding across racial lines. Crawford had the benefit of perspective gained from having seen more of the world than most in Wise County.

A year in college, World War I military service, and teenage years working in coal mines put Crawford in direct contact with all sorts of people. The way he put it, he had worked with "coal miners, with railroad men, with fishermen, with Germans, with Negroes, with Creoles, with Swedes, with Italians and with Greeks. I have mixed with the high and the low, in beautiful garden of plenty and in slums of privation and degradation."[15]

What set Crawford apart from his peers was hatred of what men could become when seduced by "some stupid order" that leads them to committing "inhumanities," in his own words. All men were good, it was groups who were the problem.[16] The best way to cleanse society of "some stupid order" was free speech. A free exchange of ideas, so Crawford's logic went, could silence the ignorant. Shine a light on poor ideas, so to speak, the idea would wither, and the stupid order that followed would shrivel on the vine. Even better if those ideas could be compared to better ideas in a forum, debate, or exchange of editorials. Crawford defended reprehensible people, including the Klan themselves, if their bad ideas were silenced. The mayor of Appalachia, Virginia, supposedly arrested a man for delivering a pro-Klan speech during the 1925 Armistice Day celebration, which prompted Crawford to write that "if the man were arrested for making a speech, then Mayor Woodward himself dropped to the level of a Kluxer. This is, theoretically, a free country. Let those mouth who will; their unwisdom, if such it be, will prove their undoing soon or late."[17]

Just before Crawford's anti-Klan campaign began in earnest, he targeted Billy Sunday—the most famous evangelical preacher of the 1920s—with accusations of being a scam artist and Klan sympathizer. To be fair, Sunday was no Klansman, yet he refused to take a public stance on the bigoted organization. Privately, Sunday accepted official Klan donations more than once, called for the jailing of Communists, and surrounded himself with men who rose to prominence in the 1930s as leaders of right-wing fascist organizations.[18] Crawford viewed Billy Sunday as a pawn of capitalists hired to distract coal miners away from union solidarity with sermons about Christian sacrifice and thinly veiled xenophobia. Sunday's anecdotal "aw-shucks" solutions to complex capitalist problems wooed the coal miner class, and Crawford's negative assessment met a frosty Wise County reception throughout 1922.

Billy Sunday did not return to Wise County the following year, likely because he did not make enough money to justify the trip. This certainly disappointed plenty of Wise County residents, but not Crawford, who celebrated the news. Instead of spending money on Billy Sunday—perhaps more than $10,000—Wise County residents could pay for the necessities of life like groceries, coal, laundry, phone bills, water bills, rents, and mortgages. Even after that was paid, one Bill Sunday payday could also pay for "churches, preachers' salaries, YMCA activities, and various community amusements."[19]

Crawford's anti-Billy Sunday campaign laced with subtle anti-xenopho-bia nearly killed his newspaper career. Local leaders threatened to campaign against *Crawford's Weekly* unless he stepped away from, in their view, overly critical rhetoric. In response, Crawford doubled down with biting sarcasm. "Some day [sic] an editor will come into being who will not be foolish enough to have a mind of his own," wrote Crawford, continuing that this imagined editor "will bury his philosophy, his humble vision of life, his convictions and his dreams beneath the old bushel hamper and join in the long procession of boys who bow at the altar of rust." Crawford was asking his community just what they would prefer—a dynamic editor who highlights the good and criticizes the bad or a lazy, supposedly objective writer who would "please the butcher, the baker, and the loafer" for a few years until their boring newspaper went bankrupt. It was never clear exactly how local leaders responded to Crawford's challenge, but *Crawford's Weekly* subscription numbers continued to slowly rise with a self-proclaimed dynamic editor at the helm.[20]

After the Billy Sunday editorials, Crawford proved he was "foolish enough to have a mind of his own" by launching a major editorial campaign against the Ku Klux Klan. Klan membership grew exponentially during the late 1910s and the first few years after World War I. Capitalizing on postwar nativism, Klan leaders brought together bigots against African Americans, Catholics, Jews, Communists, and immigrants under a single organization with a national scope. At its peak the Klan of the 1920s claimed approximately four million members. Terrorism continued to be a central component of the 1920s Klan resurgence, marked by masked public marches and cross burnings. Murders were also common, especially lynchings, as evidenced by the significant rise in lynchings in Virginia during the 1920s compared to the slow decline that had characterized the preceding twenty-five years. The Klan was no innocent social organization; it was a hate group prone to violence with significant political influence. Regular Klan meetings may have carried the air of other voluntary organizations, but as pointed out by historian Leonard Moore, the Klan repre-sented the full white Protestant community's supremacist views.[21]

In January 1923 Crawford described the Klan as "hooded roughnecks, "the dread menace," and "an intolerant confederacy of dark-minded cowards hiding under sheets."[22] By this point, Klan activity and recruitment in Wise County was growing. Locals distributed Klan recruitment literature portraying the or-ganization as little different than a local drinking club or semi-secret frater-nal order. Klan council meetings were highly secretive, as were membership rolls. For all anyone knew, the city council conspired privately to undermine Wise County's future. This was outrageous enough on its own, but even worse, in Crawford's view, was that so many others in the community appeared unconcerned. What concerned Crawford the most was that the Klan operated so cowardly as to hide their ideas away from public view, betraying a fundamental value of liberal society.[23]

Sensing his typical editorials were failing to rally locals to his anti-Klan cause, Crawford launched a new strategy in November 1923—publishing debates between himself and Frank L. Cash, a local casket maker and Klansman. The Crawford-Cash exchange began by accident. An anonymous letter dropped into the *Crawford's Weekly* office demanded Crawford "Be a Man" by republishing articles originally appearing in Klan newspapers. *Crawford's Weekly* had a strict policy of not publishing anonymous letters, so it delighted Crawford that Cash claimed authorship within a few days. Cash's letter, as reprinted by Crawford, argued the Klan positively impacted a man's character by encouraging honesty, honor, and respect. Cash claimed Klan membership, though he was technically barred because of the Klan's "Jew clause." This meant that Cash was himself a walking contradiction, a Jewish man who was also Klansman despite the Klan barring from membership "Negroes, Jews, Bootleggers, and Catholics." The rest of Cash's letter generally attacked Crawford's business, masculinity, and honor. With such an inflammatory letter in hand and in print, Crawford now had the opportunity to demolish an individual's stupid ideas on his own terms.[24]

The Cash letters proved to be Crawford's entrée into unveiling Klan beliefs as hypocritical, anti-American classism. His response to Cash came harsh and swift. He began with condemning the Klan's bigotry—"Nothing can be more unjust than to generalize about nationalities and to speak of a race as worthless or vicious simply because you have met an individual who treated you unjustly. . . . A man—the kind we hope Mr. Cash would have one be—is far above the badges of faith and of race. Good Jews are precisely the same as good Christians, and bad Christians are wonderfully like bad Jews." Superstitious religion was the root cause of such ignorance. A place existed in society for good, pious people, but demonizing another for a slightly different piety was simply wrong, even irreligious in his view. Do not be seduced by Klan picnics or school fundraisers, Crawford warned, as the "grand total of its atrocities" far outweighs any perceived social benefit.[25]

Over the next several months Crawford published at least one anti-Klan article per weekly paper, including several more exchanges with Klansman Cash. Crawford published each of Cash's letter unedited alongside a thrashing dismantling. Moving into 1924, Crawford published dozens of letters to the editor both for and against the Klan. Frank Cash always represented the pro-Klan positions, while anti-Klan statements had several authors, including local lawyer J. F. Bullitt, Bristol-based wholesaler Charles F. Hagan, the Reverend C. W. Dean, "A Reader," and Crawford himself. Crawford essentially gave Cash just enough free speech to destroy his own argument, or so it must have seemed to any reader following the back-and-forth weekly.[26]

At the same time, a potentially destructive argument developed in the pages of *Crawford's Weekly* between Crawford and most of Norton's leading clergymen. In one of Crawford's responses to Cash, he wrote, "There have been a few instances of ministers placing the Klan where it belongs. But a gift of money and the parading of the flag will cause the average preacher to capitulate." The accusation that some preachers took Klan money essentially as a moral bribe outraged the Norton Ministers' Association, which demanded Crawford retract the statement. Crawford begrudgingly agreed. In a revised article, he wrote that the "average preacher" did not capitulate to the Klan but noted none of the protesting Norton preachers publicly condemned the Klan. Crawford called upon the preachers to hold a special meeting to "take a stand for or against the Klan. . . . If they are for the Klan, they shouldn't be afraid to go on record favoring it. But if they are opposed to it, let them have the courage to say so publicly and why." If preachers commented on nearly everything else—prohibition, labor rights, tobacco and alcohol, and politics—then why not rip into the Klan as bigoted Christian pretenders? Crawford's calls went unheeded. The ministers never condemned the Klan, or at least did not do so in a public forum.[27]

Crawford's anti-Klan campaign finally met real success during May and June 1924. On May 1, 1924, Frank Cash requested permission from the Norton town council to hold a Klan parade. Public demonstrations were a common Klan tactic as a way to prove their supposed influence over local government. Commandeering Park Avenue, Norton's main street, in full Klan regalia would further terrorize African Americans, Jews, Catholics, and any other class of peoples deemed the enemy of Frank Cash and his associates. Norton council approved Cash's request for "some early date" with no ban on masks. Crawford responded to these developments with outraged mockery. He took to his paper to portray Cash and his fellow Klansman as uneducated fools seeking political power by printing a spoof on their parade speeches in exaggerated dialect:

I feel it due Dimekratik brethrin and Klamsmin that I stait the resens for takin this step. They run ez follows: 1s: I want an offis. 2d. I need a offis. 3d.

A offis wood suit me; ther4, 4th. I shood like to hev a offis. I maik no boasts uv what my speshel clames air, but I have dun the purty and the community some service and lived here the rest of the time. I hav allus rallid 2 the poles erly in the mornin and hev spent the entire day a bringin in the ajid and infirm, and in the patryotik and 100 per ct. business of knockin down the opposition voters. No man hez drunk more whiskey than I hev fer the party—none has done it more willingly. . . . Now, fell citizins, ef eleckdid, I shel sware to doo my dooty; if not eleckdid, I shel sware anyway.[28]

By the end of June 1924, *Crawford's Weekly* delightfully reported the "eternal obliteration" of the Norton Klansmen. Ethel Ould, one of the wealthiest Norton residents, refused to allow Klansmen access to the downtown Boice and Bell Building. Klan organizers initially misled her by reserving the space as the "Business Men's Club," and she quickly locked the doors once she discovered it was, in fact, the Klan. A reasonable assumption would be that Crawford tipped her off. The meeting space loss caused the Klan to fissure, as multiple factions never again came to terms on a new organizational arrangement.[29] Crawford wrote very little on the Klan or related nativist organizations from this point forward. The primary exception came a decade later with Adolf Hitler's rise to power. Crawford regularly compared German fascists to American Klansmen, for instance writing in 1933 that "we are fast drifting into a situation favorable to the emergence of Hitlerism in this country. We have all the elements for an American Hitler to work with—a Ku Kluxury, dormant or potential, with its hatred of races, its low emotionalism, its superstitious and tinfoil patriotism."[30] Either way, the death of the Norton Klan seemed enough for Crawford in 1924. Going forward, he hoped his friends and neighbors would "be ashamed to let their children know how they took part in it."[31]

LYNCHING

While Crawford wrote about the Klan, three African American men were murdered by lynch mobs in southwest Virginia. These murders outraged Crawford, so on the heels of his anti-Klan writing came an anti-lynching campaign, perhaps his riskiest to date. "*Crawford's Weekly* has shown extraordinary fearlessness on various occasions," wrote the *Richmond Times-Dispatch* in 1929, continuing, "when a lynching bee was staged a couple of years ago a few miles from Norton, Bruce Crawford investigated and printed the facts, calling the lynchers just what they should have been called, i.e. cutthroats and murderers."[32] During the early 1920s, a new wave of lynching violence swept across Virginia, especially in its southwestern counties, as white mobs rejected sham trials and legal hangings for their own nighttime gallows. No other state, Southern or Northern, experienced such a resurgence, so something was wrong in the Commonwealth.

For example, a white mob murdered David Hunt, a twenty-five-year-old Black man, in Wise County in 1920 after a woman accused him of assault. Just up the road in Wytheville in 1926, Wytheville law enforcement declined to protect Raymond Byrd, a Black man accused of sexual assault, from a murderous white mob. And in 1927, a lynch mob formed in Wise County after the killing of Herschel Deaton, a white man employed as a mine foreman. The mob accused two Black women and Leonard Woods, a Black man, of killing Deaton and, without providing any evidence, murdered Woods in cold blood. The David Hunt lynching horrified coalfield progressives because of its violence, but also because eighteen years had passed since the most recent Wise County lynching. Many who believed lynching days were coming to an end suddenly awoke to their harsh reality. Further horrifying these same progressives was law enforcement's total capitulation to mob violence. Some hope could be found in jail sentences doled out to a few lynch mob participants, a first in Virginia, so maybe it was possible to leverage the court system in finally stamping out these evil acts.[33]

The Raymond Byrd murder was what really set Crawford off. *Crawford's Weekly* immediately joined voices with the editors of the *Richmond Planet*, the Commonwealth's largest African American newspaper, to condemn the lynching. In issue after issue in the following weeks, Crawford lambasted Wytheville's white leadership both because they facilitated brutal violence and because Byrd was an innocent man. Crawford conducted some on-the-ground reporting and concluded that Byrd's accuser, a white farmer named Grover Grubb, invented the sexual assault charges because Byrd was dating at least one of Grubb's daughters. Further reporting uncovered one of the Grubb women and Byrd had a child years earlier that was cared for by a local African American woman, likely because Grover Grubb did not approve.

Crawford's Weekly took the Byrd-Grubb story, an open secret in Wytheville, statewide by calling for legal intervention. Wythe County leadership clearly had no intention to follow up on the crime, so in Crawford's view "Governor [Harry F.] Byrd should waste no time in ferreting out those lynchers and, in the name of the State of Virginia as a whole, establish a precedent for upholding duly constituted law."[34] Louis Jaffe, the esteemed editor of the *Norfolk Virginian-Pilot*, also called on the governor to "make every lynching a matter of direct state concern and to arm the Governor as chief law enforcement officer, with the unrestricted power to initiate and prosecute investigations in to lynching's and to employ every power at his disposal to bring perpetrators to justice." [35]

A month later, Crawford successfully escalated his campaign by drawing connections between lynching and the Klan, again challenging Governor Byrd to prove he was "intelligent enough and courageous enough" to do something about both problems. If Virginia's leadership chose to do nothing about either lynching or the Klan, then the Commonwealth would remain "in a class with the most ungoverned State[s] of the backward South." [36] Weeks later, with no action from anyone in Virginia's leadership class, Crawford sarcastically wrote, "Is it not a terrible reflection on a modern civilized community that it has within its borders fifty murderers it cannot catch?" [37]

Surprising virtually everyone in local media, a few months later Wythe County organized a grand jury at with Governor Byrd's support. The grand jury of all white men then indicted Floyd Willard, a white Wythe County man, for murder in January 1927. With bond posted, Willard waited six months for his trial to begin, though the outcome was never in doubt. Willard's defense produced witnesses to vouch for his whereabouts, so the jury voted quickly to acquit.[38]

Six months after Floyd Willard walked free, a white mob in Wise County murdered the African American Leonard Woods. Woods's death deeply upset Crawford. In the following weeks, *Crawford's Weekly* published several articles on Woods, with such titles as "The Mob," "A Deplorable Affair," and "Virginia Again Disgraced." Crawford's direct reporting on the event likely provided the most accurate account of events leading to Woods's murder. It all began when Woods allegedly shot and killed Herschel Deaton, a white man, supposedly because Deaton refused to give a ride to Woods and two unnamed Black women. The three fled the scene. A massive lynch mob formed in both Virginia and Kentucky in the hopes, according to white observers, that a "necktie party" would be held that night. Officers eventually arrested Woods and, likely to guide the lynch mob, announced Woods would be held in Whitesburg, Kentucky, just an hour's drive from the border and far less secure than larger cities like Lexington or Frankfort. Two days later, spurred on by emotional displays at Deaton's funeral, the lynch mob formed again. Crawford witnessed a convoy drive away from Norton bound for Whitesburg to kidnap Woods from jail and bring him back to Virginia to be hung. Crawford depicted a harrowing scene as he lingered near the Virginian mob:

> At Fleming thirty-six cars with Virginia license tags stopped, turned, and line up, ready to start back. They waited. . . . It was decided that the

delegation would just wait here until the larger mob, composed mostly of Kentuckians, brought the Negro from the Whitesburg jail.

The Kentucky mob had been gone toward Whitesburg for quite a while. Nearly one hundred cars were in the procession. The Virginia line waited, lights lit. They wore no masks. Some smoked. They stretched their legs.[39]

Kentuckians seized Woods and the two women from the Whitesburg jail with no resistance from law enforcement. The mob returned to Jenkins, where Woods supposedly killed Herschel Deaton, only to be met by local police. Rather than protect Woods, Jenkins officers requested Woods be killed elsewhere, specifically Pound Gap, because "[Jenkins] is [Consolidated Coal] Company property—we have lots of Negro laborers here—and we don't want any disturbance in these camps." Finding the police's logic correct, the mob carried Woods to Pound Gap, murdered him, and viciously mutilated his body. A large rock behind the lynching site that was scarred with over five hundred bullets was just part of Crawford's description of the lynching scene:

> Around a hill on the Virginia side, not a hundred yards from the lynching scene, a newly worn path meandered through a freshly burnt woodland. At the end of that path stood men and women looking down at the ground. They were staring strangely at a new grave—a carelessly shaped mound of clay, with two dead stumps stuck in it, as if by some humorous fellow, departing late. Visitors had been sounding the grave with pointed sticks to find out how far down the wooden box was. "Hear it?" one would say, tamping the box with a long stick. Thump! Thump! Ten inches below the ground.
>
> There lay the mutilated remains of Leonard Woods—until Negro friends from Kentucky came later in the day and removed the body. Thus ended the "neck-tie party."[40]

Crawford's Weekly had much more in common with the Black press than other progressive newspapers in responding to lynchings at this stage. Crawford, unlike most of his white journalist peers, possessed no faith that the system would provide justice for Leonard Woods. Other responses to the 1927 Woods lynching were all too familiar—outrage from progressives, nihilism from many, and half-hearted opposition mixed with indifference from the Right. Against this backdrop, Crawford kept up his anti-lynching campaign, publishing a few essays in national publications, including articles in the *New York World* and the nation's largest African American newspaper, the *Pittsburgh Courier*. "Bruce Crawford, a young white editor of Virginia, is an example of the slowly awakening conscience of Southern whites," wrote the *New York Amsterdam News*, an African American newspaper. "In this [anti-lynching] fight he has learned some things that people outside the South have always known . . . the falsity of the saying that the upper class of Southern white people are against lynching, that they deplore it, but are helpless before the rush of the lower class mob." [41]

Crawford soon learned that all classes of white people in his neighborhood deplored his anti-lynching campaign. Over one hundred locals signed a petition calling on him to desist. The *Chicago Defender* quoted Crawford, never one to back down, as saying, "I have learned that a surprisingly great number of supposedly enlightened people, while unwilling to participate in a lynching, will openly advocate mob law or mildly defend it. And some of them will attempt to mob an editor by the petition method." [42] In response to the petition, *Crawford's Weekly* amped up its anti-lynching coverage by calling for systemic social changes such as laws outlawing judicial racial bias and better racial education in public schools. Also included was an explicitly anti-police viewpoint. Crawford strongly asserted that no amount of police presence or law enforcement would have prevented any of Virginia's lynchings of the previous few years, so any addition of officers would do no good. Law enforcement men "worship money" and thus are prone to corruption, so Crawford argued. Still, "corrupt as things are, better a half a loaf than none. The courts afford the only civilized approach to justice." White men received jury trials expected to be fair and impartial, so why shouldn't Black men?[43]

To the delight of many in the Black press, Crawford also started a fund to support the prosecution and conviction of the Woods lynching's leaders. Both Virginia and Kentucky had no intention of pursuing any charges, so again locals pushed back, on the grounds that starting such a fund would only further divide their community. "Our fund stands," read *Crawford's Weekly* the next week. Crawford again lambasted his neighbors as perfunctory, hypocritical, and permitting their "murderous impulse" to take over the community. Deeply ashamed of his neighbors, Crawford felt that at a minimum the laws should be enforced lest the community return to a "primitive state that gives the lie to all our claims to Christian enlightenment and human progress." [44] The *New Journal and Guide*, a Black newspaper in Norfolk, especially came to Crawford's defense. When the *Roanoke Times* bashed Crawford's position, the *New Journal and Guide* asked readers to publicly support him. Crawford's editorials on the Klan and lynching appeared regularly in the *New Journal and Guide* pages, positioning as one of very few allies among white editors.[45]

Crawford's writings, alongside the campaigns of Black newspapers and Louis Jaffe, editor of the *Norfolk Virginian-Pilot*, finally caught the attention of Governor Harry Byrd in late 1927. Byrd's office organized a December 1927 conference so newspaper editors could provide him direct advice on solutions to Virginia's lynching problem. Jaffe was the primary agitator for the meeting, having developed a long-standing relationship with Byrd and his political allies. The meeting group, about three dozen in total, did not include any members of the Black press. While a full attendee list has not yet been discovered, Crawford and Jaffe were the only ones present to engage in anti-lynching campaigns targeting lynching's brutality and racism.

Two weeks after the meeting, Governor Byrd called on the General Assembly to pass new anti-lynching legislation. The core of Byrd's agenda, which would become known as the Barron-Connor Act, would allow for state payouts to lynching victims' families and would establish a fund for special gubernatorial lynching investigations. Lynching would also be made a state-level offense and no longer subject to the whims of local police or courts. Newspapermen who met with Byrd endorsed the proposal, as did the biggest voices in Virginia's Black press. With overwhelming support, the Barron-Connor Act became law on March 8, 1928. Without question, such a law never would have come to pass without pressure from Crawford and Jaffe. Though the act did not change the racist culture or educational system of Virginia, Crawford was somewhat relieved that just one more documented lynching occurred in Virginia from this point forward.[46]

After this legislative achievement, Crawford's anti-lynching campaign came to an end, though he continued to write about the evils of lynching for years to come. A few months after the journalistic clamor around the Woods lynching quieted, the Baltimore *Afro-American* asked Crawford to write a short piece on lynching. Positioned alongside much more famous writers like H. L. Mencken, Crawford used this opportunity to flex his writings skills and call for more radical anti-lynching action:

> By all means, the fight must be continued for the enactment of the Federal antilynching bill. It is useless to wait for the South—or any other area—to become enlightened and civilized enough to be shamed out of this sort of crime; just as it would be useless and foolish to have no laws against murder on the ground that murder can be tolerated until people become millennially pure of heart . . .
>
> A Federal law to protect the poor, in circumstances where ordinary laws

against murder are not enforced, is opposed largely because the rich have a good deal to gain by reason of lynching—mass intimidation of workers, both white and black.

Lynching is the convenient weapon of landlordism and industrial despotism. While it is most prevalent in the South, where Negro and white workers are pitted against each other in the struggle for work and existence, its partner in lawlessness and murder, vigilanteeism [sic], is no respecter of localities. It would be well to have a Federal anti-lynching law which would penalize mob murder of any kind.

Yes, I noticed during the agitation for the antilynching law, the mobs kept to cover. If the mere threat of passage of the bill could have such a deterrent effect, the ever-ready law on the Federal statue certainly would be more effective.[47]

Crawford, Jaffe, and their editor peers continued anti-lynching work for many more years. Jaffe was the most critically successful, winning the Pulitzer Prize for editorial writing in 1929 for his ultimately unsuccessful *Virginian-Pilot* campaign for a national anti-lynching law. Crawford meanwhile kept writing anti-lynching editorials for *Crawford's Weekly* whenever a near-lynching transpired in the region.[48] He also reprinted several essays by writer-editor Sherwood Anderson, such as "Look Out, Brown Man!," and national reports on lynching, such as the 1931 Southern Commission on the Study of Lynching report and a 1932 study produced by the Tuskegee Institute. The reality, though, was no more lynchings or near-lynchings took place in Crawford's immediate vicinity. Governor Byrd's push for state-level anti-lynching laws largely placated Crawford's less radical peers, so without an audience for his change-inducing rhetoric, Crawford moved on to another fight.[49]

POLL TAXES AND PRISONS

A theme in Crawford's anti-lynching writings was that the root cause of such racial violence grew out of systemic inequalities of the American system. Starting in 1925 Crawford launched a direct editorial campaign to eliminate flogging as a punishment in prisons. It was legal in Virginia for prison guards to beat prisoners as punishment for a range of infractions, most of which were minor, such as a failure to clean a jail cell properly. State prison officials claimed floggings were necessary to maintain order and noted other states, primarily in the South, also had such disciplinary policies. Crawford's attention on the subject was first sparked by Virginia Bullitt Taggart, president of the Wise County Federation of Women's Clubs, when the *Richmond*

Times-Dispatch published her letter to the editor condemning flogging and calling for its abolition. Crawford seized on Taggart's writing, firing off dozens of letters to newspapers across the nation inquiring as to their states' flogging laws. What he learned—and published—was that Kansas, Massachusetts, New York, Ohio, and Wisconsin had all abolished corporal punishment while Alabama still "whips her convicts." [50]

Taggart's and Crawford's efforts had an effect. The State Board of Public Welfare, headed by Secretary Joseph T. Mastin, submitted a report to the governor a few weeks later claiming prison guards whipped "only" forty-nine prisoners during the first ten months of 1925. Crawford joked that "being told that is like being served in a restaurant with a 'reasonably good' egg!" [51] Taggart despondently noted in the pages of *Crawford's Weekly* that Virginia leaders would "put their stamp of approval on this kind of legal torture; despite all of this, there remains a bitter reality to those of us who consider ourselves just a wee bit past the shadows of the dark ages . . . there remains the disgraceful fact that VIRGINIA DOES WHIP." Secretary Mastin, despite his reputation as a reformer and training as a Methodist preacher, ignored such pleas as he was also a hardline segregationist and eugenicist who believed in such treatments as sterilization of the "feebleminded." Mastin had been in his position since 1908, and both his power and perspective certainly contributed to the passage of several racist, eugenicist laws during the mid-1920s. In other words, Crawford had little chance of changing Mastin's views with clever wordplay. [52]

Over the next few years, prisoners wrote to Crawford in response to his and Taggart's campaign detailing abuses they suffered in prison. *Crawford's Weekly* reprinted about a dozen such letters, with the most impactful being written in 1927 by James Goodwin, Prisoner no. 20762 in the Richmond state prison. Goodwin told the story of a nineteen-year-old inmate who prison guards brutally whipped twenty-five times for failure to meet production quotas. According to Goodwin, prison officials failed to train the nineteen-year-old in properly manufacturing clothing destined for a private clothing company, so he failed to meet quotas and was thus subject to punishment. The superintendent ignored the real problem at hand—the training instructor skipped instruction and attempted to sexually assault the nineteen-year-old—and, upon being rebuffed, took to whipping. Making matters worse was that fellow prisoners could not report violations, or at least perceived they could not, because the superintendent had total control over the conditional pardon system. Any action against the superintendent's will resulted in more punishment, a longer prison stay, or both. Goodwin understood that he risked as much, but commented that he was "willing to sacrifice what chances of getting pardon" so he and his fellow inmates could "live like human beings" in the Richmond state prison.[53]

With no signs of change from state leaders, Crawford pivoted in early 1928 to a critical assault on Virginia's death penalty, as well as the fundamental question of incarceration. *Crawford's Weekly* took the official position that the death penalty simply should not exist. It did not prevent crime and was often implemented with heavy influence from an emotional public, so why must it continue?[54] By the following year, *Crawford's Weekly* took a position that prisons should largely be abolished in a civilized society like Virginia: "Today there is so much confusion as to the so-called criminal type that we have all grown uneasy and self-conscious about our inherent tendencies. . . . Many hold that crime is a disease . . . [and] do not think, however, that sentimental kindness is a cure. They realize that many things, cruel and painful to the patient, are essential to his recovery." Finally, Crawford placed importance on reform, arguing society should place more emphasis on social reform to prevent crime rather than cruel punishment after the fact.[55] Again, none of these essays caught the attention of elected politicians or spurred popular sympathy for prisoners. Writing two years later with no change in sight, Crawford opined, "Unless the prison problem is solved, along with many other problems the neglect of which is producing more and more criminals, all the jails will burst one of these days, in a time of social chaos, and there will be hell to pay."[56]

With his prison campaign falling on deaf ears, Crawford pivoted to a campaign against what he viewed as the next-most-important force oppressing poor people and African Americans—poll taxes and disenfranchisement. Virginia poll taxes, as of the late 1920s, applied to any voting age citizen in Virginia and remained in place until 1966, finally abolished during the civil rights movement. During Crawford's era, the poll tax was $1.50, a significant cost for an average working person. Often, an individual's poll tax was paid by a political machine with the promise that the person would vote in the machine's interest. This was especially common in the Virginia coal fields, where political favors could go a long way in company-owned towns. Crawford's analogy was that of the political angler, both Democrat and Republican, using "the poll tax as a fisherman uses a fish hook. The poor sucker gets no bait if he doesn't bite, and if he bites he loses the bait and gets the hook."[57]

In later years, Crawford developed a more sophisticated argument against all forms of disenfranchisement, including poll taxes, literary tests, and property qualifications. He also included economic factors like poverty and over policing as factors robbing poor people of their voting rights. If something did not change soon, then Crawford advocated for a revolution against this growing robbery of rights. Voting was Crawford's preferred manner of social change, but "militancy and violence" were other options. It is worth noting that he often reminded readers that the French Revolution, guillotines and all, and not the American equivalent was the most admirable revolution in Western history.[58]

After the 1934 elections, Crawford noted that McDowell County, West Virginia, counted over twenty-eight thousand votes that year compared to about thirty thousand across the entire Virginia Ninth District. Altogether, roughly four times more West Virginians than Virginians voted statewide, simple yet provocative evidence that Virginia disenfranchised poor people at an alarming rate.[59] But Crawford had no illusions of success, recognizing that "the Virginia political machine will not consent without a fight." He was right, as in both 1938 and 1940 Governor James H. Price proposed lowering the tax amount only to see proposals defeated in the General Assembly by Democrats. It would take U.S. Supreme Court intervention to ultimately repeal Virginia's poll tax by finding it unconstitutional in 1966, ending ninety years of poll tax disfranchisement in the Commonwealth. Crawford could claim no personal role in these victories, but certainly he was a voice in the early campaign.[60]

ANGLO-SAXONS

Considering that most of Crawford's early campaigns all focused on causes benefiting African Americans—anti-Klan, anti-lynching, prison reform, and expanding voting rights—it would be reasonable to assume Crawford was a civil rights leader of sorts, especially given the praise he received from the largest Black newspapers. However, Crawford's greatest shortcoming as an editor, writer, and intellectual was his lack of perspective on race. Two related themes appeared commonly in *Crawford's Weekly*: tacit support of or failure to condemn Virginian white supremacists not explicitly allied with the Klan and unquestioning repetition of Lost Cause interpretations of the Southern past. Such themes make for jarring reading, as Crawford would publish his own articles on, for example, a need for African American voting rights legislation alongside delighted praise for the military genius of Thomas "Stonewall" Jackson. As with anyone, there were blind spots in Crawford's worldview that become clearly visible when stepping away from his various progressive campaigns.

The racial demographics of southwest Virginia were much different in Crawford's era than they are in the twenty-first century. The population of some coalfield counties, especially those in southern West Virginia, peaked at about 30 percent African American between 1900 and 1930. By the late 2010s, this population had declined to roughly 8 percent after decades of job decline and outmigration. Wise County, Crawford's home, was an outlier in 1930 with just 6.2 percent of the population reported as African American.[61] There was no immediate explanation for such a difference between Wise County and its neighbors. Perhaps such a low comparative minority population was due to the local Klan, fears or lynching, or fewer coal companies willing to hire African Americans. Whatever the case, Crawford certainly aided African Americans in his campaigns, but his record on civil rights issues disintegrated in the face of challenging structural racism.

Crawford's writings on Anglo-Saxonism, a eugenicist term invented to describe "pure white" individuals, best demonstrate how progressives like Crawford were seduced by the pseudoscience peddled by race science of the era. Anglo-Saxonism was nonsense and many of its proponents knew as much, but it held great sway amongst powerful, educated Virginians who thought extensively about how to draw thicker lines between terms like "white" and "negro." An individual's "blood," meaning their race and ancestry, mattered intensely to Crawford, though he never explained exactly why. The term "Anglo-Saxon" appeared often in *Crawford's Weekly* during the 1920s, most often as casual shorthand for "white" or paired as the racial opposite of "Negro." Crawford on occasion deployed "Anglo-Saxon" as a loaded term defined by eugenicists as a person of European ancestry, preferably British or northern Europe, who exhibited desirable traits like honor, honesty, and hard work and could claim a supposedly pure lineage. Crawford was not alone in his preference for the term "Anglo-Saxon" as Virginia's elite, namely Governor Harry Byrd, Governor Henry Stuart, and *Richmond Times-Dispatch* editor Virginius Dabney, were all quoted in *Crawford's Weekly* using the term at least once.[62]

One of the first examples of such editorial behavior came in in 1921 when Crawford published a letter to the editor containing a subsection entitled "Anglo-Saxon Ancestry." The letter's opening paragraph described why, in the author's mind, the nearby town of Coeburn was worthy of industrial investment:

> But our glory is not in our church buildings, nor in our system of public schools, nor yet in our strong banks and business houses, but our glory lies in the very character of the inhabitants of the Appalachian Range— here are to be found the truest, and the only real, types of Anglo-Saxon civilization. Our educational system is good because our teachers are building on integrity, honesty, industry; our banks are safe and strong, not because they have millions of dollars in resources, nor even because they

are protected by modern devices and precautions against burglary—they are safe because our business men have learned from their Anglo-Saxon ancestry that "honesty is the best policy." We have no labor troubles, due in great part to the fact that we have no mixed multitudes.[63]

Crawford's publication of the "Anglo-Saxon Ancestry" letter was odd because it contained several outright falsehoods. The claim that Coeburn had "no labor troubles" was simply untrue. There may have been no strikes within the borders of Coeburn, a community of about eight hundred people, but coal mining residents absolutely engaged in labor struggles elsewhere in the region. If Coeburn did not have any strikes, it was definitely home to strikers. Even more ridiculous was the claim that Coeburn's important citizens were all pure Anglo-Saxons, a truly meaningless statement asserted by any white person drawing a line against their Black neighbors.

Crawford's Weekly also published many reports written by eugenicists with no challenge or criticism but plenty of Crawford's own Anglo-Saxon commentary. One of the more egregious was his reporting on a Dickenson County Board of Education meeting, which began with a basic county demographics overview: "Here is found some of the purest Anglo-Saxon stock in America. . . . There was not a negro in this country until the mines came a few years ago it is said. Today two Virginia counties have no Negros: Craig and Buchanan, it is understood." In quoting this statistic, Crawford was objectively wrong: in 1930 there were just 15 African American residents of Craig County, by far the lowest such numbers in the Commonwealth (at 0.4 percent), but that population was 230 (8.4 percent) and 261 (6.0 percent) in 1870 and 1900 respectively. Crawford was obviously unaware that such an "Anglo-Saxon" county had experienced a rapid demographic shift within his lifetime.[64]

Three years later, on March 1, 1924, just days before Virginia's Racial Integrity Act became law, *Crawford's Weekly* published a front-page article titled "Color Line Is Fast Fading in Old Dominion." The article, almost assuredly written by Crawford, outlined several eugenics-driven conspiracy theories that preyed on peoples' poor understandings of race, evolution, and integration. The article began with the seemingly innocent title question—"Is the color line in Virginia fading?" From there, Crawford descended into eugenic buzz words like "race mixing." He provided anecdotes supposedly from educators in Richmond, Norton, and Lee County who claimed they could not enforce segregation in their schools because they could no longer tell white students from their "colored" peers.

The article included quotes from white supremacists like musician John

Powell, who argued that "there is not a county in Virginia which has not at least one community where the color line has almost disappeared." Despite its obvious falsehood, such a statement would have instilled terror into the heart of any racist white folks. Crawford clearly took Powell's statements to heart and sought out a real-world example in his own backyard. An educator in Lee County supposedly told Crawford of a community in which there was a large family—or as Crawford wrote it, "a large tribe of the same surname"—of mixed-race individuals, with some claiming to be white, others colored, and "some [. . .] neutral." On this, Crawford somewhat hedged his bets, noting that any "fine old family" in Virginia would have at least one Black member of the family tree and that classic Virginia writers like James Branch Cabell often included mixed-race families in their stories. Yet Crawford's conclusion read like pro-eugenics propaganda:

> Now we want a law to fix the [color] line. We would lock the stable when the stallions, many of them pure white, are already disappearing over the skyline of history. If a law can undo the sins of our fathers then, in God's name, the law and quickly! We now know that a reversion to KKK barbaric mob law can never save our race from the yawning maw of barbarity. Let us then have a law and orderly statue, passed by our Anglo-Saxon representatives at Richmond, forever fixing the line. But let us omit restrictions against those having 1/64 Indian in their veins, for the most aristocratic families in the state are proud of this blood.
>
> The cardinal principles of the Anglo-Saxon race—which exists in its purest in our mighty mountains—as a fair field for all and special favor to none. We must fix the blame for the racial catastrophe which John Powell and Ernest Sevier Cox see looming up in the near future. Did the ignorant and repulsive African male impugn the color line? We'll make a ghost of him who says so. Was it the male of the notorious "white trash"? Partially, only. In many and many a case, ad nauseam, it was the white male with a thousand years of blood and culture behind him. Let the axe and the chips fall wherever Newton has inferred they must.[65]

A close reading this extended quote perhaps hints at a bit of sarcasm or mockery, as was so common in Crawford's writing, but the reality was that his argument was largely based on an interview with John Powell about the Anglo-Saxon Clubs of America and the Racial Integrity Act of 1924. Legal historian Paul Lombardo referred to the Anglo-Saxon Clubs as "an elitist version of the KKK," and the official organization stance centered on "the preservation of racial integrity; for the supremacy of the white race in the United States, without prejudice or hatred; and for all principles of liberal Americanism conceived in the spirit of broad patriotism." Just one year earlier, Powell had delivered a speech at the University of Richmond in which he claimed that African Americans were being "absorbed by the Anglo-Saxon," resulting in the "degradation of the strong race."[66] *Crawford's Weekly* promoted a local chapter of the Anglo-Saxon Clubs even as its editor chastised the Klan and lynching, an inexplicable contradiction in itself.[67]

Anglo-Saxonism was closely related to the Lost Cause, a catch-all term for a variety of ahistorical pro-Confederate viewpoints that sought to justify secession and denied that the Civil War's primary cause was slavery. Lost Cause rhetoric commonly appeared in *Crawford's Weekly* despite Crawford himself regularly and correctly identifying the Civil War as having been fought over "cheap black labor" and noting that the conflict's "battle cry was slavery."[68] For instance, about a year after the publication flirted with Anglo-Saxonism, Crawford reprinted an article from the *Richmond Times-Dispatch* detailing the funeral of an African American man held at St. Paul's Church (nicknamed "the Cathedral of the Confederacy"). The key paragraph of the essay was not a eulogy to the man but a cynical take on segregation and racism through the lens of the Lost Cause:

> They say the War Between the States was fought to preserve slavery; they say the South hates and is cruel to the negroes; they say that true freedom and true kindliness are to be found by the negro only outside the South. Without bitterness and without spleen, it is asked: Can there be hatred and cruelty and oppression here, when in the capital of the Confederacy, in the church which was its chief temple an old negro man who has died in service draws together at his death the very flower of the South to join in sorrow and in hope to do him honor?[69]

Not once did the essay share the thoughts of the African American man or his family; nor did it even print his name. Instead, grand conclusions about race relations in Virginia were made based on his funeral location. That Crawford reprinted this essay with no commentary suggested that he too believed that southern African Americans enjoyed freedom in the twentieth century and harbored no ill will toward the South for its enslaving past.

Confederate imagery also regularly appeared in *Crawford's Weekly*, usually in relation to some tourism initiative. Images of Robert E. Lee, namely a portrait and the recumbent Lee statue at Washington & Lee University, dominated the *Crawford's Weekly* front page on October 3, 1925, in an effort to promote a new Virginia Chamber of Commerce motor tourism campaign. The statue was identified by the Commonwealth as a major attraction, and Crawford supplied his own support for this interpretation via a brief summary on Lee titled "South's Peerless Leader" and a second essay praising historian Douglas Southall Freeman's recently published Lee biography.[70] Crawford's praise of Lee can best be seen in another article a few months later on the 1925 Stone Mountain Half Dollar, a U.S. Mint coin depicting Stonewall Jackson and Lee with the words "Memorial to the Valor of the Soldier of the South." The coin was intended by President Calvin Coolidge to raise money for the Stone Mountain Confederate Monumental Association's efforts to kick-start construction of the Stone Mountain carving, though the coin was ultimately a failure as a fund-raiser.[71] Crawford's assessment of the coin was simple—"Every American, Yankee and Rebel alike, should be proud to be a citizen of a country that could produce a coin like that," he wrote, adding that Lee was "a great gentleman, a great soldier, a great citizen, a great American."[72]

Crawford's Lost Cause writings continued to appear throughout most of the *Crawford's Weekly* lifespan. An editorial dispatch on the forty-first and last reunion of Confederate veterans in Montgomery, Alabama, depicted "graying and thinning veterans" and "aged heroes" gathered for "banquets, balls, and patriotic speeches" alongside "belles . . . marching military units, and brass bands." "Sentiment misted the eye and when the band struck up 'Dixie' a madness touched the crowd for the moment," wrote Crawford, concluding, "Our hat is off to you Johnny Reb, in a respectful salute. You made history that will last forever, but after all 'The paths of glory lead but to the grave.'"[73]

Crawford did not write in this way about any other group in America's past. For other historical figures, Crawford emphasized "the human side of the heroes we worship in bronze and stone" and avoided hero worship. For instance, Columbia University historian Meade Minnigerode wrote a *Saturday Evening Post* essay that was, at the time, one of the first popular attempts to examine the many flaws of President Andrew Jackson, such as his "volcanic, cantankerous, scrapping character." Reviewers lambasted Minnigerode for denigrating the former president, but not Crawford. Instead, *Crawford's Weekly* celebrated Minnigerode's essay as a triumph because it represented Jackson as a "historical character vividly human," in contrast to "the pallid figures as statues in parks for the birds to roost on."[74]

Linking the Anglo-Saxon Clubs and Lost Cause was white supremacy, often represented in public during the 1920s and 1930s as "Anglo-Saxonism." Crawford himself deployed "pure Anglo-Saxonism" generalizations whenever it suited his goals, despite his intense hatred of stereotypes. In 1927 he published an essay that asked a deceptively complex question: "What is happening to our Anglo-Saxon stock?" In doing so he intended to explore how authors depicted Appalachia as a place full of Americans with the purest white ancestry. In short, was their depiction correct? The answer, according to Crawford, was that the "average hillsman" in his part of Virginia was of degraded stock. "He is runty, scrubby, and somewhat 'run out,'" continued Crawford, alluding to "vestiges of glorious manhood" that have been eroded by the difficulty of mountain survival. The only indication that such people could escape their plight was the civilizing force of the state. Roads, education, and public services purged mountaineers of their "backwardness and ignorance," and "their children" were getting educated and getting out. Ironically, despite an interest in Anglo-Saxonism, Crawford often depicted mountaineers as wholly uninterested in such definitions, simply writing a few years later that "if the dwellers of Piney Ridge are Anglo-Saxon, few if any of them know it, and it doesn't matter."[75]

Squaring the circle between Crawford's Anglo-Saxon writings and the biting anti-stereotype satire of "The Mountain White" penned just a half-decade earlier is a difficult task, but the most likely scenario is simply that Anglo-Saxonist rhetoric influenced Crawford's thinking on race and ethnicity. In the 1890s the president of Berea College articulated a difference, in his mind, between "poor whites" and "mountain whites." The former was a degraded group described with terms like "poor stock"; the latter was a group that had "not yet graded up" to being "poor." It was a hierarchical view in which "mountain whites" were mythological innocents untouched by capitalism. Only time would tell if "mountain whites" became "poor whites" or something better.

In Crawford's view, ignorant, innocent communities of "mountain whites" were indeed a myth, but "poor whites"—or "hillsmen" in *Crawford's Weekly*—were abundant in southwest Virginia and east Kentucky. Crawford proposed a simple solution to solving the "hillsmen" problem. Exposure to education and technology would allow people to overcome problems brought on by their "poor stock" and backwardness. Many eugenicists believed such peoples to be beyond hope, but many others, such as the authors of *Hollow Folk*, would have largely agreed with Crawford. A common eugenicist theme in Appalachia was that geography created isolation, and isolation begat devolution. Removing the mountaineer from the mountains could solve the problem, in theory. The only major difference in Crawford's procedure would be to bring education to the mountains rather than attracting mountaineers to educational institutions. In this way, Crawford was more practical and compassionate than mainstream eugenicists and politicians. Speaking as a Virginia senator, Harry F. Byrd stated that ignorant "simple mountain people"—meaning Crawford's "hillsmen"—did not deserve modern amenities like electricity, indoor toilets, or factory-made furniture. Therein lay the difference between Crawford and Anglo-Saxoners, albeit a small one—Crawford believed change could be brought to the mountains, while the rest viewed class and caste differences as immutable and the mountains as a decivilizing force.[76]

Ironically, Crawford's Anglo-Saxon writings appeared alongside his advocation for integrationist and racial equality organizations. In the same year during which Crawford republished John Powell's Anglo-Saxonist views, he also supported the recent formation of the Appalachian District for Interracial Cooperation, an organization co-managed by equal parts white and Black members to improve health and economic conditions in the mountains. The organization's primary means for achieving its goal was slow desegregation through education. If both whites and Blacks could be brought out of mass ignorance, so the thinking went, then racism and segregation would simply fade away. Such thinking was common among both white and Black progressives, many of whom followed the lead of Booker T. Washington, as well as among Communists, who largely believed an educated populace would recognize that true social strife was due to class, not race.[77]

Though *Crawford's Weekly* rarely expounded on race specifically, Crawford regularly endorsed ideas that aligned with his own. One of Crawford's favored speakers on race was lawyer Clarence Darrow, who had just come to national prominence for his role in the Leopold and Loeb murder trial and the Scopes Monkey Trial. Darrow generally advocated education and hard work while also recognizing which white men were allies and which were enemies as major factors in improving African American life. Crawford reprinted Darrow's speech given to the Negro Industrial School in 1927 as a near perfect representation of his own perspectives on race relations, which emphasized education and camaraderie while disdaining ruling elites and religion:

> I can't help you, you will have to help yourselves, but I advise always an attitude of defiance toward the white man who calls himself "your friend." How has he manifested this friendship? By hanging and burning you, by making you do his work, and use his back door, refusing to let you enter the best hotels and to use his best coach in the train, and by making you sit in the rear of the street car. The only front place the white man has ever given you is in the battle line. There you can stop the bullets, but when you return home you cannot use the sidewalks, you have to use the road.
>
> What can the colored man do to help himself? I see you pray, but I

don't know why. Your God must be a "white" man, considering the way he treats you. No doubt there will be a Jim Crow law in your heaven when you get there. You can sing—I heard you sing—"Sweet Land of Liberty," but I don't see how you can. I don't sing it because I know it's not true. But you can work and gain a place for yourself if you can do your work better than the white man. You are being recognized and you have some friends who are not afraid to sit at the table with you. I have done so and even drank bootleg liquor with you, and in what better way can friendship be manifested?[78]

While performing double-speak on some racial topics, Crawford eloquently linked race and labor time and time again. In 1932 a predominantly African American sharecropper strike in Tallapoosa County, Alabama, turned violent when police raided a union meeting and killed one man, arrested three dozen others, and released four others to a lynch mob. "It is a war for bread . . . being met with an army of terror," Crawford wrote as he chastised local law enforcement and lambasted sharecropping as modern-day slavery.[79] Such a perspective had been developing in Crawford's writings and public speaking for years. Three years earlier, Crawford was an invited speaker on southern labor and race at the UVA Institute of Public Affairs. In the speech, he opined, "Labor can expect no more than the Negro received from the [Republican] party." Laborers supported Republicans despite this out of an old-time allegiance, much like African Americans voted Republican because of Abraham Lincoln. The problem facing southern workers, white and Black, was that the freedom granted by Republicans was imagined. Slavery, for instance, may have been ended, but freedom hardly replaced it when held in the balance of discrimination, segregation, disenfranchisement, and lynching. It would do all workers good to abandon Republicans, in Crawford's view.[80]

While Crawford's vision of long-term equality and Democratic-voting poor people was readily evident, in the early 1920s, he still blamed many structural problems on African Americans themselves—African Americans in the North "had the ambition to strike out"; those in the South were "lethargic." He wrote on race in 1924 that southern whites deserved more educational and economic opportunities because, in part, it was shameful that African Americans from northern states typically performed better on intellect tests than southern whites. Like segregationists of his generation, Crawford firmly believed that African Americans in his time and place were inferior to their white neighbors. Paradoxically, like many progressives of his generation, he argued that mass educational programs could eventually close the racial divide. This was the progressive racial future envisioned by previous generations of leaders like President Woodrow Wilson, not the views of Crawford's peers in the Black press. Also of note is that Crawford was not particularly interested in racial uplift among white Appalachians except as it applied to the poorest of the poor.[81]

While Crawford's attitudes toward race were hardly unusual for the era, he still deserves criticism for his failure to challenge Virginian white supremacists. Crawford was, after all, a self-proclaimed radical progressive and budding socialist, not a run-of-the-mill Democrat. It is useful to compare his position with that of radical editor Louis Jaffe's attitude toward Virginia's eugenics movement. Jaffe used his newspapers to openly challenge the state's eugenics laws. By the time Crawford printed his first newspaper, eugenicists occupied positions of power within Virginia's prisons, mental health facilities, and state universities. It was simply impossible for an intellectually curious person like Crawford to not encounter the worst of Virginia eugenicists. Yet, he avoided criticizing eugenicists even when given multiple opportunities. Even worse, Crawford himself published several articles in support of eugenicist thinking beyond those favorable to Anglo-Saxon Clubs. For example, in 1933 eugenicists celebrated the publication of *Hollow Folk*, an ethnographic study of multiple supposedly deficient families in the Blue Ridge Mountains. The study's authors recognized the deep poverty in which these families lived but rather than propose systematic reform, they instead concluded their subjects were beyond help. Many families documented in *Hollow Folk* were ultimately removed from their land against their will to make way for Shenandoah National Park, with *Hollow Folk* used as evidence they would never positively contribute to society.[82] Crawford wrote an essay for the *Virginia Quarterly Review* about the community of Piney Ridge just months before the publication of *Hollow Folk* that could have been pasted directly into that eugenics-informed sociological study:

> Probably three or four of them know that their ancestors were a mixed lot: pre-Revolutionary settlers of good blood who were marooned from progressive regions, fugitives from the law in eastern communities, and slackers who evaded service in the War Between the States and found sanctuary in this secluded highland corner wedged between the North and South. But, remote as Piney Ridge is, it knows there was a war with Germans, for the nearest draft board yanked out of the community a dozen of its young men and failed to return several of them. Owing the world nothing, Piney Ridge is at a loss to understand why this sacrifice was necessary.
>
> And the perplexed inhabitants have learned that there is, besides a

county treasurer's office, a county jail-house. But, for the most part, they have lived remote from the world, marrying and intermarrying when wed-lock was necessary, some of them drinking incredible corn liquor, some shooting their way home from blind-tiger or church, and most of them letting their children grow up with equal opportunities with the domestic animals.[83]

This was Bruce Crawford's vision of race and science in the 1920s and 1930s. For as much as he fought the Klan and lynching, he did just as much to pro-mote their pseudo-intellectual cousins in white supremacy. However, for every uneven article on race, Crawford published multiple articles on labor and capitalism displaying a clarity unmatched in his time.

COAL BARONS AND CAPITALISM

At the height of the Great Depression and in the hopeless final months of Herbert Hoover's presidency, Crawford was driving home one day after an unproductive meeting with Wise County officials. The local economy was a mess and administrators feared a total collapse if the county failed to pay its bills. As Crawford drove through Norton, an overflowing coal train pulled out of the depot. Crawford was reminded in this moment of one Appalachian fact—miners ship coal out the mountains, but the revenues from coal sales never return. "What is the future of this county so long as its chief resource is being exploited and hauled away and so little being left to show for it?" specu-lated *Crawford's Weekly* the following week. Everyone in Wise County knew that coal profits were siphoned off to major urban centers like Philadelphia and New York while the county infrastructure collapsed. What nobody knew was how to solve this problem.[84]

Crawford's Weekly was generally recognized as a friend of miners and regu-lar enemy of coal barons. The relationship between coal companies and labor during the 1920s and 1930s was tense and had been so for decades. Coal com-panies controlled southwest Virginia's economy and held a massive popula-tion in a state of oppression. The only means to breaking coal hegemony were either a full political revolution, a highly unlikely possibility given both po-litical parties supported Big Coal, or joining a union to fight for incremental gains. Naturally, Crawford favored revolution but understood union politics stood a better chance of success. Once *Crawford's Weekly* began publishing pro-union articles, coal company owners and their proxies, also known as opera-tors, soured on Bruce Crawford. Coal companies neglected basic infrastructure needs, created a debt peonage system through company scrip, and dominated the legal system. In Crawford's view, operators in particular stood as the enemies of progress; he also believed the high point of coal was in the past and that therefore the existing oppression operated in the interests of an incredibly short-sighted money grab. "What is the future of the coal industry? It is not at all promising unless new uses for coal and its by-products are developed," he wrote. Crawford knew coal was not southwest Virginia's future; he also knew that coal operators would not give up their power quietly.[85]

In southwest Virginia, the coal mining industry had created horrid conditions rivaling those in West Virginia and eastern Kentucky. The state of Virginia rarely, if ever, conducted legally mandated mine inspections. Workers' compensation laws skewed in the company's favor by operating on a sliding scale based on income levels reported by the company. Virtually every coal company cooked their books, so injured coal miners received a pittance of what they were owed. Masses of disabled ex-miners were in this way condemned to a life of poverty. Coal companies also resisted infrastructure projects, especially roads. From the corporate point of view, the necessary rail lines were already in place and any new roads would only allow a captive workforce to escape company control or to ally with their unionizing neighbors. On numerous occasions, if a coal company failed to defeat a road project in the political stage, the company would then purchase the required land and refuse all future offers. Sometimes this involved farmland, further compounding the abuse heaped upon poor Virginians. Virginia lagged in protecting workers through legislation even when compared to Kentucky or West Virginia, two other states hardly known for pro-labor politicians. For Crawford, the situation was urgent as "coal company lawyers" were quite literally writing the Commonwealth's labor laws.[86]

Crawford's first foray into challenging coal operators, in the early 1920s, centered upon road projects in Wise County. A road construction project to connect Norton and Lynch, Kentucky, came under threat in 1922 due to typical political opposition. Crawford, perhaps innocently, interviewed locals and reported that coal operator opposition hampered the project. In response, coal operators responded vociferously that *Crawford's Weekly*'s reporting was inaccurate and that they held no such anti-road position. Crawford, already refusing to back down, shot back in his newspaper with the first of what would be a long volley:

The position [*Crawford's Weekly*] took unlocked an avalanche of criticism in certain quarters, although it was highly approved by the citizens generally. Attorneys and agents for certain coal interests got invisibly busy in an effort to discredit our charges, and one newspaper grabbed up the cudgels in their defense. But Appalachia's live citizens are hard to fool, and a few days ago they published, in the *Independent*, a report of their investigation of the road fight, which report substantiates us on practically every point. Hereafter, when you hear some one [*sic*] calling a newspaper "radical," "mischievous," or "not responsible," give a thought to who he is, how he earns his living, and what interests he is friendly to or associated with.[87]

Challenging coal operators was dangerous, perhaps as much so as targeting the Klan. Coal controlled the local economy, so the newspaper could easily be pressured financially; most companies employed violent groups of enforcers, usually referred to as private police or detectives, who targeted union members to coerce them into capitulation. "Out with the private detectives!" read an editorial in *Crawford's Weekly*. "Not for the good of the country do they work. They cater to a class and engender class struggle. . . . They cause hatred for law rather than respect for it, because they toady to a bunch that seeks to control the law." [88] Most other newspapers published whatever coal companies desired, so anti-union propaganda ran wild. Many people believed private detectives to be protecting local interests and not just coal companies. Crawford though wrote on the truth: "Some [coal companies] are already broke and long have been doomed because of economic trends that have nothing to do with unions . . . their surpluses having been drawn off by absentee owners." Local banks and governments were, in his view, thus stuck holding debts that companies never intended to pay off, as "profits go East" never to be seen again.[89]

Such writings about coal often blended seamlessly into Crawford's long-running campaign against capitalism. Unlike other campaigns, *Crawford's Weekly* essays targeting coal and capitalism never had a true beginning or end, a specific goal or philosophy—just a general aim of helping workers. For a few months, Crawford might target coal, jump from there into tirades against unjust agricultural economics, and then outline how clever socialist legislation might alleviate such problems. For instance, Crawford's reporting often explored new labor struggles throughout the South, wherein former agricultural workers, having turned to New South industry for better pay, were rapidly becoming a new oppressed class. Unionized workers began striking in pre-Depression 1929 in places like Elizabethton and Gastonia, North Carolina, a phenomenon Crawford saw as the beginning of "industrial war" in the South. He likened New South industry as a "Trojan horse," whereby abusive capitalism invaded the South only to create class and race tensions. Other local newspapers, namely the *Pulaski Times*, denounced the unions as the products of

Northern meddlers and insisted the police put them down. Crawford, ever the ally of the working man, accused his own neighboring newspaper peers of committing "mob-it is," drawing an intentional parallel to lynching, in the hopes that shame would awaken their best sensibilities.[90]

The market crash of 1929 set Crawford's writings on capitalism into overdrive. Disparity shone through as the most common theme, as the already thick class lines became even thicker in southwest Virginia. Things were so bad in Wise County that, according to Crawford, two visiting journalists exclaimed, "I can understand why an editor out here would go red, I have never seen such poverty!" and "God, I'd go Bolshevik too if I ran a paper out here. Can't something be done for these people?"[91] While Crawford struggled to identify any specific solutions to society's problems, he had no problems ripping into political leaders. Both major parties advocated hard work and bootstraps to get the economy back on track. Crawford found the concept of bootstraps, especially since it never applied to the "middle-men parasites and the big bankers" who profited off economic crisis in the first place.[92] As Crawford gazed upon Norton in the first few months of the Depression, he saw families suffering and near starvation. Even homeowners experienced an illusionary success with no retirement savings, no education, and no vehicle, just four walls to "finish the night and to clear out from in the morning."[93]

Crawford asked his readers: just who offers help in capitalist system during a depression? Not the local government, for police selectively enforced laws against the poor. "We arrest the lowly wage-earner who lot prohibition was supposed to improve, and wink at the influential citizen who has such liquors as he wants and does pretty much as he chooses," Crawford wrote in the *Outlook and Independent* magazine.[94] The only organizations in Wise County with the immediate ability to help the poor were corporations, and of course they were not interested. Hoover-led capitalists promised charity, but instead austerity ruled in the mountains:

> These chain stores should come across and help out in the relief work. Many of their customers have been among the very people who are now in sore straits. The independent merchants are helping them out in their distress, and many of them doubtless will continue to trade with the chain stores. The chains should help out in this work. They make their profits here in our midst. Those people of the community who trade with them, and yet are called upon to help the distressed, should think about this. It's a matter of fairness and of community conscience. Do the chains have a community conscience? It remains to be seen.[95]

As worker unrest grew in 1929 and 1930, Virginia's Depression-era governors, all Democrats allied with Harry F. Byrd, also pushed anti-labor legislation that would eventually fall under the umbrella of "right to work" laws. Large strikes broke out in the Commonwealth during the Depression's early years, at the Dan River Mills, a major textile plant outside of Danville. Owners increased quotas throughout the 1920s without worker consent, forced workers into company-owned housing, and severely cut wages when the stock market crashed. When owners banned union organizers from mill property in September 1930, approximately four thousand workers went on strike. Beyond a tepid offer for mediation services, government officials clearly favored mill operators, who rejected a union outright. Governor John Garland Pollard ordered hundreds of militiamen to Danville, ostensibly to calm tensions but in practice to break the strikes and defend Dan River Mills property. Workers held out for a few months but ultimately returned to work as a defeated force after four months. "This is justice in New Virginia," Crawford wrote, utterly furious that the governor's office so blatantly opposed workers' rights in such difficult economic times.[96]

"The right to work! We get damn well tired of that hypocrisy," responded Crawford to Governor Pollard's Dan River Mills actions.[97] As of late 1930, the "right to work" was a novel term. Politicians typically used it to opposing pro-workers' rights laws. "Right to work" legislators believed the capitalist theory that open markets and free labor naturally sorted out economic problems, like depressions, and that therefore avoiding the passage of laws that intervene in the market was the fastest way to end the Depression. While capitalist-leaning politicians dominated state politics, the opposite was true at a federal level. The 1935 passage of the National Labor Relations (or Wagner) Act, President Roosevelt's hallmark pro-labor legislation, codified union rights such as closed shops, collective bargaining, and collective strikes, among other protections.[98] The legislation passed within the backdrop of concerted efforts by anti-labor capitalists to develop a coherent "right to work" agenda as a counter to Roosevelt's policies.

In mid-1934, the "right to work" cause was taken up by the *Bristol Herald Courier*, a pro-business newspaper and one of Crawford's bigger local rivals. The Bristol editor called for Virginia to pass laws allowing for union formation so long as the new union rejected "lawless acts"—meaning closed shops—against nonunion workers. The paper's language was carefully worded so a casual reader would the argument to be solidly pro-labor, for instance reading "the right of the workers to work should be upheld at all times by whatever means the responsible public authorities deem necessary. . . . [Nonunion] workers have the same right to work that union workers have to strike." Crawford recognized this tactic for what it was, a clever propaganda effort to reshape labor discourse by using "right to work" phrasing. The goal of the *Herald Courier*, according to Crawford, was to drum up anti-union, pro-company sentiment to drive a wedge between union and nonunion workers. *Crawford's Weekly*'s published response thoroughly trashed the Bristol paper's editor, concluding that "right to work" should instead be named "right to work—but on condition that [the worker] is willing to be a scab, strike-breaker, and a sell-out." [99]

Governor Pollard's suppression of workers in Danville, the breaking of other strikes, and backlash to the Wagner Act led to the spread of the "right to work" movement in Virginia despite Crawford's energetic opposition. In 1937 Crawford took to the offensive. In the pages of *New Masses*, a socialist magazine, he published an essay on the struggles of Virginia and West Virginia labor and how the Commonwealth ignored federal protections. The U.S. Supreme Court narrowly upheld the Wagner Act in April, but Virginia's government opposed it regardless. Crawford again focused on a single instance of injustice, surrounding the vote of rayon workers in Covington, Virginia, to unionize under the Congress of Industrial Organizations (CIO). The Industrial Rayon Corporation, in open defiance of the Wagner Act, declared that any communication between union and nonunion members constituted "coercion," even if it occurred away from work. Union workers voted to strike and began protesting on March 29. The strike lasted over three months but ended much like the Dan River strike. Governor George C. Peery leveraged anti-lynching laws, of all things, to order state police into Covington to "keep the peace." In the end, officers escorted about fifty nonunion workers into the rayon plant, effectively destroying the unionization movement. In announcing the police order, Governor Perry preached "right to work" gospel, stating, "Strikes are legal, but any man who wishes to return to work certainly has the privilege and right." With the Commonwealth's actions in both Danville and Covington, it was clear "right to work" had become entrenched in Virginia. [100]

Strikes and pending legislation occupied many of Crawford's writings in the early Depression years, but if there was no news on that front, he often wrote about the broader topics of capitalism and poverty. Particularly offensive to Crawford was how conservative writers typically blamed poor people for their own poverty, often accusing them of being wasteful, lazy, or dumb and thus responsible for their plight. "I boil every time I see a freak item in the papers to the effect that a beggar was found buying ice cream or a drink of whiskey or taking a sight-seeing tour," he wrote of nearby conservative papers. "These exceptional cases are told and retold by sanctimonious folk who like to look down on people." Big Money leaders, Crawford came to realize, would never admit fault in the Depression; nor would they express empathy. The Depression provided Crawford with proof of what he had long believed to be true—the "lazy poor" were a myth. People were poor because of capitalist inequality and oppression.[101]

Capitalism's impact upon daily life in Norton was felt most in access, or lack thereof, of two basic elements of life, specifically electricity and water. During the 1920s and 1930s, debate raged as to whether or not electricity and water should be protected by government as public-owned utilities. Corporations in Virginia generally opposed public utility plans, led by the Old Dominion Power Company (ODP), a corporation built on the privatization of electricity and water throughout southwest Virginia.[102] ODP lobbied state legislators while also, starting in late 1931, mounting a media campaign to undermine confidence in Norton's public water works. According to Crawford, ODP water meter readers lied to Norton customers that their bills were much higher under public water than they would be with ODP. Angered, Crawford called his readers to action lest water become another extractive Appalachian industry: "Every citizen should resent this attempt of the power company to undermine public confidence in his own water business." *Crawford's Weekly* later cited Chapel Hill, North Carolina, as an example of privatization gone wrong. In that case, a private water company cut water to poor families for failure to pay bills, so these families drew water from unclean streams and rivers. Predictably, Chapel Hill residents suffered through a typhoid outbreak. This was "typical of a society that thinks it can save itself by impoverishing its workers," read *Crawford's Weekly*. Crawford's anti-ODP campaign had some effect apparently, as ODP never overtook Norton's water supply. Even after ODP left town, Crawford continued writing about other industries he believed should be made public, namely farms and coal mines, though these campaigns were largely ignored except by some of Crawford's conservative newspaper rivals.[103]

By about 1933 Crawford's anti-capitalist campaigns coalesced into something resembling a philosophy: "The government is really the instrument of capitalism to control labor."[104] He called on readers to question government at all levels, to assert their rights as workers, and monitor corporate greed. Key to Crawford's focus on government was a call for better education. "It has been said that Americans are the most gullible and long-suffering people in the world," he wrote. "We haven't really known of anything better than an economic system of special privilege and jungle-like competition. With no conception of a more intelligent society, no knowledge of attaining it, we are denied the benefit of contrast."[105] Americans—and especially southwest

Virginians—needed to educate themselves about the world beyond America's borders. For example, if they understood European trade unionism, this would help them achieve better conditions in Appalachian coal mines. However, Crawford also presented a caveat to his argument. Barring a true revolution, either involving violence or mass education, the existing system would remain in place indefinitely.

Crawford never decided which was preferable in his view, education or revolution, but he knew capitalism had to go. "There are no reforms that will save capitalism," Crawford wrote in 1933, adding that "we need revolutionary changes—a clean sweep—and not mere reforms. All these reforms are mere branches grafted on a tree that is hollow and dying in the truck. We need a new tree." [106] He took issue with the biggest figures of corporate capitalism like Andrew Carnegie and Henry Ford and corporate descendants of nineteenth-century magnates like J. P. Morgan, Jay Gould, and Cornelius Vanderbilt. "Whose prosperity and whose progress?" asked Crawford. Why does society follow titans of industry to the ends of the earth with their "comment on anything from nutmeg to fiddles considered oracular"?[107] In early 1931 conservative editor Merle Thorpe claimed in a Roanoke speech that the ongoing economic depression was "a state of mind" and people should just work harder. If this was the capitalist response to depression, then Crawford asked, "Where is the end of this downward trend? . . . Always before we have said that human nature is against socialism; now it is going to be against capitalism. And for the same immemorial reason—survival." [108]

African American and liberal newspapers often republished Crawford's writings during these years while conservatives typically ignored him unless he presented a direct challenge. Powell Chapman, the *Roanoke Times* editor, regularly poured on the criticism. Typically, Chapman resorted to personal attacks, calling Crawford a "coward" and labeling him a paranoid, irrational doomsayer. According to Chapman, the Great Depression was but a small blip in American progress and anyone to doubt the American system was a borderline traitor. Crawford pushed right back, arguing that Chapman dozed while society crumbled. "Maybe the [*Roanoke*] *Times* is too dead asleep to even have a nightmare," Crawford wrote. "Better a saving pessimism than ostrich optimism or this jabbering in unknown tongues to conjure back prosperity." [109] A year later, Crawford was even more fired up, referring to the *Roanoke Times* as "sophomoric" and possessing "intellectual adolescence." This type of feuding continued throughout Crawford's entire newspaper career but never developed into anything more than editorial slap fights.[110]

By the end of the 1920s, Crawford's political philosophy had significantly evolved but was no closer to solidifying. Even as his views on capitalism hardened by about 1933, he was no closer to outlining an anti-capitalist or pro-socialist program to his readership. He had begun the 1920s as a bright young editor ready to take on challenges in his hometown. Whether it was against the Klan, lynching, disenfranchisement, or prisons, self-contained campaigns represented a reliable, though potentially dangerous, way to sell newspapers. Crawford's sojourn into writing supporting Anglo-Saxonism demonstrated a mind still seeking truth. Crawford valued logic, science, and free speech, but he was also young and untrained. The implications and wide effects of big ideas often eluded Crawford in his earlier years, especially when the topic was white supremacy and eugenics. Still, his interests at this time were more pragmatic than anything else. Crawford wrote on October 19, 1929, just five days before the market crash, that "the question down South is not whether strikers or police are guilty of violence and murder, nor whether communism, atheism, and free love imperil the state, but whether wages and living conditions are in line with the state's much trumpeted progress." [111] Philosophy could wait—an economic war raged throughout not just Norton, Wise County, or southwest Virginia, but the entire American South. The young Bruce Crawford believed economic oppression manifested primarily in coal mining areas. By 1930 he saw oppression everywhere and leaned heavily into anti-capitalism. As Crawford wrote, he continued to read, think, talk, and correspond with more experienced writers. These experiences pushed him slowly toward socialism and Communism, but it would take a dramatic, life-changing event for him to make the leap from entrepreneurial newspaperman to Communist activist.

CHAPTER 2

GETTING SHOT IN HARLAN COUNTY

In the early twentieth century, few writers commanded fame of the magnitude attained by Theodore Dreiser. A college dropout, Dreiser worked as a journalist in Chicago before becoming a prolific writer of both popular fiction and nonfiction, including the renowned works *Sister Carrie* and *An American Tragedy*. He was also one of Crawford's closest friends and colleagues during the 1930s, with the pair having been drawn together by similar backgrounds and politics. Crawford once interviewed Dreiser for the magazine *Real America*, in which he described the older writer as "an individualist, but an individualist in the highest sense. . . . Yes, he is a dinosaur of his period, or a literary mastodon whose bones will be something for coming generations to marvel at."[1] After such sly praise, Crawford—in a method so true to his developing brand—made certain his political point was driven home in a final description of Dreiser's disposition:

> Dreiser, away from the jam and noise of Manhattan, was basking in this spring day with dreamy contemplation. Was he thinking, like the caged lion, of a lost glory? Or was he envisioning a society in which individualism would be, not for a parasitic few as under capitalism, but for all who worked and added to the abundance and quality of living?[2]

Anyone reading *Crawford's Weekly* in 1935 would have plainly recognized that Crawford had become an open socialist and Communist after years of flirtation. Crawford's embrace of Marxism was no sudden transformation but a gradual process spanning a little under a decade. From 1928 to 1931, Crawford regularly sought news beyond Wise County that would lay bare the contradictions inherent in America's capitalist system. He also began writing for other newspaper and magazines, some of which had a national audience. Respected academics started to invite Crawford to conferences and to write articles about politics, economics, and industry. Through these ventures, Crawford met new people and received adulation that he personally desired. Crawford's ego grew so much that *Crawford's Weekly* mused its editor was in the process of receiving a metaphorical public intellectual's baton from someone like Louis Jaffe, writer-scholar H. L. Mencken, or University of Virginia President Edwin Alderman. Those three thinkers would be great mentors, but Crawford's greatest admiration was reserved for his friend Dreiser and his colleague and neighbor, another famous fiction writer and activist, Sherwood Anderson.[3] Popular acclaim for Dreiser and Anderson came from their writing, of course, but also their political activism. Both dedicated significant portions of their lives to championing the rights of the oppressed, especially workers and African Americans in the South. They were also avowed socialists, though not quite Marxists, Communists, or as radical as critics accused.

Between 1928 and 1935, articles appeared in *Crawford's Weekly* that were far more radical than in previous years. Nearly all were written by Crawford and represented his desire to join the ranks of Dreiser and Anderson as America's (or at least southwest Virginia's) next great public intellectual. Articles regularly appeared in *Crawford's Weekly* to rationalize Crawford's shift to the political left, with many packaging radicalism, revolution, and socialism into simplistic, sometimes folksy terms. One such example appeared as a brief editorial titled "Parable of the Potatoes":

> Just now our colleges are grinding out new candidates for the non-producing upperclass [sic] of society, notwithstanding, offices are full up, and pulpits are being consolidated. The top is getting too heavy, too rich at the expense of the bottom, and the surplus is beginning to decay.
>
> Which recalls a little personal experience in our back lot. We planted a few rows of potatoes. The ground was very rich. And how those potatoes grew. The tops flourished. They consumed all the available carbon, hydrogen, oxygen, or whatever it is potatoes must have. We were proud of them, for they were rank and rich and good to see.
>
> Thinking that such prosperity should be to some purpose, we dug into the hills. Well, we didn't find any spuds to speak of. Just starved, runty things that never had a chance. Perhaps it was the wrong time of the moon, or something.

The wife and I went Bolshevik and turned those superfluous tops under. For fertilizer. And the next year we had fine potatoes. That may not be much of a parable, but it seems to us that what is needed in this country is a great turning under of the parasitic and decaying top. For fertilizer. And it is about the right time of the moon.[4]

Crawford published "Parable of the Potatoes" in May 1931; two months later, a Harlan County police officer shot him. To understand this transformation—from folksy Communist writing in Norton to being physically harmed and de facto banned from the entire Commonwealth of Kentucky—it is helpful to trace Crawford's move away from day-to-day local reporting into broader forms of activist writing typically labeled as being on the political left.

Throughout most of the 1920s, Crawford struggled to define his own politics publicly, though detractors and allies alike would have probably labeled him a leftist radical. During the 1920s, the Left was in shambles nationally, with no clear platform. Progressives lost the White House in 1920. The subsequent three conservative presidencies and anti-Communist backlash to the Bolshevik Revolution in Russia effectively killed progressivism as a national political movement. Left-leaning politicians responded in a myriad ways. Most progressives who stuck with Democrats shifted to a more moderate political stance, having been placated with labor rights victories during the Woodrow Wilson presidency, or openly supported less "socialist" progressive policies such as conservation, public electrification projects, and providing economic relief to small farmers. The latter of these paths could best be represented by Robert M. La Follette, whose failed 1924 presidential campaign as the Progressive Party nominee earned him 16.6 percent of the popular vote and thirteen electoral votes. La Follette died the following year, but his progressive political mantle was taken up by his son, Robert M. La Follette Jr. Broadly speaking, these progressives would bide their time until it was safe to emerge, so to speak, when the Great Depression clearly signaled that conservative austerity and charity were not the answer.

A smaller set of progressives, such as Dreiser, writer-editor Max Eastman, and Crawford, maintained their faith in Communism, socialism, or some other radical pro-worker position. Both the Communist and Socialist Parties in the United States were hampered by internal squabbling, so many leftists focused their efforts locally or regionally instead, knowing that national political victory was highly unlikely. They favored direct action, such as providing support to striking workers or fighting against racial injustice throughout the South. These writers maintained that capitalism was, at its core, a flawed and immoral system that had led much of the nation into economic ruin. Crawford himself focused on the plight of southwest Virginian workers, namely their exploited and almost hopeless status. To Crawford, the primary remedy was radical change, though he never seemed to agree even with himself just what that change may look like.

Crawford himself identified that his first embrace of left-wing radical politics came as a result of a trip to Elizabethton, Tennessee, to report on striking rayon workers in April 1929. When Crawford arrived in Elizabethton, he realized that all the strikers were women, many standing on the picket line with their young children. Crawford stayed in Elizabethton for a few days among the working women, perhaps the farthest he had yet traveled for a story. He returned to Norton invigorated, having witnessed what he called the beginnings of an "industrial war." [5] Crawford viewed the unrest both in Elizabethton and in his hometown as connected to a broader labor movement that was national or even international in scope. His articles thus placed coal miners, coal operator oppression, and company towns within the broader political landscape. No more would Crawford spend his days reporting on every small-town meeting; instead, he would focus on everyday reporting that connected, for instance, a handful of striking Virginians to a global socialist movement, or so hoped an optimistic Crawford. Capitalism was the ill that oppressed all, with some form of socialism being the best cure. Yet, Crawford's goal by the summer of 1929 was much less egalitarian—he wanted to become a major player in national political discourse on the subject of labor, capitalism, socialism, and politics. This ambition led Crawford briefly into academia and, more specifically, the University of Virginia (UVA), as he honed this new voice. *Crawford's Weekly* still hit the presses weekly, but the allure of academia's ivory tower was calling.

TO THE UNIVERSITY OF VIRGINIA

In August 1929 Crawford participated as an invited speaker in the third annual meeting of the Institute of Public Affairs (IPA), a multidisciplinary academic conference hosted by UVA and focused on solving society's many problems. UVA president Edwin Alderman commissioned the IPA as a special organization within the university "to advance the popular understanding of current public questions . . . particularly the domestic problems of the United States and to have them discussed in a broad and competent fashion by men charged with the task of public administration and by those who are actively engaged in public affairs." [6] Alderman hoped the IPA would be another step toward professionalizing UVA as a modern, nationally important university. In 1929 experts throughout the nation received invitations to present their thoughts on rural America at the two-week event. Each day began with round table discussions, a lunch social, and concluded with a series of invited individual addresses in the evening. Featured speakers included Sherwood Anderson, Louis Jaffe, Virginia state senator Carter Glass, Maryland governor Albert Ritchie, and numerous other professors, lawyers, judges, preachers, and business leaders. For Crawford, who was barely thirty years old and still working as a small-town editor, to even receive an invitation, much less an offer to speak, must have been a thrilling proposition. He even doubted the invitation at first, initially responding that "as a speaker I have always been a dud" and suggesting he only speak for five minutes lest other, more famous speakers be deprived of their time.[7]

Crawford's IPA open forum address was one of the first at the event and titled simply "Labor Situation in the South." Crawford's presentation lacked a bit of the zip typical of his newspaper editorials—he made no mention of tearing down coal barons—yet it was one of the furthest to the left politically of the addresses heard at the IPA that year. After citing the dire situation of workers throughout the South, Crawford condemned capitalist practices that tore apart the social fabric of coal towns all while defending actions of labor unions:

We hear much about "agitators" and outside labor organizers, as if they were as noxious as carpet-baggers. We are told that labor leaders bleed the workers, first putting radical ideas in their heads and causing them to quit good jobs and distress prosperous communities. This no doubt is sometimes true. But we hear little about company labor agents sent into communities to lure workers to other fields, where wages, however good they may at first appear, are in the final analysis inadequate compared to the boosted price level. We hear little about corporation attorneys and land agents who go as forerunners into a new territory and prepare the way for its exploitation and the economic enslavement of its people. Those who cry "agitators" are generally the real exploiters.

Crawford's final argument was that southern workers were exploited by the combined force of corporate capitalists and moderate political parties seeking to stay in office instead of working toward a better society. While Crawford largely stuck to a straightforward argument, a few of his concluding statements drew from his newspaper's typical sarcasm. On southern labor conditions, Crawford concluded that things had to improve soon because "the situation in itself is intolerable. It cannot last."[8]

An important observation from Crawford's IPA talk is that when granted his first major opportunity to speak publicly to a range of important, intelligent people, he took a decidedly less radical tone than was typical of *Crawford's Weekly*. Crawford never explained why he dialed back his radicalism for the UVA setting, but two factors likely contributed more than any other. First, Crawford knew how to read his audience and adjust his approach as necessary. The IPA comprised obviously not just radical writers or Wise County coal miners; the event brought together a banquet hall full of economically conservative white men, most of whom were business owners or academics. Through employing a balanced, objective tone, Crawford hoped to impress them that labor movements were simply the result of a logical choice made by individuals acting in their best interests. Within this framework, labor's interests could be modified to include business owners too, so long as southern workers received a wage increase to bring their livelihoods in line with those of their northern counterparts. How Crawford's speech was received broadly will never be known; at the very least, however, he earned Sherwood Anderson's respect. Anderson, a resident of Marion, Virginia, not far from Norton, wrote Crawford a few weeks later inviting him to visit any time, an offer Crawford accepted several times over the next decade.[9]

The second and most important revelation from Crawford's IPA speech was that he believed the only way to engender major, systemic change in America was through the two-party democratic system. Despite his eventual radicalism and anti-capitalism, Crawford was never willing to tear down democracy, no matter how flawed it may have been, but instead demanded that workers and politicians alike awaken to political realities. To politicians, Crawford said that if both Democrats and Republicans opposed labor unions, they risked the emergence of an American Bolshevik revolution. As for workers, Crawford drew a parallel between labor rights and the rights of African Americans. Both groups voted mostly Republican in the late 1920s out of a decades-long loyalty based on that party's previous support of their interests, support that was now generally nonexistent. Crawford articulated as much at UVA: "The Republican party gave the Negro a mythical freedom, as a by-product of an economic struggle that ended in bloodshed, and has since used him to stuff ballot boxes, and it has given the white laborer a mythical economic freedom in return for his vote for the tariff." Briefly showing his radical hand, Crawford continued, "Both the Negro and the white working man have gained what they have through organization—in spite of the party rather than because of it." Such a statement must have resonated with any politically minded listener no matter their partisan affiliation, as Crawford suggested that the combined strength of labor and African American organizations could shift political allegiances and power to Democrats within a few years.[10]

Regardless of his intent, many Virginia newspapers reported that Crawford's IPA speech delivered a radical analysis of labor conditions in the South. Virginius Dabney of the *Richmond Times-Dispatch*, one of the most powerful voices in the state, wrote that in "condemning Southern labor practices as archaic, inhumane and unjust, Bruce Crawford . . . entered into a denunciation of government protection of industry and oppression of labor in a speech today." Dabney highlighted Crawford's criticism of Republicans for roadblocking workers' rights but placed it in the context of Crawford's known support of striking workers and disdain for "business attitude." Less than a month later, IPA organizers wrote Crawford for input on next year's session and encouraged him to participate again. It's not clear why Crawford did not speak at subsequence IPA events, but this single event garnered him attention beyond academia. Perhaps most important to him, a union—the United Textile Workers of America—reprinted Crawford's speech in their official publication. He got what he wanted in terms of the respect of his peers, statewide attention for his political ideas, and a platform to agitate for progressive electoral politics. Midway through 1929, it looked like Crawford was well on his way to joining Virginia editors like Dabney and Louis Jaffe in influencing state politics.[11]

GETTING SHOT

Living and working conditions for coal miners in late 1920s Appalachia were already poor and threatened to deteriorate further. A faltering coal industry beset by declining national demand, the opening of new coal fields in the West, and the failure of Appalachian companies to invest in new mining technologies meant sharply reduced profit margins. Rather than proactively adapting to the new fossil fuel economy, coal companies lazily passed on their economic hardships to coal miners and their families. Appalachian miners in 1930 received wages that only allowed for a subsistent living, if even that. A further problem was that new mining technologies led to more automation in coal mines for those companies willing to make such an investment. Automation meant the replacement of labor-heavy mining jobs with credentialed workers like engineers, mechanics, and other professionals requiring extensive training largely unavailable to poor miners. Historian Ron Eller wrote of the Appalachian mining in 1930 that "unemployment, destitution, and despair stalked the coal fields," as smaller operations closed and larger coal operators implemented austerity measures. Staring poverty in the face, union-affiliated miners organized and led strikes as they—not the operators—bore the brunt of coal's economic collapse.[12]

Striking miners in Harlan County, Kentucky, featured as the biggest news item in *Crawford's Weekly* during the spring of 1931. Throughout 1930 had written bleak stories about the Depression's effect upon coal country. Most coal communities in Appalachia suffered, and Harlan coal miners lived in some of the worst conditions of all. During the winter of 1930–31, Harlan coal operators unilaterally cut wages by 10 percent for all workers. Miners represented by United Mine Workers (UMW) went on strike, and the company initiated harshly enforced mass evictions from company-owned housing during the year's coldest months. With roughly 85 percent of Harlan County miners out of work, homeless men and their families congregated near what few non-company-owned spaces existed, primarily in the town of Evarts, when not on the picket lines. Coal companies hired private guards, all of whom were deputized by Sheriff J. H. Blair, supposedly to protect company property but in reality to act as strongmen hell-bent on breaking the strike through intimidation, harassment, and violence. The uneasy peace broke on May 5 in Evarts when miners and private guards exchanged gunfire. When the violence calmed, three coal company guards and one miner lay dead in the streets. Kentucky governor Flem Sampson responded by ordering National Guard units to Harlan County. The UMW, fearing government violence, ordered miners back to work with no concessions gained from their months-long strike. Local UMW members were furious. Harlan County's UMW cratered as miners dropped their membership in favor of the National Miners' Union (NMU), a much smaller, Communist organization, in part because the NMU sponsored soup kitchens and promised renewed direct action.

Crawford first traveled to Harlan in April 1931 and published a lengthy article on the strike the following month that clearly showed his growing radicalism. This essay, titled "Harlan: A Study in Futility?," carried a theme of hopelessness from all sides. Miners deserved to be supported, but union-driven economic gains were largely impossible from Crawford's point of view. The economics of the coal industry just could not support workers any longer, not to mention that coal companies received full backing from state courts. The Kentucky government, through its heavy-handed National Guard response, prevented mass violence (as was seen a decade earlier with the Battle of Blair Mountain in southern West Virginia) but also worsened Kentucky miners' lives by enforcing antiworker court injunctions. Coal companies legally evicted miners and filed suit against them on trumped up charges, such as trespassing in their own homes, but this only angered local communities and scared off potential nonunion replacement labor. From every viewpoint, the Harlan situation was an exercise in futility—all sides were bound to lose. The only hope in Harlan, according to Crawford, could be found in aggressive union militancy and tactics, including the willingness to accept bloodshed. Harlan miners, absent any power through democracy or protest, could only challenge the system through violent martyrdom:

> I am anxious to see widespread unionization as a part of a clean-sweep program of socialization. . . . I am for revolutionary change, brought about peaceably if possible. There should be a general staff composed of insidious men who could be as lawless as the State. For whatever the workers do, which is effective, is ruled as lawless anyway. In short, I'm for revolution. You can't wait on universal enlightenment and democracy.
>
> With democracy a long way off, there may be the next best thing—seizure of power by the producers, after their eyes have been opened to the ghastly scheme that enslaves them. The only alternatives are Fascism and world war. The only good thing that can come out of Harlan is a scandal, red with sacrificial blood, which will stir workers everywhere to a sacred madness that will light their way out of the darkness of confusion and exploitation.[13]

Crawford's writings got the attention of Harlan's coal elite by the middle of 1931. Other newspaper editors going into Harlan County that year generally catered to coal companies. These writers typically entered the county under company protection, escorted by private guards, and wrote stories depicting miners as a bunch of violent hillbillies. In contrast, during May and June, Crawford wrote more about Harlan as a company town, focusing on local wages, costs at the company store, and justifications given for firing union miners. *Crawford's Weekly* also published a dispatch by Tess Huff, the son of a miner's lawyer, accusing Sheriff J. H. Blair of beating striking miners. In response, Sheriff Blair traveled to Norton and threatened Crawford with a libel lawsuit. Not concerned by a frivolous lawsuit in the least, Crawford made two promises to Blair—his Harlan stories would include printed corrections if errors were discovered and *Crawford's Weekly* would publish Sheriff Blair's retorts to Huff. No reporting errors were ever discovered, Blair never published in any Crawford newspaper, and Blair never filed a lawsuit. Seven years earlier Crawford had praised Blair specifically for his policing in Harland, indicating that the two had no long-standing grudge. Most likely, Blair was a coal company pawn doing the operators' dirty work.[14]

Not one to drop a story so easily, Crawford traveled to Harlan County again in late July to report on the ongoing violence and Communist union organizing. He also hoped to meet with Tess Huff. Crawford, along with *Crawford's Weekly* employee and "hardware merchant" E. S. Fraley, arrived in town on July 27. The pair first met with the Reverend Allen Keady, a Christian pastor fresh out of jail on charges of providing relief for jobless miners, and other religious leaders. Within minutes of Crawford entering Keady's home, someone reported to Sheriff Blair that *Crawford's Weekly* was in town. Sheriff's deputies followed Crawford and Fraley around the county for the rest of the day. In an effort to avoid Blair's surveillance, the pair ditched their vehicle in a closed garage before hurriedly walking across a foot-bridge to Huff's home in Evarts. After they chatted for an hour, some of Huff's Harlan friends arrived to warn everyone not to leave the home that night, as unknown men with guns, possibly deputies or coal company–funded strongmen, had positioned themselves above the bridge. Crawford, Fraley, and Huff took the advice. The trio hunkered down for the night in the hopes that all would be clear in the morning.[15]

It is best to allow Crawford's own written account of what happened next stand on its own. Details would be questioned by political opponents, but one fact was undeniable—someone shot Crawford in the leg:

The bridge is high over the river and exposes one up there clearly against the sky. The next morning about nine o'clock, Fraley and I were coming across the bridge and we heard two shots, but didn't pay any attention because a car had been running up and down the railroad and some boys had put some torpedoes on the track, but I felt the third shot at the same time I heard it. I stopped and looked at my white sock and saw blood stains. It felt like a barrel-hoop or something had flipped up and hit me on the shin, and I called to Fraley and said that I was shot and he turned to come back, and the fourth shot splintered up the boards between us, and we realized then that we were targets and we looked at each other and started to run. We were about 200 feet from the end of the bridge on the Harlan side. The shooting seemed to come from back that way on Huff's side of the river, but it turned out that it came from the side we were running toward and it was the echoes from the other side that made up think the shots were coming from there. There must have been seven or eight more shots fired, and we ran over the end of the bridge into a resident section and people were all along the street, we passed two or three men at the end of the bridge who seemed to be cool and unconcerned about the noise, but people were scattered around on the other side of the river and there was a good deal of excitement there. I didn't know who these men were, but we went to town and hunted out a sympathetic doctor [Dr. Harry Linden] and had my leg swabbed and dressed, and we went around to the front of the courthouse and saw Sheriff Blair looking out.[16]

A brief Harlan police investigation, unsurprisingly, found bullet holes in the bridge and casings about four hundred yards away but failed to identify a shooter. Investigating officers then forcefully suggested that Crawford and Fraley leave town, preferably via bus or train as their car was likely now a target. Disregarding the advice, the pair milled around Harlan a few more hours before safely driving home to Norton. In this moment, what angered Crawford most was not the bullet that pierced his leg but the fact that "neither Sheriff Blair nor Commonwealth Attorney [W. A.] Brock made any effort to speak to [Crawford] or investigate the shooting," despite Crawford intentionally loitering near the Harlan courthouse "in plain view of the sheriff." A further outrage was that nobody identified the shooter even though Crawford recalled a dozen Evarts residents witnessing the shooting.[17] While Sheriff Blair and a few coal company owners denied any involvement, nobody countered Crawford's published version of events. However, Blair and his allies used the event to take digs at Crawford's integrity and engage in a little red-baiting. An oft-repeated rumor driven by the sheriff was that Crawford was in Evarts for a Communist meeting at Huff's home and that "Communist literature was found" in the area.[18]

Crawford took well to his newfound fame of being shot by, from his perspective, a corrupt sheriff—he loved attention after all—but he also reminded his readers that Harlan County miners suffered far more than he. Miners would continue to suffer if coal companies continued their reign of terror in the Kentucky mountains. Over the next few weeks, Crawford leveraged his wound to grow his celebrity and continue his campaign against the corruption in Harlan. "The first bullet-hole is a luxury if you get it in the right place," he wrote, essentially confirming newfound celebrity. Some viewed him as a somewhat new pro-labor journalist, but most of his neighbors simply wanted to know "how it feels to be shot."[19]

Other newspapers reported on Crawford's injury and responded with reports and editorials of their own over the following weeks. The *Tidewater News*, *Radford News-Journal*, *Central Virginian*, and *Gloucester Gazette* each published editorials admonishing the Harlan coal operators, criticizing Kentucky officials for red-baiting, and praising Crawford's brave professionalism in reporting the news. Exemplifying these editorials was Louis Jaffe's essay praising Crawford for "bringing to light the essential facts and has a bullet-hole in his ankle as a souvenir of his efforts." Jaffe's essay continued:

> One slug punctured his foot. It might just as easily puncture his heart. It did not puncture his spirit. The ugly facts about the Harlan coal war are still appearing in *Crawford's Weekly*, while many larger Kentucky newspapers preserve a discreet silence.
>
> We need Bruce Crawfords in these days of industrial travail more than ever. Among Virginia editors, he is king of a gallant Don Quixote, breaking perilous lances in duels that are sometimes, strictly speaking, no concern of his, always intransigently on the side of the underdog, the ill-used, the exploited, and the oppressed. In the prevailing fat-cat American press of the Hoover-prosperity era these knights errant willing to take chances for human rights are few in number. May their tribe increase.[20]

Even though Jaffe called upon others to follow Crawford's lead, very few journalists traveled the dangerous road to Harlan County or other centers of coal town violence. Where was the story to go from here, with no support? Crawford could not return to Harlan County on his own or even with a small entourage—doing so would be fatal. Eastern Kentucky newspapermen were hostile to Crawford; both the UMW and NWU declined in membership and threatened to fold in Harlan; and political elections in Harlan County were absolutely not free and fair. All of these factors together meant there were few journalists, union leaders, or politicians who could have protected Crawford had he chosen to return. And so, instead of going at it alone, Crawford turned to his new friends in academia. His brief trip to UVA for the IPA conference inserted him into a new community centered at the intersection of writing, intellectualism, and activism. It was in this world that Crawford found his solution to fighting corruption in Harlan County.

DREISER COMMITTEE

Theodore Dreiser called on Crawford shortly after the Harlan shooting. Other than a scar on his leg, the biggest personal outcome of Crawford's Harlan reporting came when Dreiser invited him to take part in the National Committee for the Defense of Political Prisoners (NCDPP), better known as the Dreiser Committee. The NCDPP was a Communist organization founded to protect workers, especially those on strike, from violence, oppression, and suppression of their right to free speech. Dreiser's newfound affinity for socialism, which emerged in the late 1920s after his visit to the Soviet Union, greatly impacted the NCDPP. Three months spent in Soviet Russia—all at the Russian government's expense—led to Dreiser's belief that America was destined either for socialism or abject ruin. Upon returning to the United States, Dreiser dedicated himself to working-class causes and expended personal wealth on NCDPP actions in support of the working class and African Americans in the South.[21]

NCDPP administration was partially handled by the International Labor Defense (ILD), a Communist legal advocacy organization for victims of class warfare, especially African Americans, political prisoners, and oppressed workers. Dreiser was involved with both organizations in the early 1930s. ILD leaders invited Dreiser to lead the NCDPP as "a sort of intellectuals' auxiliary." As head of the committee, Dreiser provided an arena for theorists and writers, according to Dreiser biographer Richard Lingeman, work that grew increasingly important to socialist thinkers as fascist regimes came to power in Europe. Mussolini's move toward fascist governance, the rise of Adolf Hitler and the Nazi party, and increased authoritarianism in both the United States and United Kingdom greatly worried Dreiser and his NCDPP colleagues. In their view, the NCDPP could, in theory, provide philosophical and activist support so that actual ammunition would not be necessary in fighting fascism. The NCDPP's work under Dreiser developed into far more than stuffy academics debating socialist theory. Dreiser took the committee's show on the road, so to speak, to raise awareness and strike at the heart of American oppressive forces, which were in his mind represented by racists and greedy capitalists throughout the South.[22] Just before Crawford got shot in Harlan, Dreiser took his committee to Scottsboro, Alabama.

The Dreiser Committee's first major action was in support of nine young African American men in Alabama—nicknamed the Scottsboro boys—accused of raping two white women. The Scottsboro boys were innocent, yet trials overseen by racist judges and decided by racist jury members (or "race-hating white men" as Crawford put it) resulted in convictions and death sentences. Dreiser and celebrity author John Dos Passos led a team of socialist writers and labor leaders in publishing dozens of newspaper and magazine articles raising awareness of the injustice. The goal was to awaken the sympathies of white urban liberals who would cast a judgmental eye upon Alabama justice, thus forcing new trials and ultimately acquittal. Crawford, not on the Dreiser Committee yet, wrote several pieces along these lines in *Crawford's Weekly*, leading to praise of both from Black newspapers for their "bitter protest" against the Alabama injustices.[23]

Over the next few months, the National Association for the Advancement

of Colored People (NAACP) and ILD viciously debated Scottsboro legal strategy. Mistrust and deep disagreements grew, which certainly was not helped
when both Dreiser and Dos Passos published articles criticizing the NAACP
for inaction. In actuality, NAACP legal counsel Walter White had been working back channels for months developing a sound case. White, even after he
no longer served on the defense, told *Harper's Weekly* that the Communist
ILD played a minor role compared to the NAACP. Meanwhile, legal appeals
drafted by ILD-funded lawyers wound through the judiciary. Federal courts
overturned several Scottsboro guilty convictions throughout 1932, including
the ultimate Supreme Court case *Powell v. Alabama*, in which justices reversed
all nine Scottsboro convictions. As Dreiser was wont to do in his high-speed
activist life, he took off for another project well before the Supreme Court filed
its decision (though not until he was confident the Scottsboro boys would be
freed). Dreiser spent a few days near Pittsburgh interviewing striking miners,
visiting picket lines, and speaking with local officials. Within a matter of weeks
though, the ILD made a direct request to Dreiser—re-form the committee and
take them into the Harlan County coal fields. They asked him to file a report as
soon as possible, because conditions in Harlan County were quite possibly the
worst in the country.[24]

Dreiser's Harlan mission was to evaluate working conditions much as he
had just done in Pittsburgh and, more importantly, investigate rumors that
the police threw miners and their families out of their homes and sometimes
into jail with no charges. On-the-ground reporters, mainly Bruce Crawford
and Communist organizer Boris Israel, contradicted coal companies, police,
and company-allied media claims that striking miners had turned violent and
committed a host of crimes. Crawford and Israel both described dynamited
soup kitchens, murdered community leaders, and police shootings. Peaceful
mediators, such as clergymen, were useless in resolving the conflict, many finding themselves jailed simply for offering food or lodging to homeless miners
and their families. With no independent newspapers in Harlan County, the
only information came from sources bought and paid for by coal companies
or from radicals who had their heads cracked and legs shot by Harlan police.
Dreiser spent a large amount of money on the committee's Harlan trip, hoping
to pierce the fog of class warfare and get the real story out.

Harlan posed several new challenges to the Dreiser Committee, not least
of which was the total lack of allies in the area and apparent disinterest in coal
country by America's progressive Democrats. Scottsboro was largely a fight
for the lives of nine Black men and judicial reform for African Americans in
the South. In Harlan, the desired outcome was not so clear. The conflict was

also clearly marked by the threat of violence, anti-Communist sentiment, and the wealth of coal companies. Dreiser recognized that a committee of outsider writers and academics much like himself could be received poorly by miners themselves, so he invited a range of distinguished leaders who, despite their outsider status, carried a national reputation. Among the invited were Senators Robert La Follette and George Norris, Harvard Law School professor and future U.S. Supreme Court justice Felix Frankfurter, president of the Baltimore & Ohio Railroad Daniel Willard, and other writers, journalists, and educators from the region. Of these, only Bruce Crawford responded to Dreiser's initial call.

With such a response, or nonresponse, Dreiser welcomed Crawford and then asked NCDPP to find some volunteers. Dreiser also recruited Sherwood Anderson and John Dos Passos, both increasingly popular socialist-leaning authors, to act as his de facto seconds in command. Contemporary journalists and later historians writing on the Dreiser Committee in Harlan focused on Dreiser, Anderson, and Dos Passos largely because of their fame, while ignoring other committee members. This is a shame, because the other nine members represented an impressive collection of talent, some of whom possessed significantly more understanding of Appalachia, coal, leftist politics, and labor than the three famous authors combined.[25] In addition to Dreiser, Anderson, Dos Passos, and Crawford, other official contributors to the Dreiser Committee report included the following:

1. Anna Rochester, an original founder of the Labor Research Association, a Communist labor statistics bureau. Her book *Labor and Coal* was notable primarily for exposing corrupt judges who owned stakes in coal companies and coal-producing land. Rochester did not travel to Harlan but contributed significantly to the final report.[26]

2. Adelaide Walker and Charles Rumford Walker, a married couple who wrote about socialism, technology, and society both together and separately. Charles edited *Atlantic Monthly* during the 1920s and published books, both fiction and nonfiction, on the steel industry. Most notable was *Bread and Fire* (1927), a loosely autobiographical novel following a New York socialist editor's foray into work at a Pennsylvania steel mill. Adelaide worked as an actress in the 1920s and wrote occasionally for outlets such as *American Mercury*.[27]

3. Lester Cohen and Melvin P. Levy both worked as screenwriters and playwrights. Cohen's work before the Dreiser Committee largely comprised books and plays about capitalism and immigration. After, he struck fame

by writing the screenplay for *Of Human Bondage* and eight other major motion pictures. NCDPP secretary Levy was a novelist who wrote more screenplays after his time in Harlan, most notably *The Bandit of Sherwood Forest* (1946).[28]

4. Boris Israel, whose legal name was Blaine Owen and who also went by Israel Berenstein, worked as correspondent for the Federated Press, a news agency that supplied daily dispatches to radical, labor, and left-wing newspapers. He primarily wrote in Communist serials, including the *Daily Worker*, *New Masses*, and *Sunday Worker*.[29]

5. Arnold Johnson represented the American Civil Liberties Union and was a student finalizing his degree in Christian education and divinity in New York. He would spend six weeks in jail with striking miners, an experience he later cited as his reason for leaving the church and dedicating his life to labor rights and the Communist Party.[30]

6. Jesse London Wakefield represented the International Labor Defense League based out of Harlan County and was, according to other committee members, the bravest woman they had ever met. She was just twenty-three-years old and had already survived car bombs, prison, and innumerable death threats with hardly a scratch.[31]

7. Samuel Ornitz was from New York and worked as a writer. A few years after his work on the Dreiser Committee, he would become one of the Hollywood Ten, a group of writers, actors, and produces accused of harboring Communist sympathies and blackballed from working in the film industry. He did not contribute to the published report but his groundwork, such as organizing venues and securing interviews, was considered invaluable to the committee.[32]

A series of problems beset the Dreiser Committee within minutes of their November 1931 arrival in Kentucky. Most pressingly, several committee members faced open criminal warrants. Dreiser knew Harlan police could arrest the entire committee or individual members thereof at any time, with their only defense being the press and Dreiser's wealth. Another major problem that escaped from the notice of Dreiser and other key organizers lay in the fact that the committee's Harlan work was poorly conceptualized from the beginning. At the suggestion of Ornitz and Cohen, Dreiser set up a testimonial space for miners, the companies' representatives, and law enforcement in rented hotel conference rooms, first at the Continental Hotel in Pineville and then at the Lewellyn Hotel in Harlan. The goal was to evoke a courtroom, with Dreiser at an elevated table in his "blue suit, bow tie, white shirt, his grey-blue eyes surveying the miners and newsmen, looked for all the world like a judge." Additional hotel rooms were also rented as multipurpose lodging and staging areas for those testifying. The Dreiser Committee sent out a public invitation to miners in the region, with individual invitations sent to local leaders in government, police, business, and unions.

Much like a twenty-first-century reality competition, brave miners or miner family members first spoke with a committee member and, if their story was deemed worthy, would be would be escalated to the main testimony room, with Dreiser as judge and Ornitz as scribe. The pair listened, asked questions, and made an official record. Historian David C. Duke noted how such a system likely placed striking miners in even more danger. In order for a miner to participate in the committee events in Pineville or Harlan, they had to walk through town, passing by hostile figures, including company guards and unfriendly police, only to arrive at what resembled an inquisition before a seemingly powerful but temporary committee. Some miners were members of the UMW, or at least not affiliated with the Communist NWU, so there were further practical reasons not to want to meet with an openly Communist organization. Furthermore, Dreiser himself was generally unprepared, a common criticism he faced throughout his career. A dramatic committee event came to pass when Herndon Evans, a coal company–friendly Pineville newspaper editor, simply asked Dreiser how much he earned from his most famous book, *An American Tragedy*, and how much of those earnings Dreiser donated to charity. National newspapers printed Dreiser's answers— approximately $200,000 profit and zero to charity—which made Dreiser look like a hypocritical cheapskate. And no matter what happened with the Dreiser Committee, Harlan County miners would still live in Harlan County long after Dreiser's train, hypocritical or not, left town.

Despite such problems, at least forty miners, family members, and friends—or "victims of this local reign of terror" as the report later named them—testified before the Dreiser Committee. Dreiser personally described Harlan testifiers as "those who had been shot at, or shot, including the wives or relatives of those who had been killed, also of men who had been present when soup kitchens, seeking to feed hungry miners, their wives, and children were dynamited, as well as of men who had been arrested and jailed for collecting food or money for starving miners." [33]

Testimony was heart-wrenching, to say the least, with stark, nearly unbelievable details. Jim Grace, an unemployed UMW miner, described the police raiding his house because of his union membership. He then fled the county fearing for his life, only to be arrested in nearby Letcher County. There he was held in a jail cell owned by Consolidated Coal Company with another miner, NMU representative Tom Myerscough. Later that first night, armed men removed them from jail and shoved them into a car. In Grace's own words, he first thought the men were taking them to jail in Harlan County to stand trial, but he quickly understood their destination was a lynching. He recalled saying to Myerscough, "They're not taking us to Harlan, but to the Big Black Mountain. They're taking us up there to kill us." By about 2 a.m., armed men forced Grace and Myerscough from the car at the Virginia border, took their money, and beat them bloody. Myerscough desperately ran into the woods chased by at least twenty gunshots. Grace was certain Myerscough died on that mountain and even more certain he would be next. The armed men turned their frustration on Grace, beat him again, forced him to run into the woods, and then fired another dozen shots after him. Miraculously, Grace stumbled through the early morning woods over ten miles to Big Stone Gap and caught the morning train home. *Crawford's Weekly* published that Myerscough was alive a few days later, though Crawford shared few details. About a week later, Grace's rational fears got the best of him. He fled to New York and applied for public relief rolls as being unemployed and unskilled.[34]

Other testimonials were no less dramatic. Flora Shackelford, the wife of a miner, described her treatment when trying to find food for her children:

> When we would go to different places the law would follow us and when we got to church the law would be parked along the front and would blow their horns. The gun thugs are the law in this country now and not the judges and juries. At a mass meeting to be held here at the courthouse we were ordered away and hand grenades and tear gas were thrown.[35]

Robert Dean described the realities of opening a soup kitchen to feed unemployed miners and their families:

> This was at two-thirty in the morning. We heard the explosion and my wife said, "There goes your soup kitchen." I jerked my clothes on as quick as I could, the smoke hadn't cleared away but it was certainly riddled.[36]

And driving home the point that the power structure in Harlan oppressed the entire community, Caleb Powers shared an exchange he had with Judge D. C. "Baby" Jones in open court after his arrest for unknown charges:

[Judge Jones] said to us, "Well, Mr. Powers, I have had several conversations concerning you for the last week" and he said, "You have the reputation of a good man, a mighty good man and we don't want to see a good man in jail," and I said, "Judge, I have always tried to conduct myself that way," and he said, "We will turn you loose if you will leave the county," and he said, "This here [the NWU] is an unlawful organization."

I said, "I didn't know that, Judge," and I said, "I have always been a law-abiding citizen and I ain't done nothing," and I said, "I am paying taxes over here and I have got children in school and maybe I can't leave the county," and he said, "Of course it is bad to take the kids out of school," and he says, "I will turn you loose, but if I turn you loose, will you go out to stirring up soup kitchens again and doing all you can to aid this organization around here?"

Powers agreed to Judge Jones's demands that he stop organizing soup kitchens, and just like that, Jones ordered him released from county jail.[37]

Villains in the Dreiser Committee's story also testified, including Sheriff Blair, newspaperman Herndon Evans, and Harlan County's Commonwealth Attorney William E. Brock, though the most powerful political figure in the county, Judge Jones, publicly refused to do so. Judge Jones initially promised an appearance, so his reneging particularly irritated the committee. At the time scheduled for his testimony, he was conspicuously absent from Harlan, Pineville, or anywhere else in the county.[38] In response, the Dreiser Committee crafted a public letter accusing Jones of abusing his office. Of course, the letter had no legal authority, but it caught the attention of liberal-minded judges in Kentucky.

That you [Judge Jones] sat in judgment in cases in which your wife and your wife's relatives have financial interests. That you [Judge Jones] used your judicial position to control or change the political opinions of the prisoners arraigned before you. That you [Judge Jones] used your judicial position to exile citizens from their native county and state. It was our intention in going to you to give you an opportunity to refute or contradict the statements made by Harlan citizens. Inasmuch as we are going to submit the record of our inquiry to the Kentucky State Bar Association and the Government of Kentucky, we feel it is our duty to advise you of our intention.

We have taken an interest in your citizens because they are penniless and hungry and yet they have the spirit and courage to make in public charges against the judicial and police officials of your county. We would not be here in their behalf if they were not starving and if they did not believe themselves deserted by their own community.[39]

After three and a half productive days of testimony in Harlan County, the committee left town quickly because of a supposed sex scandal. Local muckrakers published newspaper articles claiming Dreiser was sleeping with his much younger secretary. This was the last straw for most of the committee. Threats of physical violence and now character assassination drove members out of town, especially once national media picked up on the Dreiser sex story. Crawford wrote privately that the accusations were "a story after a bourgeois reporter's own heart . . . played up to the exclusion of anything concerning the crimes against the miners." Crawford also noted that "it is a terrible commentary on newspapers and public that a sex scandal can obscure such inhumane and tragic conditions as exist in Harlan, but the powers that be usually meet social challenge with personal scandal."[40] Dreiser himself denied the charges and claimed to be impotent. Regardless, the Harlan coal powers got what they wanted—Dreiser and company out of town.

Even in the shadow of the Dreiser sex scandal, the most dramatic event of the testimonies involved rivals Sheriff Blair and Bruce Crawford. Sheriff Blair implied he would testify and, to the surprise of Judge Jones, actually showed up at the hearing. However, instead of offering a full testimony, Blair issued a summons to Bruce Crawford to appear in court on charges of slander and libel, for which he faced $50,000 in damages. Crawford was required, if he chose to obey, to appear at the Harlan circuit court within ten days, a truly unthinkable proposition. In response, Crawford simply left town with the Dreiser Committee. Safe at his Norton home, he used *Crawford's Weekly* to publicly mock Blair's weak complaints over the next few weeks.[41] Privately, Crawford was concerned that he might lose the lawsuit if it were to go to trial; he was also worried because the summons effectively banned him from crossing the state line into Kentucky. After an unsuccessful appeal to the ACLU for assistance, Crawford complained that "a red has no rights and deserves no quarter [in Kentucky]." The ACLU declined to help despite Dreiser's personal lobbying on Crawford's behalf, claiming a lack of funds. Not one to give up so easily, Dreiser wrote to ACLU membership directly via telegram on Crawford's behalf, appealing for assistance of any kind:

Bruce Crawford, miner sympathizer, of Norton, Va., wounded July 28th in Harlan. Now sued by Sheriff Blair of Harlan fifty thousand for slander based on Labor-Coalfield editorial. Hear offer within six days. Suit a frame. Object possibly to kill him. . . . Your organization should defend him and at once. . . . Could your organization name me shrewd attorney who will delay and get this case out of Harlan. All enemies, no friends there.[42]

Even with these problems, and on his own now that the Dreiser Committee had left town, Crawford continued to flirt with disaster in Kentucky. Since the ACLU refused to act, Crawford hired a Kentucky lawyer who successfully transferred the lawsuit to federal court in London, about forty miles from Pineville and outside of Sheriff Blair's jurisdiction.[43] The added benefit of the venue change was that Sheriff Blair regularly abused his connections by filing retaliatory criminal syndicalism charges, with no evidence, against Communists in Harlan courts, a problem that soon confronted Dreiser. Sheriff Blair argued that the very nature of Communist philosophy meant a conspiracy against Kentucky government. The charges were obviously bunk, but serious nonetheless—criminal syndicalism carried a potential twenty-year sentence in Kentucky. Nobody in their right mind would risk such a jail sentence at a trial presided by Judge Jones. Sheriff Blair never indicted Crawford for criminal syndicalism, but still Crawford told Dreiser he would never return to Harlan County, lest "the 'law' will nab [him] whenever [he goes]."[44]

Ever the daredevil, Crawford reneged on his promise and returned to Harlan County just six months later. In May 1932 and by the cover of night, he stopped in Pineville on the way to the London federal court to reassess the labor situation in town. He wandered about the courthouse area talking to locals before listening to a preacher, likely Primitive or Old Regular Baptist, speak to an interracial crowd. Politicians followed and Crawford marveled, in comparison to Harlan, at the lack of violence and relative freedom. "The affair was fantastic," Crawford wrote. "The country was beautiful, fresh in its new foliage and pleasing in its carefully tilled fields . . . it was on the whole an enjoyable sojourn in Kentucky. Nothing disastrous happened to me. I stole a march on them over there this time." He couldn't resist taking a dig at Sheriff Blair either: "It was a little stimulating to the blood pressure. For whom, seeing the Virginia tag, might not recognize the editor who was shot in the leg nearly a year ago? Representatives of the Punctured Press are not welcomed back in the Kentucky coal field."[45]

Crawford again returned to Harlan County in November 1932 for a new story, though this trip was less successful due to stresses caused by the Sheriff Blair lawsuit. Crawford accomplished little and likely spent more time with his lawyer than in the field interviewing miners. By this point it looked as though

Blair might win, an outcome Crawford literally could not afford. His mental health suffered. Crawford wrote to Dreiser that his nerves were so bad that he could only work "two or three hours a day" due to a poor stomach and "an evangelist belaboring me for my Communism." In the end, and much to Crawford's relief, the case was never reached trial. Sheriff Blair lost interest and withdrew his lawsuit after Crawford's Kentucky lawyer simply filed delay after delay.[46]

Slander and libel lawsuits behind him, Crawford kept tabs on his Kentucky enemy Sheriff Blair. *Crawford's Weekly* reacted gleefully when Blair lost support of the local coal operators, in part because of the undue attention brought upon the area by Dreiser and Crawford. Without operator support Sheriff Blair lost his bid for committee chair of the Harlan County Republican Party. Blair avenged the perceived betrayal by firing 126 mine guards paid for by the companies but deputized by the sheriff. Consequently, miners' lives improved drastically, yet another victory celebrated by *Crawford's Weekly*.[47] The interstate feud came to an end just two years later, as Sheriff Blair died in May 1934 from complications stemming from appendicitis. He was fifty-two years old and no longer sheriff by this point, having lost the election for county judge the previous year. Crawford, in a moment of dark humor, mailed Dreiser a *Knoxville News-Sentinel* article reporting Blair's death. Crawford made a small note above the article reading "one murder less," a cryptic inside joke neither he nor Dreiser explained.[48]

HARLAN MINERS SPEAK

Returning to the immediate months following the Dreiser Committee's Harlan County work, the committee members corresponded regularly about what actions to take next, with most agreeing it should be some sort of written report or book. The committee had no more momentum, thanks to the Dreiser scandal, so all agreed to complete another action to cap off their work. Crawford specifically advocated taking their case to Congress. "I wonder what plans, if any, have been made for laying the matter before Congress," Crawford wrote in a *Labor Age* article before concluding, "It would help further embarrass capitalism—which should be given a good push while so near the edge."[49] Dreiser organized a speaking forum in New York for December 15, 1931, to raise money for Harlan miners as a stopgap measure while the group planned its next steps.[50] Other committee members wrote short articles for newspapers and magazines, with Crawford himself writing an essay titled "What Have We to Lose? The Story of Harlan, Kentucky" for *Labor Age* and quite a few others in *Crawford's Weekly*.[51]

Ultimately, the Dreiser Committee decided to publish a book. *Harlan Miners*

Speak, a series of essays and interviews by most of the committee members, became the Dreiser Committee's testament to their time in Harlan County. It was also one of the first published academic works on labor strife in the Kentucky coal fields as well as one of the first to argue that Harlan County miners were worth the fight. In contrast to the "culture of poverty" trope, the book portrayed a community built on resistance, advocacy, and organization. Harlan County miners hoped that life could be better and were willing to fight for this future.[52] Published by Harcourt, Brace. less than a year after the committee's work, the book sold well enough to raise awareness. Divided into three sections, the volume opened with eight essays penned by committee members describing their time spent in Harlan County. This was followed by a much longer section with transcripts of Harlan County testimony, first of the miners and then of Sheriff Blair and Commonwealth Attorney William Brock. The finale contained writings by John Dos Passos and Sherwood Anderson. Concluding the book was an addendum of congressional testimony from novelist-activist Waldo Frank, who was assaulted by unidentified coal company men in Pineville and Cumberland Gap three months after the Dreiser Committee visit.[53]

Contributors to *Harlan Miners Speak* genuinely hoped to improve miners' lives, though several essays unfortunately fell short due to some authors' weak understanding of regional labor politics, sensitivity to Kentucky culture, or reliance on stereotype. For example, Lester Cohen, who authored the second essay, noted eastern Kentucky had only been civilized in the past few decades. Per Cohen, "When they weren't fighting," Kentuckians "lived simple lives in sparsely settled mountain districts. Because of their isolation, they had been allowed to preserve the last frontier. . . . They remained a primitive people past the turn of the twentieth century." Cohen went on to describe a Kentuckian community of "four principle stocks—English, English-Irish, Scotch Highlanders, and Scotch-Irish" who had only recently discovered currency, wage labor, grocery stores, and "wearing 'store clothes.'" In other words, Cohen encouraged readers to view Harlan County's striking miners as innocents of the purest white bloodlines.[54]

Another example displaying the Dreiser Committee's poor understanding of eastern Kentucky could be found in Melvin Levy's essay. Levy touched on similar themes as Cohen, though with a bit more depth and romanticism. To him, Kentuckian miners represented "one of the last strongholds of the pure old-American blood" directly descended from the "first ancestors of the hill people drifted in almost 300 years ago." Kentucky became their home because the mountains appealed to their independent streak, pioneering soul, and desire for solitude, he argued, not to mention their aversion to farming. Levy claimed to have met Kentuckian and Virginian mountain men who still talked as if Daniel Boone were still alive, had never seen a map, and never read a single book. How these pre-Revolutionary Kentuckians fed their families, Levy did not elaborate; nor did he explain how "among some of the miners Lenin has become a kind of hero." All they knew was that Lenin would fight alongside workers like them, and that was good enough. It is easy to imagine Bruce Crawford, who authored "The Mountain White" a decade earlier, simply shaking his head at his city-based Communist peers.[55]

Despite such shortcomings, other writers' essays provided new insight into the region's economic woes within the context of American capitalism and labor. Anna Rochester, who had just published *Labor and Coal* in 1931, outlined how wealthy capitalists came to own so much eastern Kentucky land. In her analysis, the oppression in Harlan began decades earlier when "Wall Street and capitalists in Chicago, Detroit, Baltimore, and Cincinnati" came to "dominate the coal fields of Harlan and adjacent counties." The forces that pressed Harlan miners into deep poverty—namely J. P. Morgan, Andrew Mellon, and Henry Ford—were doing the same to others nationwide, all for the sake of profit. In this way, the struggle of Harlan miners was the struggle faced by American workers broadly. Other writers drew similar connections: Adelaide Walker outlined general housing conditions and food security issues, Charles Walker placed the formation of Harlan labor unions within a regional context, and Johnson and Israel both documented personal experiences that had been ignored by journalists for years. All successfully illustrated what so many Appalachian historians struggled to depict decades later—Appalachia is American and so are the region's ills, capitalism and all. However, they still shied away from discussing the Harlan miners themselves, instead choosing to speak about labor abstractly.

Crawford was one of few contributors to represent Harlan miners are they really were—a heterogeneous group suffering because of extractive capitalism at its worst.[56] The focus in Crawford's essay was propaganda. Local and regional press, and even on occasion the Associated Press, presented the Dreiser Committee as un-American. Supposedly neutral, AP reporters exhibited a "phony air of impartiality" owed either to malice, coal operator bias, or outright ignorance of Appalachia in Crawford's view. He described an interaction between an AP reporter and a Harlan County woman who worked as a midwife. The woman stated that during the previous summer, at least seventeen newborns died of dysentery. Such deaths were largely preventable if Harlan County had had modern hospital facilities, but cheapskate coal companies refused to purchase even the most basic needed supplies. The AP reporter's next question was, "Can we see the graves?" Crawford also lambasted the Harlan *Enterprise*'s decision to ignore the Dreiser Committee's activities outright and instead publish an eight-column story on local football. Outraged, but not defeated, Crawford concluded that all is not lost in Harlan, as this type of thing happens everywhere under capitalism in every country of the world.[57]

For all that, *Harlan Miners Speak* did not have the impact desired by the Dreiser Committee. While both Dreiser and Crawford were proud to have produced the publication, conditions for the Harlan miners and miners' unions worsened after the committee's work concluded.[58] The NMU, once so promising, collapsed both in terms of union finances and membership. Things only got worse when, on February 10,1932, a Knox County (Kentucky) sheriff's deputy working as a mine guard shot and killed Harry Simms, a twenty-year-old NMU organizer. Within days, novelist Waldo Frank led the Communist-funded Independent Miners' Relief Committee deliver food and clothing to miners in Harlan County and other eastern Kentucky communities. A mob intercepted the group and ferociously beat Frank, NMU lawyer Allan Taub, and others. Frank and Taub, finding themselves stranded and alone, hitched a ride to Knoxville, Kentucky, only to discover they had been charged with criminal syndicalism and disorderly conduct in Harlan County. They chose to flee Kentucky, rightfully fearing for their lives.

The primary accomplishment of *Harlan Miners Speak* was, in conjunction with these other incidents, bringing awareness of eastern Kentucky conditions to a broader political audience. Crawford praised Frank, Taub, and others for their success "in proving, once again, that the coal industry and the 'law' are fused into one in Kentucky and that constitutional rights are mythical indeed." *Harlan Miners Speak* and the Frank and Taub incident also caught the attention of Senator Robert La Follette Jr., who ordered hearings on conditions in the Harlan and Bell County coal industry for May 1932. These hearings, which included testimony by Dreiser Committee member Melvin Levy, provided details of one of the worst economic situations in Depression-era America. One other post-Dreiser Harlan event followed when students from "about thirty universities" traveled to eastern Kentucky for a firsthand look after readings *Harlan Miners Speak* and articles published by Crawford. Crawford wrote of the students' observations but failed to report any lasting changes achieved by this action. Meanwhile, in Washington, DC, New Deal legislation provided some labor union protections with the Wagner Act and the La Follette Civil Liberties Committee, but change was slow coming to the mountains. Needless to say, eastern Kentucky conditions never improved to a level desired by the Dreiser Committee or other allied groups.[59]

Perhaps the greatest beneficiary of the Dreiser Committee was Bruce Crawford. About a month after the conclusion of the Harlan work, Crawford exchanged a series of letters with Dreiser regarding Crawford's hope to publish essays and potentially a book. Dreiser generously provided revisions and eventually distributed one thousand copies of an essay to his New York City literary friends free of charge. The pair stayed close, exchanging dozens of letters until Dreiser's death in 1945. In most of this correspondence, Dreiser acted as Crawford's peer and mentor. In one exchange the two discussed international politics, for instance, followed by Dreiser answering Crawford's questions regarding the publishing industry. Comparatively, Dreiser developed a similar relationship with Sherwood Anderson, but their letters were brief, businesslike, and never veered from the publishing and writing industry. "I think that when we are together there is a natural shyness and then we are both writers who have written a great deal and for a long time," wrote Anderson to Dreiser in 1934. "The true thoughts flow more freely through the fingers than through the lips." This may have been true for Anderson, but there was clearly no shyness in Crawford.[60]

As for any long-term impact of *Harlan Miners Speak*, veterans of the Harlan County violence interviewed in the early 1970s claimed to have no memory of Dreiser, the committee, or even the miners who testified in 1931. At least some Harlan veterans, namely UMW organizer George Titler, recalled the Dreiser Committee with outright hostility. "The Communists tried to seize control of the union spirit in Harlan," he wrote in his memoir. "The famous novelist, Theodore Dreiser, then a Communist tool, wrote nationally syndicated newspaper stories about Harlan County coal miners."[61] Crawford did not even appear as a footnote in Titler's book, though to be fair Titler did not arrive in Harlan until 1937 as a UMW organizer, so his recollection of Dreiser was not firsthand. By the time Titler published his memoir in 1972, the Dreiser Committee's actions in Kentucky were largely unknown outside of activist circles and university classrooms. This changed in 2008 when the University Press of Kentucky reprinted *Harlan Miners Speak* for the first time since its original publication with a new introduction by Appalachian historian John Hennen. Now more accessible, *Harlan Miners Speak* is a reminder to twenty-first-century Appalachian activists and writers that such work is never in vain. Spiritual predecessors laid the field's groundwork nearly a century ago. Even though the Dreiser Committee was not successful in its time, the publication of

Harlan Miners Speak highlighted the importance of bearing witness and shining light on injustice. If nothing else, the committee's work contributed to miners' short-term well-being in getting people fed, housed, and not shot by the police.[62]

APPALACHIAN COMMUNIST

Crawford's Dreiser Committee experience brought him closer in contact than ever before with some of America's leading Communist voices and placed him firmly on the track of advocating for the rights of poor people in Appalachia and the South. He would still, on occasion, dabble in other causes, but by the end of 1931 Crawford's gaze was focused squarely upon Communist activism and bettering the lives of poor people. Communist organizing took up much of Crawford's attention whenever he could step away from *Crawford's Weekly*, with the first such post-Harlan venture involving a leading role in the Southern League for People's Rights (SLPR), a subsidiary of the National Committee for the Defense of Political Prisoners. The SLPR was a new organization organized in Atlanta for two purposes—to unite radicals and liberals fighting for poor people in the South and to specifically aid Angelo Herndon, an African American worker who had been arrested for leading biracial labor demonstrations.[63] Police arrested Herndon for insurrection, after which a search of his hotel room turned up Communist publications. Two ILD-funded African American attorneys defended Herndon to no avail. A jury found him guilty on January 18, 1933, and recommended a "merciful" sentence of eighteen to twenty years. The judge agreed on the length, sentencing Herndon to hard chain gang labor.[64]

The nascent SLPR organized quickly around the Herndon case with the election, some in absentia, of three white and two Black officers—Sherwood Anderson (chair), Crawford and the Reverend R. W. Coleman (vice-chairs), historian C. Vann Woodward (secretary), and accountant J. B. Blayton (treasurer). Alabama-based sociologist and University of North Carolina PhD student Olive "Polly" Stone was not elected to an official position, but she published the SLPR newsletter and attended more meetings than most.[65] Unfortunately, SPLR members in Atlanta were unsuccessful in advocating for Herndon. As Herndon appealed his conviction, the SLPR shifted attention to other concerns and membership splintered. Woodward, who would become perhaps the most esteemed white southern historian of his era, quit SLPR the following year, "as communist influence increased." Crawford, Polly Stone, and others grew membership to around fifteen hundred dues-paying members primarily in Virginia and North Carolina. By 1934 Stone's role as a recruiter had garnered her significant influences, allowing her to steer the group toward her primary causes: fighting sharecropping, corrupt police officers, strike-breakers, and lynching. For whatever reason, Crawford and Anderson both drifted away from the group during the mid-1930s, as did Stone. By 1937 membership was nearly nonexistent. What began as a promising new venture turned into nothing nearly as quickly as it began.[66]

At about the same time as the foundation of SLPR, Theodore Dreiser contacted Crawford with a proposition. They, along with a few other handpicked Communist writers and journalists, would form a new organization to manage a pro-Communism, pro-socialism public relations campaign. Dreiser described his mission simply: "Communism as practiced by the Russians, at least most of it, can certainly be made palatable to the average American if it is properly explained to him and if the title Communism is removed." Both Crawford and Dreiser believed Americans—especially those mired in poverty—would strongly support Communist policy if only they understood that Communism was not a dirty word and that many popular New Deal programs were highly similar. For instance, most Americans supported, and still support, higher taxation on the wealthy and lower or no taxation on the poorest, but attaching the word "Communist" or "socialist" to such policies resulted in a significant loss of support.[67]

Dreiser's method for achieving American acceptance of Communism or socialism was vague and gradualist by design. Americans could, in his view, be convinced that socialist government was in their best interest through the gradual introduction of individual policies. A sudden revolution would be rejected, possibly even leading to civil war, so the new organization—which he tentatively named the American League for National Equity—would lobby politicians behind closed doors to pass socialist legislation and publish supportive essays in prominent newspapers and magazines. Exactly how this would be achieved Dreiser left to the imagination. He tapped a few prominent progressive voices to join the effort, including founders of the ACLU Morris Ernst and Arthur Garfield Hays, businessman and peace activist Fisher C. Baily, Broadway actor Ralph Holmes, New York lawyer and statistician H. H. Klein, and Russian immigrant and Revolutionary writer Ivan Narodny, but none of these possessed enough political capital to unlock the halls of Congress.[68]

Crawford hated the proposal. In a lengthy private letter, Crawford's sharp words cut into Dreiser's ideas while openly calling for a full Communist revolution, a far cry from the gradualist position Crawford himself had possessed just a few years earlier. This marked an important shift in his philosophy and a clear sign that three years of Hoover, the Harlan bullet wound, and the

Dreiser Committee had transformed his politics. He first let down Dreiser easy by agreeing that writers should serve as "support" and not as leaders under Communism, but they should work directly with workers rather than on their own. Crawford's new philosophy was clear—writers like himself must provide education and communication for workers, both white and Black, and could link somewhat isolated workers to the international Communist movement. The end goal was a workers' revolution:

> I believe, and conversation with you at Pineville indicated that you too believe, that there can be no scientific, equitable, or just organization of a new society unless the ground is completely cleared of capitalist debris. That means revolution. In no other way, in my opinion, can we begin with a clean slate. The new society should not be handicapped and corrupted at the start by having to compromise with the old order. Revolution is the placental covering that makes possible the birth of the new society free from the diseases of its predecessors.
>
> And it is further agreed, I think, that the revolution will have to be won by the workers. Because they are coming to be more precariously situated, both white and black, than were the Negroes before the Civil War, the workers will most easily and most quickly understand the class character of the capitalist state. By use of the club, the gun, and the jail, the state in cooperation with exploiters makes the issues crystal clear. The trade union organizer will be aided by the economic crisis in precipitating industrial conflicts. The workers will, and must, because of their numbers, bear the brunt of the revolutionary struggle. They will suffer most from the violence of the powers that be; they will be beaten and jailed and shot.
>
> It is true that our capitalist society does not like the name Communism. It would dislike as bitterly any other organization no matter what its name, which had for its purpose the socialization of the machinery now used for exploitation. . . . Red as I am, I believe the writers should not sponsor a program less militant or less revolutionary than that of the Communist party. . . . The only way a writers' organization can serve the revolutionary movement, from what I have been able to observe, is to support the workers who are, and must necessarily be, the foundation of that movement. If the program of the writers is divorced from the struggle of the masses, that program can have little practical effect.[69]

In this letter, Crawford also suggested to Dreiser a few other ideas for a writers' organization. First, all members must be Communists and must join the party. Anyone unwilling to do this was either a capitalist or a potential fascist, so may as well get those people out of the way right away. Next, group membership must be kept secret. Members would only be able to exercise full intellectual freedom if their membership was not broadly known. In Crawford's view, a leaked membership list could lead to blacklisting or writers' unrelated publications could be labeled Communist propaganda and careers could be ruined. Finally, the organization must have a staffed central office through which all work flowed to ensure stability, consistency, and accountability. Framework in place, a long list of mandatory "duties and purposes" for the group followed, such as:

> To write books, articles, and reviews which set up a standard of judgement, of criticism and value, based on the philosophy of communism and class struggle.
> To clarify issues in industrial conflicts.
> To reply to newspaper and magazine articles which seek to prejudice the public against the cause of the workers in their industrial struggles.
> To keep the public informed, though every available source, of the achievements of communism in Russia. To see that the public gets a true and an accurate, rather than false, report of what is happening in the land of the Soviets.
> To convince the public of the inherent contradictions in capitalism and of its inevitable collapse.[70]

Crawford encouraged Dreiser to heed these suggestions, draft an organizational framework, and formally issue a membership call as soon as possible, though ultimately the organization floundered under Dreiser's sporadic leadership and general inaction. A few months later Dreiser again wrote to Crawford, this time with a proposal for the creation of an Intellectual Workers League (IWL) that followed all of Crawford's advice. The only problem was the name. If the IWL consisted of only "intellectual workers," Crawford reasoned, then it implied workers who were not members were not intellectuals. Setting the name aside for the moment, Dreiser's first goal was to contact "writers and editors all over the country with the view of having them correctly publicize every struggle between owners and workers and answer newspaper editorials that attack the workers." Crawford again urged Dreiser to act with urgency. It had been over three months since the original idea and America drifted slowly toward capitalist dictatorship or fascism. "Drastic times are ahead of us," read *Crawford's Weekly* during this time. "But they are going to be exciting and full of high doing, however God-awful."[71] Dreiser formed the IWL, led by himself and writer Dallas McKown, future director of the Federal Writers' Project in Arkansas. The group never found its footing and faded away at some point in 1933, just a year after formation.

Crawford and Dreiser connected one last time in 1935. By then, the elderly Dreiser had grown despondent over the prospects of Communist organizing in America. "There are too many groups, too much quarrelling, and the mass sentiment of America seems to be more anti than pro," he wrote to Crawford, ironically not noticing he himself was partially responsible for the proliferation of Communist groups as he suggested an IWL revival. Crawford's response reveals a major change in his personal politics. Just as suddenly as it all began, he disassociated himself with formal organizing. Revolutionary Communism still best described his worldview, but he dropped all political memberships and ceased most regional travel, instead focusing attention on Norton and his newspaper. On one hand, Crawford could have grown irritated with ineffective Communist organizing, getting chased out of Kentucky, or growing anti-Communist sentiment in America. But more likely, he was finding it difficult to square his radical Communism with running a successful local newspaper in a small town with very few Communists. Crawford the journalist-editor and Crawford the Communist bullhorn were no longer in harmony, and something had to give. In the end, two things gave out—Crawford's brief career in electoral politics and shortly thereafter *Crawford's Weekly* itself.[72]

CHAPTER 3

A CRITIC FAILS AT POLITICS

NEW DEAL CRITIC

Just four months into FDR's presidency, Crawford soured on the Democrats' new approach. "The New Deal is a middle class revolution," proclaimed *Crawford's Weekly*, arguing that most New Deal programs did nothing for poor people. A far greater danger, one that Crawford would write about often, was that by ignoring the needs of poor people FDR risked creating right-wing populist movement. Liberal Democrats, themselves marching lockstep with other Democrats and Republicans in their anti-Communism, failed to see that the choice was not between "romantic liberalism and communism . . . but between fascism and communism." The only praise set aside for FDR by *Crawford's Weekly* at this early point was that at least FDR acted more swiftly in comparison to Hoover, who hardly acted at all.[1]

FDR and the New Deal met plenty of challenges from left-wing critics, but Crawford was unique in that he was one of very few who was both from the South and focused on what should be done for the South and the Appalachian region. The loudest left-wing criticism came in 1934, when editors of the new magazine *Common Sense* published *Challenge to the New Deal*, a collection of thirty-nine anti–New Deal essays written by thirty-five radical politicians, critics, writers, and activists. The book was one of, if not the, first book-length publications critical of the New Deal. From the authors' perspectives, the New Deal was a once-in-a-lifetime opportunity to reorient America's runaway capitalism, yet Democrats squandered the chance by pandering to conservatives and capitalists who had created the economic mess in the first place. Diverse opinions appeared in *Challenge to the New Deal*, yet a common theme ran across most chapters—the federal government must wrest control from the wealthy and redistribute to the masses. Some essays focused on specifics, such as the Wisconsin Progressive Party's successes, how to build a new leftist political party, or methods for uniting rural agricultural and urban industrial peoples, but a common critique of liberals drew all authors together.

The *Challenge to the New Deal* contributor list read like a 1934 celebrity yearbook for left-wing intellectuals, including John Dewey, Theodore Dreiser, John Dos Passos, Phillip La Follette, Lillian Symes, Lewis Mumford, Upton Sinclair, Mary Van Kleeck, Edmund Wilson, and James Rorty. Overall, a striking lack of diversity characterized the book in that most contributors came from the same Ivy League background and lived in Boston or New York. A handful of others represented progressives in the northern Midwest, with two others being Russian immigrants living in New York. *Challenge to the New Deal* was essentially a regional, class-specific intellectual exercise of New York socialists and Communists rounded out by Wisconsin progressives. Crawford represented the one exception to this characterization.

Out of the thirty-five authors, Crawford was the only one with no formal education, no connections to elected officials, and no Ivy League connections and the only one representing the working class in Appalachia or the South. Crawford's chapter, "The Small Town and Depression," was also the lone contribution on rural communities with an economy not dependent on agriculture. Blame for ignoring the South and Appalachia can largely be placed with the editors, who simply recruited authors within their social network and remained ignorant to regional writers, only knowing of Crawford due to his Dreiser connections.[2]

Crawford's essay, originally published in *Common Sense* a month after the 1932 election, touched on all strata of everyday Norton life during the Depression. Bankers, farmers, merchants, and coal miners of both Democratic and Republican persuasions were generally putting food on their table, but plenty of other Norton residents were suffering. The argument was simple—life cannot go on in this way unchanged for much longer. Even clergymen turned desperate for financial survival, as church tithings were below subsistence level. Compounding the problem was that while nobody, whether Washington politicians or regular Norton residents, offered any real solution, faith in the capitalist system had not yet faded. "They are not getting cynical," Crawford wrote of his neighbors. "Rather they are naïve enough to believe something can be done." People retained confidence in American capitalism, American electoral politics, and in their own selves despite going on three years of financial suffering. In Crawford's view, these faithful Norton people should not be shamed for this confidence. Instead, blame must be placed upon Republicans for failing to act and, more importantly, upon FDR-loyal Democrats for their insistence on using the New Deal to repair a floundering capitalist machine.[3] For a brief period before the 1932 election, Crawford believed FDR advocated radical change but ultimately admitted he too was duped by the candidate's progressive rhetoric. In the end, the New Deal did not bring hope; instead, it renewed the promise of future disaster.[4]

After the publication of *Challenge to the New Deal*, Crawford published dozens of anti–New Deal essays in *Crawford's Weekly*, cementing his reputation as one of the South's most prolific left-wing critics of FDR. By mid-1933, Crawford became convinced that liberals, who had what he called "a nostalgic eye to Jefferson the Great Democrat," were using the New Deal and electoral support to duplicate German and Italian fascists' rise to power. Other Communist writers regularly criticized Democrats in this way, but few targeted "reformers" with Crawford's level of vitriol. Reform protected the status quo. Liberal policies like "economical councils" and "government regulation" tended toward reconsolidating power into the hands of those who caused the disaster of 1929.[5]

As for specific New Deal programs, Crawford focused on the Tennessee Valley Authority (TVA) and the National Recovery Administration (NRA). On February 8, 1933—a full twenty-four days before FDR took office—*Crawford's Weekly* took aim at the sketch plan of the proposed TVA: "The Tennessee Valley vision will appeal to capital looking for cheap resources, cheap power, and cheap labor. The major project of the government would furnish both means and stimulation for development by private interests." This essay even went so far as to paint early TVA plans as a militarization project. The logic was that the TVA would bring electricity to the mountains, electricity would bring federally owned factories, and those factories would produce goods for the United States military, especially munitions. "The American Ruhr" was how *Crawford's Weekly* depicted the TVA's vision for the Tennessee Valley, a reference to Nazi Germany's increased industrial development of the region around the Ruhr River in preparation for military aggression.[6] For several weeks, Crawford's editorials warned conditions were right for an American dictator. FDR's popularity combined with a complicit Congress made for a fearful combination.[7] Still, *Crawford's Weekly* had not yet abandoned all hope, just most of it: "Roosevelt, who was going to 'redistribute wealth' but who yachts with the Astors and fraternizes with the Morgan crowd—this same Roosevelt will soon prove to the country whether there is more to him than a camera conscious smile." Here, Crawford imagines a future of either fascism or plutocracy, hardly an optimistic outlook.[8]

The formation of the NRA briefly yet drastically softened *Crawford's Weekly* on the New Deal. FDR personally favored the NRA, his administration's first major effort at achieving full economic recovery, above most other New Deal programs. To Crawford's approbation, the NRA's core goal was to reduce capitalist competition. Private businesses voluntarily adopted NRA "codes," which were broadly accepted rules—not laws—governing minimum wage, maximum workweeks, and price controls. The idea was that if companies mutually agreed to NRA codes, customers would patronize NRA-supporting companies, leading American industry would recover. Customers would know which businesses supported the NRA because they would post the NRA "Blue Eagle" logo prominently. Just two years after the NRA formed, the Supreme Court found it unconstitutional, but for that brief two-year window, the NRA was ubiquitous in the American economy. *Crawford's Weekly* was initially supportive of the NRA. No real reason was provided, just a leap of faith really, though the NRA's protection of some workers' rights had appeal to Crawford.[9]

Still, while initially supportive of the NRA—a Blue Eagle proudly appeared in the *Crawford's Weekly* office window—Crawford soured on the program after just a few weeks. "The NRA and its codes are definite fascist beginnings . . . fascism is the radicalism of the money powers in their extremity," read the first of many Crawford editorials, most of them carrying the same theme. For Crawford, Americans were divided on the NRA because it meant different things to different people. To coal operators, it meant intrusive government. To railroad companies, it was a government bailout. To the wealthy, it meant corporatism and a chance of permanent financial relief. And finally, to the informed public like himself, the NRA curated a cooperative economy that, despite the risk of fascism, strengthened labor standards and helped working people. Ultimately, Crawford failed to reconcile his contradictory views on the NRA before it was found unconstitutional by the Supreme Court.[10]

Gloomy writings on other New Deal programs regularly dotted the pages of *Crawford's Weekly*. The Civilian Conservation Corps (CCC) was an agency that hired unemployed young men and put them to work on conservation projects in forests, farmland, and parks. Out of all New Deal programs, the CCC was perhaps the most popular both in its time and from the perspective of historians ever since. Yet, Crawford found aspects of it to criticize, arguing the CCC would accomplish three things: a reduction in unemployment for young men, significant reforestation, and extreme militarization of America's youth. A "Civilian Army" trained by Army officers, as critics including Crawford described the agency, spooked those hoping America could avoid the expanding war in Europe. Socialist Party spokesman Norman Thomas, Father Charles

Coughlin, and numerous Republican Congressmen were just a few out of many who lobbed charges of "fascism" or "Bolshevism" at the CCC.[11] "Buy American" campaigns also incensed Crawford as a waste of time. He regularly argued such campaigns were destined to fail under capitalism as consumers acted rationally and typically bought the best products at the best price.[12] The FDR administration also pushed through Congress a series of coal recovery bills meant to generate immediate miner employment. The problem was the new laws did not restructure the industry, so abusive operators stayed in power. As may be expected by now, Crawford called this "a definite step toward the Fascistization of American industry."[13]

Despite such regular criticisms, some *Crawford's Weekly* readers accused Crawford of favoring the New Deal. One specific complaint came when Crawford refused to publish a letter to the editor critical of the Civil Works Administration (CWA), a New Deal agency that lasted just four months. Crawford never provided a clear reason for his refusal, beyond tepid excuses that the letter was "too long." Readers called the *Crawford's Weekly* office decrying the perceived censorship. In response, Crawford promised he would publish any CWA criticisms so long as they were grounded in political or economic reality.[14] A few weeks later, two new *Crawford's Weekly* essays ripped into the CWA. First, Crawford accused the CWA of being a new Democrat tool to cynically court voters for the 1934 election. Second, Crawford questioned why the FDR administration eventually cut the CWA, arguing that America's civil infrastructure was in dire need of improvement and that the CWA could be reformed. Instead, the FDR administration favored rebuilding "economic infrastructure," meaning favoring industry and commerce over regular people. To Crawford, industry was not a "recuperative power" and the administration's actions in this case smacked of Hooverism.[15]

Crawford totally gave up on the New Deal by the middle of summer 1934, when it became public knowledge that leaders of the U.S. Chamber of Commerce—"the biggest business lobby in America"—were responsible for both the NRA and the Agricultural Adjustment Act (AAA). Wall Street financier Bernard Baruch, along with many of his colleagues, were now undeniably in FDR's inner circle, further convincing socialists and Communists that the New Deal offered little hope. As both the NRA and AAA ambled toward Supreme Court rejection, FDR admitted publicly, as reported by *Crawford's Weekly*, that he had little control of the situation.[16] Once optimistic, Crawford believed that New Deal programs meant to supplement income—or "rehabilitate" out-of-work laborers as Crawford wrote—would soon be defined by an "economy of scarcity," meaning poor people would be trapped in a paycheck-to-paycheck, subsistence lifestyle. *Crawford's Weekly* now argued the New Deal encouraged state dependence, not individual independence, for regular workers, businesses, and farmers.[17] In one of Crawford's final articles on the New Deal, he essentially threw up his hands in disgust:

> Redistribution of wealth was a major New Deal promise. Many people have supported the Administration because they believed it really intended to spread the wealth out. This newspaper has never been among those who entertained such a belief. We have contended that the machinery of our economic system so functions to further concentrate wealth.
>
> Recently, President Roosevelt, who promised redistribution, appointed M. S. Eccles, Utah banker, as Governor of the Federal Reserve Board. Time Magazine says Governor Eccles "is a thoroughgoing New Dealer who will do what the President wants him to do." Yet when Eccles was putting his idea into the Congressional Record nearly two years ago, he declared: "Such measures as I have promise may frighten those who have wealth. However, they should feel reassured that it is to save the rich and not to soak them."
>
> Last week Governor Eccles stepped to the stage front to pooh-pooh any radical impression his Senate testimony may have created. "I have certainly, for instance, never advocated the redistribution of wealth," he said. "That is perfectly impossible under the capitalistic system."
>
> Here's a capitalist agreeing with Karl Marx! The laws of capitalist economy operate not only to prevent redistribution but to increase concentration. New Deal premises of spreading out wealth, while New Dealers are trying to "save the rich" are sheer demagogy. Capitalists themselves are not going to part with their wealth, but through their New Deal government they are trying to keep the people hoping for redistribution. Meanwhile concentration goes on, accelerated by monopolistic freedom which the capitalists have gained under their New Deal.[18]

This was the Bruce Crawford of 1934—openly socialist, anti-capitalist, and one of the most vocal critics of the New Deal in the entire South. And then, he decided to run for Congress.

A CONGRESSIONAL RUN

Crawford's Weekly, while technically a politically neutral newspaper, generally supported Democrats, but Crawford's shift toward Communism by the early 1930s indicated that such support was tenuous at best. Generally, Crawford wrote editorials heavily critical of the Democratic Party and its legislation while including smatterings of support for individual Democratic politicians as he saw fit. This was true even before Crawford's Communist turn. "My way of seeing the situation is this," he wrote in 1924. "The two old parties are carrying on a mock scrimmage at the behest of the powerful financial interests for the befoolment of the masses . . . their political differences are not sufficient to make them real enemies."[19] In 1928 Democrats lost big, and in the aftermath Crawford called upon Virginia Democrats to stay true to pro-labor party values. Conservatives dominated Election Day, so plenty of Virginia Democrats, roughly one-third of the caucus, demanded pro-business candidates or they would defect to the Republicans. Crawford wrote that it was a hoax—"they're going to peter out before primary time"—so progressive Democrats should not back down.[20]

Just two years later, in 1930, *Crawford's Weekly* presented an opposite argument, that Democrats should rally behind pro-business candidates in order to purge Republicans from Congress. Virginia's junior senator, Carter Glass, was up for reelection in 1930. Glass was a pro-business conservative Democrat and seen as a growing political titan within the Byrd Organization. Despite Glass's apparent electoral invulnerability, rumors swirled that Virginia's progressive Democratic governor E. Lee Trinkle intended a primary challenge. Crawford, for reasons of party unity, urged his readers to reject the Trinkle rumors and rally behind Senator Glass. *Crawford's Weekly* read, "To oppose Glass would be to risk hurting one or the other, either by the defeat of a former governor whose tail feathers are still perked up, or by the toppling of a Senator who has preserved Virginia a conspicuous place in the governmental affairs of the nation." Apparently, Crawford's views of them Democratic Party shifted on a case-by-case basis.[21]

As for Crawford's own politics, his belief in Communism and socialism peaked around the time he got shot in the leg by a Harlan police officer in 1931. About a month after taking the bullet, *Crawford's Weekly* both contested and embraced accusations that Crawford himself was a "Red." Here for the first time, Crawford clearly articulated his personal political philosophy in its entirety:

I believe the law should apply equally to all people and should not be an instrument of employers for keeping underpaid workers in subjection.

I believe public authority should not be usurped by private interests and enforced by Chicago gunmen and ex-convicts.

I believe the government through its county officers should not turn gangster and bomb soup kitchens, dynamite workers' cars, and shoot representatives of the press from ambush.

I believe striking miners should be allowed to go to the United States post office on company property for their mail without being intimidated or manhandled.

I believe that a worker should not be charged with criminal syndicalism and held without bond for having in his possession a copy of the Survey Graphic.

I believe the state should not send a man to jail whose only offense is an attempt to visit the sick and feed the hungry.

I believe a coal miner should not be compelled to pay $1.59 for a bag of flour at the company store when he can get it elsewhere for 60 cents.

I believe that a coal company should not compel Negro workers to support a white Baptist church which they would be lynched for entering.

I believe a preacher in sympathy with striking miners should be allowed to quote Moses to them without being jailed for criminal syndicalism.

I believe workers should have the same right to join unions to keep wages up as employers have to join associations to keep wages down.

I believe friends of imprisoned miners should be permitted to work up their defense without being jailed or run out of the county by officers of the court.

I believe a judge with coal company connections and violent anti-labor prejudices should not be permitted to sentence miners to long prison terms or death for rebelling against peonage and conditions which mean perpetual starvation.

If this be red, let the yellows make the most of it.[22]

With these politics clearly articulated, Crawford's consistent inability to either condemn or embrace the Democratic Party stemmed both from his Communist politics and his disdain for his own House representative, Democrat John W. Flannagan Jr. It is fair to say that Crawford's Communist politics and loyalty to Democrats were inversely related, especially in the late 1920s, but his disdain for Flannagan became a greater interest after Flannagan's successful 1930 House of Representatives election campaign. Flannagan, an attorney and banker, narrowly focused his congressional agenda on agriculture, hustling a membership on the House Agriculture Committee. Such activity led to Flannagan being shortlisted for secretary of agriculture on occasion, though he declined each time claiming no ambition to serve in a presidential cabinet. Flannagan leaned toward the conservative end of the party but was not a Byrd acolyte and generally supported the New Deal, often breaking with the Byrd machine and congressional Democrats on farm bills.[23]

What Crawford hated about Flannagan was his utter failure to address poverty relief in any serious way, as well as his failure to use his power to improve New Deal legislation. At first, *Crawford's Weekly* supported Flannagan because of a promised "poverty first" legislative packet. "Doles to the big bankers" would end, proclaimed Flannagan, and in exchange *Crawford's Weekly* carried a full-page Flannagan endorsement the week before the 1930 election. This all changed during Flannagan's second term. Flannagan positioned himself as a New Deal champion—"foursquare and flatfooted with Roosevelt," in Flannagan's own words. No singular moment drove Crawford against Flannagan. It was instead the compounded factors of Flannagan's unthinking support for FDR, unwillingness to address constituents, and lies about pro-union coal bill proposals. The latter was the most egregious, as unionized coal miners threw support behind Flannagan only to be rewarded with inaction on Flannagan's part. Rumors also spread throughout southwest Virginia that Flannagan's old banking friends had essentially bribed him. "Why is Congress so futile?" Crawford wrote in 1932. "For one thing," he continued, "it couldn't be truly representative if it tried to be. It is preposterous to expect any considerable degree of popular government in a capitalistic society." Republicans did not challenge Flannagan's seat in 1932, the final point needed by Crawford to determine the congressman was nothing more than a capitalist stooge.[24]

And so Crawford decided to take matters into his own hands and newsprint: the June 27, 1934, issue of *Crawford's Weekly* read, "Crawford Announces for Congress." Republicans again indicated they would not challenge Flannagan's seat; nor would Flannagan face a Democratic primary challenge. Presented with an unsatisfactory choice of who to vote for, Flannagan or nobody, Crawford decided to run himself, as an Independent. Weeks before, the pages of *Crawford's Weekly* joked that friends encouraged Crawford to run, so much so that they stopped him on the street and cornered him in hotel lobbies. This was not a hasty decision, evidenced by Crawford's concise, yet deep platform. Three days before the *Crawford's Weekly* announcement, Crawford distributed a campaign statement press release outlining his positions. At its core, the platform would "demand that the laborer, farmer, and small business man get all they were promised by the New Deal—and more."[25]

The full Crawford campaign platform was solidly progressive, though not quite embodying the revolutionary Communist policy proposals that appeared in the pages of *Crawford's Weekly*. First, Crawford highlighted new agricultural policy packages—farm relief programs, the elimination of New Deal crop destruction policies, and a moratorium on farm debts, taxes, and fore-closures—to correct the shortcomings of the Agricultural Adjustment Acts, of which Flannagan was a heavy supporter. Other Crawford platform points touched on consumer protection laws, unemployment insurance, and better hospitals for southwest Virginia. He was also explicitly antiwar and sought to reduce the federal budget for any "war purposes." Pro-union labor laws were the most complex points of Crawford's platform and were powerfully pro-union and likely familiar to the regular consumer of *Crawford's Weekly*:

> I stand for organized labor and for collective bargaining. Collective bargaining was promised by the recovery act, but labor is still fighting for it, in most cases without success.
>
> I am against the use of troops in labor disputes, since under the ruse of protecting property the troops are used to break strikes, protect scabs, and intimidate workers. I am opposed to any labor legislation which might construe a strike as an act of rebellion against the government.
>
> I am for a moratorium for labor on all mortgages, debts, and taxes so long as the working man income is below that required for health and decency.[26]

Crawford's platform also included creating a new version of the TVA, the New Deal agency he most frequently trashed, in southwest Virginia. Electricity costs would be driven down by the proposed Southwest Virginia Authority throughout the region while providing better pay for industrial workers and better markets for farmers, though Crawford never expanded in writing just how the new agency would differ from the much-maligned TVA.[27]

Newspapers in the Ninth District welcomed Crawford's candidacy, though few offered an endorsement, and plenty offered reasons to be a little wary of Crawford. The *Coalfield Progress*, Crawford's competitor in Norton, did not offer an endorsement but took a wait-and-see approach. "Bruce may harbor a critical doubt about too many things and may want to try to make it all over again," read *Coalfield's* take on Crawford's New Deal platform, continuing, "and we don't want him to do that, not quite yet at least." A host of other Ninth District newspapers—*Big Stone Gap Post, Clinch Valley News, Marion Democrat, Smyth County News, Roanoke Times, Southwest News, Bluefield Daily Telegraph, Radford News-Journal, Lebanon News*, and *Bristol Herald Courier*—welcomed Crawford's candidacy. If nothing else, Crawford promised a compelling race with his writing style and radical politics. A handful of newspapers outside southwest Virginia also took notice; for example, a glowing profile appeared in the *Baltimore Sun* documenting Crawford's action in the Virginia and Kentucky coalfields.[28]

Crawford harbored no illusions about the election's outcome. Electoral victory was likely impossible. *Crawford's Weekly* readily admitted as much in print but always pointed out that a good radical candidate was sure to push a conservative Democrat like Flannagan further left. Crawford also hoped his campaign would serve as a new platform for socialism and Communism that could reach more people than he or Dreiser ever dreamed possible. The "Virginia Democratic machine," headed by Senator Harry Byrd, stood as Crawford's largest barrier to victory. Senator Byrd would obviously not support Crawford. The pair were already mutual enemies by 1934, with *Crawford's Weekly* often running articles anxiously clamoring for Byrd's eventual downfall. "Politics at best is a game proverbially unclean. . . . We have government of, by and for gangs," wrote Crawford, with the Virginia Democrats serving as one of several "gangs."[29] But even as Crawford publicly claimed he had no belief in victory, he privately exchanged letters with intellectuals, usually Dreiser or Sherwood Anderson, that expressed a different viewpoint.

Writing to Dreiser for political and financial advice in May, a month before announcing and a full six months before Election Day, Crawford noted detected a growing concern from "the Democratic machine crowd" regarding his candidacy. With no Republican candidate, the pair reasoned that Crawford may actually have a chance. Crawford best figured that he could potentially capture "75% of the labor vote, 75% of the Republican vote, and 20% of the Democratic vote," thus ensuring a landslide in his favor. Dreiser also provided feedback on Crawford's platform, which he roundly approved. Both agreed that radical New Deal reform worded in explicitly pro-labor terms would most delineate Crawford's politics from Flannagan's. As Crawford put it, "If I should run, I would not oppose the Administration, but I would favor certain changes in the NRA to benefit the little man more and the monopolies less." He concluded with a hopeful "And if I got in, I'd bust loose!"[30] But, as with many other radical candidates, money was a problem. Crawford's campaign was broke, and everyone knew it. The *Clinch Valley News* wrote, "The trouble with Bruce is the same ailment that has seized many of the perpetual candidates, financial aridity."[31] *Crawford's Weekly* barely generated enough income to support the Crawford family, much less a congressional campaign, and there were no wealthy Communists ready to fund such an outsider candidate. Crawford also refused to beg for support from southwest Virginia's corporate and coal boosters despite their near limitless checkbooks.[32]

Crawford's candidacy must have spooked both the Virginia Democratic machine and Ninth District Republicans: within a week the two sides conspired to assist each other's campaigns within a week. As of Crawford's announcement, Flannagan was running unopposed. This soon changed when leading Democratic boosters in southwest Virginia, namely coal operators led by Bob Graham of Norton, met with Republicans to recruit a tepid GOP candidate. It mattered little to elite Democrats or Republicans in the Ninth District which party won the election, just so long as the winner was pro-coal or anti-labor. The GOP hastily called a July nominating convention in Bristol and nominated Fred C. Parks, a lawyer for the town of Abingdon. What had looked to be an election involving a potential big business Democrat versus a pro-labor outsider was now a three-way congressional race. Crawford's Weekly asked of its readers the following week, "Will the rank and file in the two parties stand for these shameless efforts of corporate leaders to save Flannagan?" Flannagan, Parks, and Crawford had less than four months to discover the answer.[33]

As summer turned into fall, the Crawford campaign ramped into full gear. A series of articles appeared in Crawford's Weekly during August that either accused Flannagan of being in the pocket of coal operators or showcased workers in support of Crawford. Crawford personally wrote an article that he certainly believed to be a damning exposé that would whip coal miners into an anti-Flannagan frenzy. The story was simple—workers at the Standard Banner Coal Company, partially owned by Flannagan, organized under the United Mine Workers of America and were fired for daring to ask for more pay. Flannagan stayed quiet for a few weeks, apparently unwilling to risk his wealth or the tenuous political support of miners, before bowing to public pressure and re-hiring some terminated miners. Flannagan remained on the hook though, as Crawford's Weekly highlighted Flannagan's "not satisfactory" congressional voting record on labor. It was not clear how much this campaign resonated with voters, but one problem facing Crawford was that many of the former Standard Banner employees who had been fired were forced to leave the Ninth District for West Virginia and Kentucky in search of work.[34]

Wise County's first annual Labor Day celebration was a coming-out party for Crawford, the potential congressman. As he proudly asserted, "I have lost thousands of dollars in business—yes and been shot in the leg—because I took sides with labor." This was Crawford's first large in-person audience and he used it to great advantage. For nearly an hour, Crawford appealed for greater labor rights protections and railed against the worst parts of the New Deal, especially the "anti-labor attitude" of the NRA. Southwest Virginia's vilest coal companies loved the NRA for its support of cooperative capitalism, so Crawford claimed, and all supported Flannagan. This mutual relationship only benefited coal power, not coal workers. Whenever Crawford got stuck on a complex point, he encouraged listeners to pick up any issue of *Crawford's Weekly*. It was in those pages of newsprint that they could see for themselves "for sixteen years . . . a record of unqualified championship of the working people." Specifically, readers should look for where *Crawford's Weekly* defended Virginian coal miners from abuses, then read other newspapers for where Wakenva, another of Flannagan's companies, fired workers for attempting to unionize.[35]

Radical notes crept into Crawford's speech as it developed beyond the New Deal, coal labor, and flinging mud at Flannagan. First, the speech addressed ideas shared with Democrats—raising wages, consumer protection laws, and taxing the wealth. Next, Crawford dove into expanding antifascism laws and expanding public ownership of nearly everything. "It was the big banks that caused the run on America . . . [and] that staged the world's greatest general strike in 1929," Crawford proclaimed to the crowd. His solution? Nationalize the banks: "Had the government taken over and nationalized the banking system, as it will eventually be forced to do, the Old and Disastrous Order might now be definitely behind." As for fascism, war was yet again on the horizon. Adolf Hitler had entered his second year as German Chancellor and tensions built across the European continent. Meanwhile, the U.S. government focused its attention and checkbook at expansive, interventionist military actions in China, the Caribbean, and South America. Crawford's solution? Congress should demand the recall of all American military personnel abroad, slash the military's budget, and reallocate resources to education and unemployment. Meanwhile, the military should strategize and prepare for coming war if fascism cannot be beaten back any other way.[36]

The remainder of Crawford's Labor Day speech called for nothing less than full economic socialization. The section on agriculture, for instance, could have been pulled straight from a socialist text:

It all gets back to the one problem of our time: how can wealth be distributed, how can the living standard be raised, how can distribution be geared to production, if the means and the machinery are privately owned by a few? Our present haywire situation shows that it cannot be done. The only and inevitable way out, for the farmer as for all the masses, is democratic ownership of banks, packing houses, factories, and utilities of distribution. We have a collectivism now of private capital, as seen in the trusts. This private collectivism must become a public collectivism. That should be the theme song of any candidate for office on a platform for the greatest good to the greatest number.

He continued with more socialist programs: free public hospitals, unemploy-ment relief, enhanced veteran pensions, increased public school funding, a "rehabilitation plan" for lagging wages, abolition of the poll tax, and strict opposition to proposed sales taxes. Ending his speech, Crawford once again proposed legislation that would allow unrestricted union organizing for every industry, be it public or privately owned, before offering his cornerstone Thirteen Point Platform. These thirteen succinct points were later published in *Crawford's Weekly* and presented perhaps the most radical platform among serious congressional candidates in the nation:

> A Better Deal for labor, the farm, and small business.
> Shorter work hours and higher wages.
> No more war appropriations.
> More federal funds for schools.
> Greater public works relief.
> Justice to the veteran.
> Free government hospitals.
> Jobless insurance and old age pension.
> Rehabilitation Program for Southwest Virginia to afford work, business, and opportunity to the common people.
> No taxes on those earning less than $3,000 a year.
> No taxes on any home worth less than $3,000.
> Higher taxes on wealth.
> Public ownership of banks, railroads, power, telephone, telegraph, all utili-ties, manufacturing plants, factories, armament and munition plants.[37]

Crawford's Labor Day speech won him some support. Coal miners wrote a letter to *Crawford's Weekly* the following week, published as "Miners Okay Crawford's Platform." *Crawford's Weekly* reported that "mine union lead-ers told the great crowd that Mr. Crawford is the man we want elected to Congress. We're tired of these oldtime politicians." Things were off to a good start, at least in Wise County.[38]

Yet, it soon became apparent that a poor Independent candidate could not manipulate the election like the two major parties. Both Democrats and Republicans used their power to suppress voter registration and turnout within Virginia usually by way of the poll tax. It cost $1.50 to vote in Virginia at the time, a few hours of labor for the typical coal miner, but often difficult to pay due to uncertain company schedules, the chaotic Depression economy, and anti-union politics. Both Democrats and Republicans often raised money explicitly to pay the poll taxes of those who promised their vote. Crawford obviously could not supply the same compensation, so he was already at a steep disadvantage. Pro-coal newspapers further tried to depress voter turnout by exaggerating Flannagan's electoral advantage. "Apathy and quiet organization" characterized Democrats, according to the *Bristol Herald Courier*, as all were convinced of an easy Flannagan victory. *Crawford's Weekly* predicted voter turnout could be as low as 15 percent.[39]

For the final two months of the campaign, Crawford stuck to the issues with one final major push—a special edition of *Crawford's Weekly* distributed to thirty-five thousand households throughout the Ninth District. This was a Hail Mary attempt to get Crawford's platform into as many voter's hands as possible. Each page included large block text outlining major campaign promises, such as "NO Tax on Any Home Valued at Less Than $3,000."[40] Crawford portrayed himself as somewhere between Flannagan and Parks on the New Deal but to the left on everything else. In his own words, he was "about 60 percent New Deal, but strongly anti-Republican and recorded as too socialistic by many who swallowed the apparent socialism of the New Deal." He even went so far as to predict winning 75 percent of the Republican vote, though without providing reasons for this optimistic assessment.[41] The largest headlines were reserved for accusing Flannagan of a bank loan scandal. The picture of a complex scheme involving shell companies refusing to repay small banks with Flannagan profiting was supported by accusations from officials in Dickenson County, Buchanan County, and the towns of Clintwood, Clinchco, Dante, and Grundy. Tabloid scandal was included too, as the issue republished Associated Press report that Flannagan no-showed on a court date for a drunk and disorderly charge filed in Richmond earlier in the year. Finally, Crawford reprinted supportive editorials from around the Ninth District, including by the UMWA, *Radford News-Journal*, and the *Roanoke Times*. The final letter was written by Harlan County UMW miners, who promised assistance if needed, offered as proof that Crawford's Kentucky adventures were legitimate.[42]

Money again became a concern during the Crawford campaign's final two months as it became clear that Flannagan had pulled ahead. Crawford appealed to Dreiser and other popular writers asking that they ask "liberals and radicals of means" for donations. Whether Dreiser spread the word was unclear, but little if any money came to the campaign. Dreiser personally did not donate money either, instead playing the role of friend and cheerleader. "Reading your speech and the comments of your opponents," Dreiser wrote to Crawford, "I can't imagine how you can lose. You have a personality that will certainly in the course of time, if it does not do it now, attach everybody in your district to you." Neither had any concerns over Crawford being labeled a Communist or socialist by his opponents. He wrote to Dreiser that "already I am called a Communist. My answer is that if my platform is red, if standing for the common people is red, then I certainly am red—and the yellow can make the most of it." Despite such confidence, Crawford never took out any loans; nor did he spend his savings on the campaign. He would later claim that he only spent about $300 of his own money, most of which went directly into newspaper advertisements and travel.[43]

Election Day 1934 finally came, voters turned out at a good rate, and Congressman Flannagan was easily reelected in a landslide. Crawford finished in a distant third place with just 2,402 votes (7.1 percent) compared to Flannagan's 20,532 (60.9 percent) and Parks's 12,355 (31.8 percent). Wise County was Crawford's home and the site of his best performance, but even there he only managed a paltry 785 (15.1 percent) out of 5,182 total ballots cast. This was not an unexpected outcome, and Crawford shrugged off the embarrassment easily enough. His unofficial advisor Dreiser did too, writing the following January that he was sorry for the defeat but proud of Crawford's upstanding "vision and principles." *Crawford's Weekly* blamed defeat on voter suppression and the fear expressed by Democratic voters that a vote for Crawford was effectively a vote for the Republican. Rumors swirled that polling stations randomly rejected "Republicans or doubtful Democrats" who could not immediately prove their poll tax status. Other rumors developed too that coal operators distributed pre-filled Flannagan ballots to miners. Neither rumor was ever proven to be true, but Crawford believed both of them.[44] Most Virginia newspapers reported the results as a predictable Flannagan victory, but the *Richmond Times-Dispatch* at least took notice of Crawford. "He Kept His Integrity" read the headline of an article praising Crawford's consistent radical platform. "Those who knew him knew before he began that he would tie firecrackers to the coattails of everybody whose coattails seemed to be worth that much effort," continued the article before finally comparing Crawford favorably to Upton Sinclair, whose 1934 California gubernatorial campaign drew heavy criticism from the Left for abandoning socialism for liberal capitalism.[45]

About a week after Crawford lost the election, *Crawford's Weekly* ran a blistering editorial titled "They Win Either Way." "They" referred to the capitalist oligarchs behind both Democrats and Republicans who ruled over the Ninth District, the Commonwealth of Virginia, and the United States. "The two old parties are like two pens within a large pen," read the editorial, arguing that the large pen comprised America's extreme pro-corporation capitalism. Most voters switched between blue and red pens every few years, never noticing that both write the same words. Even more confusing was individual corporations claim to be Democrat in one locality and Republican in the next: whatever it took to control poor people. "So that is how it is with big corporate wealth," concluded the article. "Wealth is for whichevery [sic] party is in office, but is primarily and always for itself." [46]

Regrettably for Crawford, the only thing he gained from the 1934 election was a severe blow to his faith in American democracy. The two-party system could not go on, simple as that. Prominent public intellectuals agreed with Crawford, such as philosopher-reformer John Dewey and Congressman Thomas R. Amlie. Calls for the creation of a leftist, socialist, or Communist third-party alternative strengthened during the mid-1930s, but Crawford's voice was not among them. He instead believed that socialist, Communist, and other left-wing radical candidates could win nomination through the two-party system so long as they stayed true to their values and treated voters as intelligent, rational, and independent thinkers. But less than half a year after the 1934 election, Crawford wrote to Dreiser questioning all forms of democracy, two-party system or not. Flannagan's victory still sat heavy with him, as did the impossibility of his victory in retrospect. He joked the only hope of victory would have been "by a fluke or a break—possibly the death of one of my two opponents!" His major gripe though was that while he had proven Flannagan to be a "bank wrecker and a hypocrite who drank wet but talked dry," this did not matter one bit. Voters voted for Flannagan because they liked FDR and the New Deal. It was impossible to separate local politics from the national scene in the age of growing mass media.[47] After a little more flirtation with radical activism, Bruce Crawford became a Democrat.

CLOSING *CRAWFORD'S WEEKLY*

Within months of losing the 1934 congressional election, Bruce Crawford would no longer be a Virginia newspaperman. Readership of weekly newspapers declined sharply by the 1930s as customers turned to dailies. A news-hungry public, facilitated by expanded car, train, and air networks and improved access to printing presses, demanded information at a faster pace. Weeklies occupied a space between fast daily news and in-depth magazines, a market that became increasingly irrelevant and struggled to adapt. Crawford understood all of this. He predicted the demise of *Crawford's Weekly* in 1931 and experimented often with other forms of print.[48] A few months after this comment, he privately confided in Dreiser that a trip to New York would not be possible because "unless business gets better—and I see nothing to indicate it—I may be emancipated via financial ruin. . . . There is little to fight for here. It seems a waste of time and energy to grapple with the situation."[49] *Crawford's Weekly* did more than limp along though, as he also told Dreiser the paper was "holding its own despite the general impression about here that I am a Communist."[50]

Sensing *Crawford's Weekly* may be ending soon, Crawford actively pursued other types of writing and speaking in the 1930s. He regularly published free-lance articles in left-leaning periodicals, such as *Common Sense, New York Times Magazine,* the *New Republic,* and the *Spectator,* for which he was likely paid a small amount. Collegiate speaking engagements also occupied his time, for instance a talk titled "Crusades of a Country Weekly" at Virginia Tech in 1932.[51] Two years later he again delivered this address as the headliner speaker of a Virginia Intercollegiate Press Association meeting, also hosted by Virginia Tech. Finding these activities promising, Crawford pressed Dreiser for a booking agency contact who could arrange for university speaking tours. This led to Crawford signing a contract with Management Ernest Briggs, which promised to promote Crawford alongside a recommendation letter from Dreiser. A Briggs publicity flyer distributed to journalism school deans described Crawford as "Inspiration without being Pollyanna / Critical but Constructive / Stimulating and Good-Humored." Included were twenty endorsements from noted journalists and writers, including Virginius Dabney, Sherwood Anderson, and Dreiser. A few speaking arrangements came through Briggs, but ultimately Crawford felt the agency neglected him in favor of more famous figures like Upton Sinclair.[52]

Crawford also dipped his toe into academic writing, most notably writing a chapter for W. T. Couch's *Culture in the South,* published in 1934. Four years earlier, the Southern Agrarians, a group of twelve white, male, conservative academics based out of Vanderbilt University, published their manifesto, titled *I'll Take My Stand.* The Southern Agrarians lauded the supposed qualities of the Old South, such as devout Christianity, agrarianism, tradition, and anti-industrialism, but their manifesto contained blind spots to slavery and embraced Lost Cause falsehoods. Couch, then editor of the University of North Carolina Press, took issue with the Southern Agrarians, writing, "Life in the South, as elsewhere, it may be repeated, is not a simple affair. . . . It is varied from class to class, and is further complicated by wide differences in political, economic, racial, educational, and religious faiths." Couch was somewhat conservative politically, a segregationist, and an anti-communist but nonetheless commissioned politically diverse writers from throughout the South in a challenge to *I'll Take My Stand.*

Crawford's essay in Couch's volume was titled "The Coal Miner" and took up workers' common struggle as its primary theme. Coal miners suffered company stores, anti-union policies, deputized company security forces, and "unspeakable poverty" no matter the specific area in the South. Coal operators forced upon their workers horrific injuries, long and varied hours, poor air, pathetic wages, no health care, shoddy company housing, corrupt company doctors, and laughable workers' compensation insurance. But after dressing down coal operators, Crawford pivoted to celebrating coal towns. Miners and their families deserved respect for bettering themselves and their communities and should be provided with a happy life because they were people. Passages such as "In Kentucky the Red Cross denied aid to miners because a strike is not 'an act of God'" likely shocked readers, as did the assertion that "most officers in a mining region are paid by the companies and given a badge by the sheriff." As of 1934, many southerners not living in coal towns would have been wholly unaware of the dire conditions just a few hills away.

Crawford did not write a sob story describing poverty but rather predicted that coal miners were pure Americans ready for revolution. Communism was already prevalent as an ideology in miner communities because of what Crawford described as "the most outstanding example of industrial despotism and official depravity." What made the situation in coal country particularly offensive to Crawford was that miners were, in his view, descendants of America's first European colonists. In Crawford's day, coal operators forced these "pure" mountain residents to turn around and exploit the land for which their ancestors died. The problem of course was that coal miners were hardly a homogenous group. Any coal town contained a diverse array of generational residents, immigrants, African Americans, and mixed families. A half-dozen spoken languages could be found in most coal camps. Still, even with this fallacy, Crawford aimed his harrowing picture at educated white southern liberals. Kentuckians, southerners, and Americans all had to choose—oppression or revolution.

> Here in Kentucky is a tribe of native Americans, whose ancestors fought in the Revolutionary War, today being exploited and impoverished. Their extinction is not an impossibility. Corralled, starved, harassed, killed, they are a doomed race—unless there is a thoroughgoing shake-up and socialization of the industry.[53]

Crawford's was the most radical essay in Couch's ultimately successful volume. For example, his essay was followed by "Appalachian American" by J. Wesley Hatcher, a weak chapter beholden to Appalachian stereotype that blamed mountain people for their poverty.[54] In the end, *Culture of the South* was a more a death stroke than a volley against *I'll Take My Stand*. Southern Agrarians faded into obscurity, or according to historian Sarah Gardner, "softened their earlier position," with several members abandoning cultural commentary altogether to write novels set in the Civil War.[55]

After Crawford's unsuccessful efforts at developing new revenue streams and failed run for Congress, *Crawford's Weekly* printed its last issue on February 8, 1935. Days later, Crawford ceased all printing operations and transferred the rights to *Crawford's Weekly* and his printing equipment, including the press itself, to his nearest competitor and former employer, the *Coalfield Progress*. "I may sell my paper in a few days," he wrote on January 12, suggesting that declining sales were the cause of these developments. *Crawford's Weekly* lost subscribers at an alarming rate in the 1930s. In 1934—the last year in which N. W. Ayer & Son had records on *Crawford's Weekly*—circulation totaled 2,042, down over half since the 1930 total of 4,140 subscribers and even further from a 1927 peak of 4,600. There was no one cause for this decline but surely the 1929 financial crash impacted Crawford's bottom line. Altogether, Crawford lost 56 percent of his subscription peak in just five years. Rival newspapers like the *Coalfield Progress* also declined sharply, from a peak in 1928 of 2,450 to about 1,400 just five years later, a 42 percent loss.[56] *Crawford's Weekly* also lost some advertising revenue based on the type and quantity of ads. By the end of 1934, all advertisements were from retail stores in Norton or Coeburn. A decade earlier, the newspaper included those same local ads alongside ads for larger regional companies like the Chesapeake and Potomac Telephone Company and for products like Good Luck baking powder, Bull Durham tobacco, and the Packard Motor Car Company. Such subscription and advertising losses led Crawford to the logical conclusion—it was time to move on with his career.[57]

There was no glorious, radical farewell for *Crawford's Weekly*. Crawford simply printed a front-page article titled "Crawford Printing Co. Sells to the Norton Press," informing readers the newspaper might continue, though under a different name and owner. Crawford also announced he would donate all the company's files to University of Virginia, though this apparently never actually happened.[58] The article included no hints regarding what would come next for Crawford. Other editors speculated that Crawford would either take an editor position with a daily paper or "join a labor movement."[59] Either way, all that was left of *Crawford's Weekly* now fell under the auspices of the *Coalfield Progress*. Crawford's readership apparently did not migrate to the new publisher. Three years later, *Coalfield Progress*'s circulation was just 1,922, still well short of Crawford's 1934 totals.[60]

Peers and colleagues across Virginia mourned the closing of *Crawford's Weekly*. Louis Jaffe described Crawford as follows: "No more consecrated soldier in the war of human rights was ever graduated from the training school of Virginia journalism. . . . [He was] the consistent enemy of humbuggery, cant, false pretense, intolerance, obscurantism, persecution, and pecksniffery."[61] Jaffe also penned a public farewell letter:

> In the end, the crusader decided that the game of righting human wrongs while tied down by the limitations of a weekly, dependent on the favor of the satellites of privilege for its sustenance, was not worth the candle. There is work for him to do—out in No 'an's Land where only the brave pickets venture, where the lines are facing each other for the new Battle of the Century. Out there he can swing his sword in a wide arc without fear of wounding the feelings of subscribers or advertisers. His less venturesome colleagues of the publishing world will hope he wins through [to the Croix de Guerre]. No more consecrated soldier in the war of human rights was ever graduated from the training school of Virginia journalism.

In typical fashion, Crawford responded to Jaffe's praise, writing, "If I am graduating, I hope it is into left-wing radicalism; and I urge my many liberal friends to come along."

That same year, Crawford confided in Dreiser why he actually sold *Crawford's Weekly*. With a dash of his typical candor, humor, and political flourish, he revealed that the sale had to do with his personal politics and a gloomy prediction of journalism's future. The Depression had all but delivered journalism unto corporations, in Crawford's view, so it was time to pull the escape cord:

> My rival here and I pitched a coin to see who would buy whom. From my standpoint, he lost! I turned over to him all that was mortal of *Crawford's Weekly* and let the rest—the name—take on what the Bible calls incorruptibility. In view of what looks like will be a fascist regimentation in this country before long, I am damned glad to get out of the business. I look for boycotts, direct and indirect. Advertisers will be intimidated into withdrawing business from newspapers that don't go along with the powers in authority.[62]

Two months later Crawford offered one of the best essays of his career, which contained a public explanation for the paper's closure. The essay, titled "Why I Quit Liberalism," appeared in *New Masses*, a Marxist magazine based out of New York closely linked to the Communist Party. Crawford wrote on hopelessness, both his own and that of his Norton neighbors, that slowly swallowed the community over the past decade. Neighbors shrugged at finding solutions to their problems, and Crawford tired of trying to help those who had lost their will to fight.[63] *Crawford's Weekly*, once a platform for Crawford's radicalism, suddenly became a burden. Crawford was forced to hold back on his most radical ideas so as not to offend or condemn loyal subscribers. This essay was Crawford at his peak, in all his fury, and merits extended quotations:

> I have quit publishing Crawford's Weekly. It was too radical for its bourgeois customers and not radical enough for me. Like capitalism, it was full of contradictions. Hence it could not go on.
>
> A flash-back on the Crawford's Weekly that was unable to survive its contradictions is in order: Seventeen years ago I started the paper with typical bourgeois ambitions for it and for myself. The name of the paper showed a desire for a career. I bought a big press that printed from newsprint rolls, and installed other costly equipment. The paper would be literary as well as the usual purveyor of small-town and rural news. It would also take flyers into iconoclasm a la Brann. It would raise hell and make its editor known. And who would object to a man being a success?
>
> To an extent Crawford's Weekly achieved most of its aspirations. It dished up local news, often too starkly for its clientele. It became literary and offered pleasurable reading when the content was of no importance. It imitated Brann's Iconoclast until the Mencken vogue set new standards of debunking. It was a Mencken disciple so long as he was "having at" religionists, Babbitts, and current idiocies. But Mencken was a false god. Having blasted a hole through the mountain, Mencken stood aside. His followers went on through and left him. Crawford's Weekly finally recognized the Baltimore critic as a Tory, who berated "the boobs" but didn't account for them. He was seen as a critic of democracy who did not attribute its corruption to the capitalist society he lives in—did not show that it was a capitalist democracy.
>
> Gradually my Weekly began to be a house divided against itself, psychological. True, it realized that in a society cracking up, there was no use trying to save the so-called democracy whose inherent faults had brought about its collapse; no use being a liberal and trying to follow a middle course when anything right of the Left would precipitate one toward the extreme Right, ultimately. So Crawford's Weekly, which had always defended labor and the poor, went farther and farther to the Left. And yet it was relying

almost wholly for its support on advertisers, small-town merchants, local dealers of General Motors, and other "satellites of privilege." Herein was the two-faced position of the paper. It found itself fighting its customers— an unrealistic, impossible attitude for a business.

So the Weekly would alternately "go berserk" in favor of the coal miners and small farmer, and lapse into community-boosting activity that, in spite of certain communal phases, did not offend the bankers and coal barons.

The essay continued with a general outline of what Crawford considered his career highlights: crusades against the Klan and lynching, getting shot by a cop in Harlan, and fighting for coal miners. He proudly noted how he "had announced in print years ago that I didn't believe in God, so why shouldn't they label me a Communist, from most practical viewpoints?" And he pointed out the hopelessness in southwest Virginia and how much he feared the possibility of an American fascist regime. Finally, Crawford concluded with an appeal to his liberal friends to let go of democratic hope and join him on the path to radicalism:

It was still possible to keep going, catering to the middle class and to labor over the heads of its misleaders. But the results, from the standpoint of radical or even liberal furtherance, would not have justified the tenacity and sacrifice. Holding a bear by the tail, without hope of reinforcements, is a waste of time, energy, and opportunity. And that's what many liberals are doing. They are holding on to the bear's tail and afraid, where their inclinations are leftward, to turn loose and apply both hands and all energy to the job of revolutionary salvation.

So I have let go! I have, for a consideration amounting to a salvage, turned over to my competitor "all that was mortal" of Crawford's Weekly— its machinery, advertising contracts, and nearly-expired subscription list— and let the rest of Crawford's Weekly go! If and when a fascist regimentation comes (and what could a weekly paper drawing support from fascist elements do to prevent its coming?), I shall not have any bourgeois attachments that can be laid hold of to cramp my style. I have joined the great unemployed. If I get into trouble and my head cracked, neither customers nor creditors can deplore my activities or accuse me of being recreant to obligations! If I get shot in the leg again, or go to jail, there won't be that damned feeling of apology to the respectable. Now, as a liberal graduating into radicalism, with the more tangible roots to bourgeois life severed, I hope to know a new and meaningful freedom, whatever the hardships.[64]

Heeding his own advice, Crawford immediately departed Norton for Alabama as part of a new investigative group sponsored by the National Committee for the Defense of Political Prisoners. Birmingham's city council had recently passed a law criminalizing the possession of more than one radical publication targeting labor organizers, so the NCDPP hoped to break the unjust law by creating a legal test case. The Alabama state legislature also passed the "Street bill," which redefined sedition such that Communists and labor activists now qualified for the crime just by virtue of their existence. Upon arrival in Birmingham, Crawford and the group stood directly in front of city hall for hours distributing copies of *Daily Worker, New Masses,* and the *New Republic.* This was directly in violation of both laws, yet Alabama police did not arrest NCDPP members, knowing their media connections and judicial intent.

After spending about a day in Alabama, the NCDPP group secured a meeting in Montgomery with Democratic governor Bibb Graves, a supporter of both the New Deal and the Klan.[65] Crawford wrote in the *Nation* that unknown men fired shots at the NCDPP car more than once during this trip, and those same men threatened NCDPP members whenever the group stopped their vehicle. The NCDPP petitioned Graves for protection, but nothing substantial was given. Rather than further risk life in Alabama, NCDPP members bypassed Montgomery and headed out of Alabama bound for Nashville. Press coverage of the Alabama events was mixed. Communist newspapers hailed the group and condemned white Alabama. Most mainstream outlets scoffed at the NCDPP as Communist troublemakers with one major exception being the *Richmond Times-Dispatch,* where Virginius Dabney worked as a senior writer, which described the NCDPP as doing good work despite their "economics [being] much farther to the Left than our own." Regardless of press attention, Governor Graves vetoed the "Street bill" a few weeks after the NCDPP departure, thus making the Alabama journey a success. More likely, Graves capitulated due to pressures from labor unions, national press, and "popular opposition," but still Crawford and his associates could claim at least a little credit.[66]

Crawford's dreams of becoming a radical professional speaker and independent journalist only held for a few short months as he suddenly settled into a much quieter life. For the first time in over fifteen years, he took a new job. The *Bluefield Sunset News,* a "strongly pro-Roosevelt and viciously anti-Republican" daily press in Mercer County, West Virginia, hired Crawford as their editor in April 1936. The newspaper owner was nothing like Crawford: a Republican "Liberty Leaguer," meaning a member of the libertarian, anti–New Deal American Liberty League, who owned multiple daily papers. Generally, the newspaper owner enjoyed having multiple papers with different perspectives because it cornered the entire partisan landscape, so Crawford was granted total freedom. After having worked in Bluefield for a year, Crawford wrote that he liked the job—"It has been fun with little or no dread and insecurity such as I was gnawed by at Norton during those hectic years." In general, *Bluefield Sunset News* editorials were far less radical than those in *Crawford's Weekly*. Crawford reserved his radicalism for other writing gigs like articles for magazines and a book on the history of Harlan County that never manifested.[67]

Crawford simply put his head down and got to work editing the *Bluefield Sunset News*, effectively a Democratic newspaper. Despite a decline in radicalism, he was no less attuned to local issues and no less petty than he had been while running *Crawford's Weekly*. A rival newspaper, the *Bluefield Daily Telegraph*, regularly hurled insults at Crawford, to which he responded that the paper's cartoonist was "prostituting his fine talent" to such a rag.[68] Crawford settled into the job in less than a couple months though, and developed a regular editorial titled "Ere the Sun Sets." The major difference with this new column was that Crawford toed the Democratic Party line. A single "Ere the Sun Sets" in the June 13, 1936, issue contained four editorials in praise of FDR, one critical of Democrat Carter Glass for platforming a Republican in the *Lynchburg News*, one on veteran bonus bonds, and one on a visit to the newsroom by Concord College students. By the end of his tenure, peers recognized that Crawford had "championed" FDR and the New Deal, a definite change since Norton.[69]

Either way, Bruce and Kate Crawford hoped Bluefield would be their new home and Bruce's last job, or so Bruce Crawford claimed. He plainly stated as much in a letter to Dreiser: "We are going to settle down here for the rest of our lives." The Crawford couple liked that Bluefield was just two hours away from Norton by car, that they had no baggage in Bluefield, and that it was a bit less populated than Norton and Wise. They saved every penny for three years hoping to buy land and build a house. The Crawfords had, by the fall of 1938, established construction plans and a builder. Their home was scheduled to be completed by January 1939. They even sent out preliminary invitations to out-of-town guests for a housewarming party, so there was every reason to believe their love of Bluefield life was genuine.[70]

But just as suddenly as the move from Norton to Bluefield, the Crawfords departed again, this time to Charleston, West Virginia, so Bruce could become the next state director of the Federal Writers' Project (FWP). Crawford was no longer a journalist or a critic of the New Deal; he was part of the Democratic machine now. Neither Crawford ever detailed why they left Bluefield, with only Bruce vaguely noting to Dreiser that he had "called off all schemes of mine at Bluefield and took a better job."[71] Maybe that's all it was, a better salary in a new field. The *Bluefield Sunset News* reported that Crawford's FWP appointment "came unsought [and] followed a recent conference with national officials in Washington," so it stands to reason that New Deal officials recognized Crawford as a talented editor at a West Virginia newspaper and poached him for those talents.[72] Maybe this was true, but another likely factor was Crawford's growing disdain for journalism alongside the promise of freedom that came with working at an innovative federal agency, as he wrote to Dreiser:

> I'm state director of the Federal Writers. We are compiling data for a series of books on West Virginia. As you may know, some of the jobs in other states have been unusual stuff, written in a lively, daring day.
>
> But I don't like the trend in national politics. The confounded newspapers, which howl about freedom of the press, are having their influence now. They confuse, lie, crucify. They abuse the freedom they do have.[73]

Having abandoned all plans of putting down roots in Bluefield, the Crawfords settled into a small home within walking distance to the West Virginia state capitol. Ironically, Crawford took this federal job because he had grown tired of having his press freedom curtailed, but the steepest challenge to his journalistic integrity would soon become all too evident in the context of his new job. In a matter of days, he stood toe-to-toe with the West Virginia governor's office just for trying to do his work and tell West Virginia's story.

CHAPTER 4

THE EDITOR AS PUBLIC HISTORIAN

Bruce Crawford was an excellent historian, though he officially produced historical writing for just three years. Never formally trained, he demonstrated a sophisticated grasp of the presence of the past in his own world. He understood how the general public and elites alike viewed society, how events in the past rippled into the present, and the exponential impact of seemingly small present events. The past was also highly political and far from decided. History, as it was written, had been made largely by those with power. The past played an important role in his life because the history that mattered most to him—that of working peoples—had been largely exorcised by the rich and powerful from official narratives. In righting the narrative, Crawford would become the first historian to publish on West Virginia labor history topics like the Mine Wars and Hawk's Nest Tunnel, but it was an arduous process that faced many powerful challengers and obstacles. In a letter to West Virginia governor Homer A. Holt, who would become the next great Crawford nemesis, Crawford explained his historical thinking in relation to West Virginia state history:

> The best way to show the great progress achieved in this state was to contrast what was with what is. We tried to show that the pistol had been supplanted by the conference table as a means of settling disputes between employers and employees. . . . We didn't think that recounting the old would make the present ugly, hence the generous space dedicated to labor's story in a state with perhaps more labor history than any other.[1]

Crawford began explicitly writing about West Virginia history during the 1930s, a time when many professional historians reoriented toward a more inclusive definition of the field. Carl Becker, in his 1931 presidential address to the American Historical Association titled "Everyman His Own Historian," called for his peers to both recognize the importance of the past in everyday life and, most critically, apply their historical skills in better understanding this importance. "History is an imaginative creation," he spoke, "a personal possession which each one of us, Mr. Everyman, fashions out of his individual experience, adapts to his practical or emotional needs, and adorns as well as may be to suit his aesthetic tastes."[2] Becker was speaking about a professionalism that had been practiced by some historical practitioners, a group loosely known as applied historians, for decades.

Applied historians recognize that while all history, no matter how big or small, is political, the same factors that make history contentious can be harnessed for change. Benjamin Shambaugh, best remembered as former head of the State Historical Society of Iowa, is generally credited with developing the idea of applied history around 1909, though Lucy Maynard Salmon taught the concept to her Vassar College students several years earlier. By the 1930s, applied history ideas filtered up to the elite echelons of the academy, as evidenced by Carl Becker's keynote address, though it would be several more decades before the idea took broad hold among academics.[3] Crawford was almost assuredly unaware of Becker, Salmon, and Shambaugh but nonetheless wrote about the past as an applied historian, always with an eye toward solving real-world problems. In his view, there was no such thing as history for history's sake, the past must serve a purpose. Another relevant applied history idea was that historians could facilitate peoples' history. Becker wrote in 1931 that "the chief value of history is that it is an extension of the personal memory, and an extension which masses of people can share so that it becomes, or would ideally become, the memory of a nation or of humanity."[4] Just four years after Becker wrote this passage, the Franklin Roosevelt administration and the Federal Writers Project put the concept to the test.

The idea of a populist applied history project became reality with the formation of the Federal Writers' Project in 1935. The FWP was federally funded project under the auspices of the Works Progress Administration (WPA), a public employment agency designed to provide a living wage for out-of-work people. Most WPA jobs involved manual labor, usually construction, but the agency set aside significant funding for white-collar workers. Writers, artists, musicians, and teachers were all out of work, just as everyone else. The FDR administration argued these folks deserved jobs too, lest their unique skills fade with disuse, not to mention the issue of poverty. New Deal officials tasked the FWP with employing anyone with writing ability—usually journalists, teachers, authors, and folklorists—with the goal of generating nonfiction books. Each state, some territories, and a few cities had FWP branches, most of which were given academic and structural independence. However, there were a few strict guidelines. FWP branches were encouraged to produce short books on folklore or history and one long travel guidebook. All materials had to be approved by staff in the Washington, DC, office, usually in accordance with pre-distributed writing guidelines. FWP projects were incredibly productive and employed about seven thousand writers over eight years, many of whom went on to incredible careers, including Zora Neale Hurston, Ralph Ellison, Richard Wright, and Studs Terkel to name a few.

Bruce Crawford accepted a job with the FWP in October 1938 and started work the following month as the director of the West Virginia branch.[5] The branch had missed several deadlines, so Crawford's primary initial tasks were to shepherd a few small projects to completion and, more importantly, to finish the West Virginia guidebook project. The guidebook was part of the FWP's American Guide Series, a book series produced between 1937 and 1941 that provided separate tourist guides to forty-eight states, forty cities, and seventeen regions or territories. State and city FWP offices independently produced guidebooks, though the Washington office provided support such as suggested structure, topics, and editorial workers. "Like a cathedral built over a long period of time by many hands," as Crawford described them, guidebooks were the product of dozens of FWP employees.[6] FWP state offices hired field workers to travel the state while producing written material, usually in the form of primary documentation and short dispatches or folklore anecdotes. Submitted field materials were then adapted into guidebook essays and driving tour scripts by state office staff while thematic essays were written by a combination of FWP staff and contracted third parties, usually experts employed in government or universities. Ultimately, the state director was responsible for the guidebook's final content, though dozens of hands went into its creation. The national office in Washington, DC, edited guidebooks, ensured publishing schedules were met, and, on rare occasion, traveled to state offices to settle disputes.

Crawford took to the new West Virginia job easily upon his assumption of leadership on October 31, 1938, though much of his early work involved cleaning up after a few of his predecessors' missteps. The West Virginia FWP office had been a thorn in the side of the Washington office since the agency's formation. West Virginia's first project directors were, simply put, not up to the job. The first state project director was named as a political favor. Less than two months into his tenure, he refused to hire enough workers and the national office described him as "stubborn, irritable, crotchety, and childish." National FWP director Henry Alsberg removed him in December 1936, ten months after appointment, with the help of West Virginia's junior senator Matthew Neely. The next director, a "reformed" Republican, lasted just a few months, and the third remained for about a year but never overcame the setbacks of the first two. All three of these project directors moved the project forward somewhat, meaning that field workers gathered materials, though most writing was of poor quality and produced at a pace unacceptable to the national office.[7] This was the project Crawford inherited, but before exploring his time with the FWP, the context of his appointment must be considered, as Crawford's political past immediately put himself and the FWP into the line of conservative political fire.

DIES COMMITTEE

Anti-communist sentiment during the FDR presidency reached its apex in national politics at about the same time as Crawford's FWP appointment. On May 26, 1938, Martin Dies, a Democratic congressman from Texas, became the first chair of the newly formed House Committee on Un-American Activities, commonly referred to as the Dies Committee and later as HUAC. The Dies Committee, formed partially out of concern regarding ongoing war in Europe and Asia, targeted supposedly subversive forces within the federal government. The argument was the Dies Committee intended to keep America safe by rooting out those who would destroy the nation from the inside, but in reality, Congressman Dies and his allies used their collective power to target political opponents and innocent people whose politics did not align with their own. Common Dies Committee targets included fascists and communists, though communists received far more attention before America's entry into World War II. Early in the Dies Committee's existence, it became all too clear that left-leaning federal arts projects were within its crosshairs.[8]

The Dies Committee came for the FWP during the latter half of 1938 and began its crusade just a few weeks before Crawford's hiring. Though Crawford's politics never received Dies Committee attention, other projects certainly did. New York's office, for example, was deemed to be too politically left-wing. National FWP officials found themselves before Congress, forced to defend against calls for Communist purges, which FWP director Henry Alsberg found frankly ridiculous and outside the agency's purview. In August 1938 Alsberg testified in defense of his agency. Seeking to placate anti-Communist fervor, he condemned the Soviet Union and admitted that a few early employees of the New York City project, but not the project itself, harbored pro-Communist views. Alsberg meandered somewhat in his defense of the Montana and New Jersey state guidebooks, both having been labeled by the Dies Committee as promoting class antagonisms. "The New Jersey State staff," Alsberg claimed, would "overstate and sharpen statements about labor . . . very often any one statement was not bad, but when you read fifty pages you began to feel these people were knocking New Jersey." Alsberg demonstrated that national FWP officials insisted on a more balanced tone but in the end, he openly admitted those two guidebooks, at a minimum, were problematic.[9]

Even though the hearing ended with Alsberg and the Dies Committee parting on seemingly cordial terms, the testimony generated plenty of negative press for the FWP. Conservative politicians came away with the sense that the national office was either wholly incapable of controlling supposedly Communist forces within FWP state offices or consciously harboring Communists themselves and promoting their ideas. Alsberg's admission of class divisiveness in Montana and New Jersey was all Dies Committee crusaders needed; they now had proof of another federal agency harboring subversive elements. As for Alsberg, his conciliatory performance alienated him from liberal and leftist circles. Other federal officials testifying about the FWP, namely director of Women's and Professional Projects of the Works Progress Administration Ellen Woodward, turned the tables on the Dies Committee by calling its actions flatly un-American during testimony. Alsberg's performance led to another immediate committee investigation, this time by the House Appropriations Committee chaired by Virginia congressman Clifton Woodrum. Despite Woodrum's more progressive values, his committee did not support the FWP in the end. Alsberg was done and he knew it, as was the FWP in its current form.[10]

Facing rapidly declining support, the FDR administration made no special provision for the FWP in its April 1939 budgeting. WPA director F. W. Harrington also had no love for the FWP or the other three arts projects within his domain, so during May and June 1939 he communicated clearly to Congress he had no interest in retaining federal sponsorship. Congress followed with the Emergency Relief Appropriation Act of 1939, effective June 30, which terminated the Federal Theater Project and canceled federal sponsorship for the other three WPA arts programs—art, music, and the FWP. However, these three arts programs could continue indefinitely provided each individually secured state sponsors that would fund 25 percent of their respective state project budgets by the end of September 1939. Most state FWP offices found such sponsors easily by appealing directly to state governors and legislatures. West Virginia was no different, as multiple state agencies volunteered, but the introduction of state funding brought with it even more state politics to the federal program. Now Crawford had to navigate at least three political avenues in his job—one familiar in the national FWP office, one to be avoided in the Dies Committee, and another new and unknown from the West Virginia governor's office headed by Homer Holt.[11]

Writing in the *Bookplate* in 1939, Crawford called the Dies Committee (rather uncreatively) the "Dies Smearing Committee" for its habit of ruining the reputations of writers "who politically part their hair left of the center."[12] Crawford, having written plainly innumerable times of his fondness for Communism, would have been an easy target. Just a few weeks prior to Crawford's 1938 hiring, Russell Stewart was hired to be the West Virginia FWP project second-in-command. Stewart and Crawford worked together for just two months. A pay dispute led to Stewart quitting after a few weeks, reportedly in a "fine spirit of cooperation," to take a new job with the Associated Press. Seemingly out of nowhere, Crawford then received a letter from Stewart that demanded the equivalent of a month's salary for work he had not done. Crawford obviously rejected Stewart's demand, so Stewart retaliated with blackmail threats. Stewart claimed to have written an exposé for "one of the anti–New Deal publications" that assuredly would force conservative politicians, namely West Virginia senior senator Rush Dew Holt, to cut FWP funding. Stewart never revealed the article's contents and never published any known article on the subject, but he likely knew of Crawford's political past and dangled the threat of exposing it to the Dies Committee. While Stewart's threat dissipated rather quickly, anti-Communist sentiment still loomed over both Crawford and national FWP leadership.[13] Either way, this was the baggage following Crawford as he worked in the FWP and eventually began working with Governor Holt's surrogates and later Holt himself.

GOVERNOR HOMER HOLT

Homer Holt desperately wanted to head West Virginia's Democratic Party machine and saw himself as the state's potential equivalent to Virginia's powerful Senator Harry Byrd. Crawford and Holt were diametrically opposed in nearly every way politically and seemingly set up to become great antagonists. Both served in noncombat roles in World War I, but there the similarities ended. Holt attended Washington & Lee University and graduated with a law degree in 1923. Shortly thereafter he opened a legal practice in Fayetteville and began to climb the political ranks. The Fayette County Democrats welcomed him with open arms, electing him to be their chair within a year of his moving to the area. From this modest position grew his Democratic political connections, eventually earning him the support of the state party in a run for statewide office in 1932. He earned the Democratic nomination for attorney general and rode the national wave of Democratic support into office alongside Herman Guy Kump, who won the governor's race. Kump was Holt's political mentor in many ways and the two formed a short-lived political machine. The clear plan all along was for Holt to succeed Kump, which he did in a landslide 1936 election.

Both Kump and Holt were conservative, pro-business, and opposed to most New Deal initiatives, but not so opposed that they would reject federal money if it meant political gain. Previous Republican governors endorsed Hooveresque laissez-faire responses to the 1929 economic disaster, which led to catastrophic state budget shortfalls in 1930, 1931, and 1932. Federal funding was unquestionably needed and virtually impossible, both politically and practically, to reject. West Virginia's economy recovered somewhat from 1933 through 1936 thanks to this influx of federal cash. Kump, though, was quick to claim credit and even quicker to condemn New Deal projects that operated outside of his control. Most notably, on June 8, 1935, Harry Hopkins, administrator of the newly created WPA, appointed F. Witcher McCullough as West Virginia's first state project administrator. McCullough had most recently sought the Democratic nomination for governor in 1932, a contest Kump won, and there was no good feeling between the two. Hopkins did not consult Kump on this appointment, so the governor's office first sought to block McCullough and having failed at that, obstructed WPA work projects at every turn. By the end of 1935, federal officials had exhausted all means of satisfying Kump and essentially gave up on securing his cooperation. Hopkins's traveling reporter Lorena Hickok met with Kump that November and, after realizing the governor truly did not grasp the purpose, structure, or function of the WPA, informed Hopkins of the real problem with Kump—"He's just dumb." Dumb or not, Kump controlled state politics and had the backing of many West Virginians with serious power and money.[14]

The Kump administration, alongside energy corporation Union Carbide, was also responsible for the Hawk's Nest Tunnel disaster and its effective cover-up. Between 1930 and 1935, an unknown number of workers, most of whom were African American men from the South, died of silicosis while constructing Hawk's Nest Tunnel in Fayette County. Anywhere between 476 and about 1,000 workers died as a direct result of unsafe working conditions, such as no face masks or site ventilation. An exact death total is still unknown because of company secrecy and because many victims were buried in un-marked graves near the construction site. Other workers developed the illness more slowly and returned home too sick to work. Without question, more men died at home or were permanently incapacitated. Union Carbide never admit-ted fault, nor did subcontractor companies or the State of West Virginia. Of more concern to Union Carbide and the Kump administration was ensuring the Hawk's Nest project was legally allowed to be completed and that the deaths were not widely reported.

While Hawks Nest workers died horrible, preventable deaths, a lawsuit between West Virginia and the federal government regarding interstate com-merce advanced to the Supreme Court. Holt, in his capacity as West Virginia attorney general, represented the state, Union Carbide, and other affiliated companies to ensure they all retained the project under federal law. Instead of arguing the case, Holt moved for immediate dismissal on jurisdictional grounds. This strategy worked, so tunnel construction (and worker deaths) continued unabated. Silica, silicosis, and worker deaths were not mentioned in the official court record. Union Carbide and the state further suppressed knowledge of the workers' deaths, going so far as to bulldoze work camps after work was completed. In their place, Union Carbide built a country club for white-collar employees. The disaster then faded from public knowledge, only known by the families of those affected, some West Virginians, and labor activists.[15]

As Kump's term neared its expiration, his administration's general popular-ity, along with Democratic dominance in the 1930s, foretold Attorney General Holt's gubernatorial nomination and easy 1936 victory. Governor Holt entered his new office with a clear mandate and supermajority in both branches of the state legislature. Believing the worst of the economic crisis to be behind the state, Holt became an even greater opponent to New Deal programs than his predecessor. Stricter economic conservatism was one thing, but Holt's ad-ministration radically politicized New Deal appointments. Senator Rush Dew Holt Sr., a distant cousin and political rival at times, conspired with Governor Holt in securing the cushiest New Deal jobs for their political allies, a scheme opposed by New Deal Democrats like Senator Neely to no avail. When the fed-eral government called for merit-based New Deal appointments, Governor Holt described the demand as "the blow at state sovereignty through the club of federal grants."[16] Labor unions also received no love from Governor Holt. He first interfered with a series of miner strikes in 1938 by demanding that workers return to work without a contract, an unthinkable prospect for union officials. Any opposition to Holt's position, no matter how slight, brought grandiose public condemnation, such as accusations that UMW leaders were conspiring to overthrow the government. Even when leaving office in 1941, Holt blamed others for supposedly destroying his legacy through the strategies of "modern-day European totalitarianism." The man simply saw an enemy in anyone who refused to bend the knee, especially those allied with labor.[17]

Governor Holt's most brazen assault on labor came with in the form of a pamphlet produced by his office on December 15, 1939, titled "A Message to the Miners of West Virginia." In this seventy-nine-page document, Holt accused the United Mine Workers and other unions of following the totalitarian philosophies of Adolf Hitler. He went on to accuse unnamed figures—likely union leaders and journalists—of fomenting "a distrust and hatred for the government of their own state." Big on rhetoric and sparse on details, Holt simultaneously proclaimed he would "protect [miners] in their enjoyment of their American rights and liberties" and that "it is one thing for you to have your union and to run it yourselves for your benefit and quite another for certain dictatorial persons to run you in the name of your union," an obvious contradiction that anyone could see. The pamphlet also included reprinted correspondences, annotated by Holt himself, supposedly clearing him of any wrongdoing in strike interventions the previous year. Of course, he blamed the UMW, specifically William H. "Bill" Blizzard, president of UMW District 17, best remembered for his leadership during the Battle of Blair Mountain. Holt's passages on Blizzard were some of his most aggressive in the pamphlet:

> These people who would dominate the miners of West Virginia and fatten upon their toil do not want to give the men a chance to hear from any one [sic] except themselves. They fear for their power when the men know the truth. It is the same reason which has prompted to Communists to outlaw religion in Russia. There is no room in Russia for God and Stalin. There is no room in Germany for Hitler's book, *Mein Kampf*, and the Holy Book. So Stalin outlawed religion and Hitler revised the Bible . . .
>
> The copying of these methods of Hitlerism by CIO leaders in West Virginia is not a mere matter of accident. These incidents reflect a study of the totalitarian methods of Europe and an effort to inject them into the political and governmental life of America in total disregard of all American traditions.[18]

"A Message to the Miners of West Virginia" was a political misstep at best and an abject failure at worst. In a concluding argument that was, at the very least splitting hairs, Holt claimed that he did not say that union leaders or federal labor officials were "Communist, Fascist, or Nazi . . . but I have shown you that they practice the methods of Hitler and Stalin, and you know that the methods of Hitler and Stalin are not American and are not democratic."[19] By all indications, the union miner audience did not take this bait. Unions, along with their membership base, turned squarely away from Holt and placed their support behind the New Deal wing of the West Virginia Democrats headed by Senator Neely.[20] Holt's pamphlet had no discernable impact upon West Virginia miners other than driving them further away from him. His hostile, irrational opposition to labor unions, assuredly stemming from his other career as a Union Carbide lawyer, would contribute to his downfall.

Aggressive anti-Communism laced with an absolutist, paranoid mindset also characterized Holt's governorship. Anti-Communism was a common position for all politicians during the 1920s and 1930s, perhaps best exemplified by President Hoover's rejection of the Bonus Army as a Communist plot. The Bonus Army was about forty-five thousand World War I veterans, their families, and supporters who marched into Washington, DC, during the summer of 1932 demanding financial relief. U.S. Army intelligence claimed the veterans sought violence as a "signal for a Communist uprising in all large cities," which was total nonsense, but nevertheless Hoover, in what historians identify as one of his greatest presidential mistakes, ordered the military and police to "determine more accurately the number of Communists and ex-convicts among the marchers." Unsurprisingly, this joint military-police action turned violent. In the resulting melee, the police shot and killed two Bonus Army men—William Hushka and Eric Carlson, both of whom were World War I veterans and not "Communists" or "ex-convicts." Even in the aftermath, Hoover claimed without evidence that the Bonus Army harbored Communists, the assault continued, and the Bonus Army was driven out of Washington without any payment. Most participants were forced to leave behind their belongings, which were then burned by the U.S. Army.[21]

Holt was an anti-Communist conspiracy zealot cut from the same cloth as President Hoover and Congressman Dies. He saw a Communist in anyone who had ever joined a union, read a liberal newspaper, or supported the New Deal with too much enthusiasm. A 1939 speech given in Lewisburg, for instance, included a declaration that "the future usefulness of the organization of labor must depend upon labor's choice of methods and means." A few weeks later, speaking in Wheeling, Holt defined "methods and means" as a choice "a democratic and totalitarian state . . . right and might, truth and perversion, consent and coercion" where the future of the national hung in the balance.[22] In contrast, Holt's mentor Kump was anti-Communist but hardly a conspiracy zealot.

Kump, speaking during his 1932 gubernatorial campaign, rejected the broad net of anti-Communist red-baiting projected by the Hoover administration. "The claim has been made that the company which moved upon Washington" (speaking of the Bonus Army) "was made up of Communists and anarchists; but the fact remains that the two men who were shot down by the Washington police were World War Veterans." Kump continued, "My friends, the World War veterans are not communists. They are not 'red.'" Kump also supported labor unions on occasion, such as when, in October 1934, he ordered McDowell County to fire all coal operator-funded deputies.[23] Both the Socialist Party and Communist Party recognized Holt was different from Kump as well. They combined forces before the 1940 election to campaign against whichever candidate earned Holt's endorsement.[24]

Despite Holt's divergence from Kump, his aggressiveness was never sharp enough to split their anti–New Deal coalition. Holt's opponents denigrated his actions as carried out by the "Kump-Holt aristocracy," going so far as to parallel between Holt's administration and "the iron rule of Hitler . . . that has sought by every scheme to politically enslave the citizens of West Virginia."[25] The loss of union support ultimately spelled doom for Kump and Holt. Unions broke with the Kump-Holt regime after Holt's ill-conceived 1939 pamphlet and formally called upon Senator Neely to run for governor in 1940. With no successor strong enough to challenge a sitting senator, Kump and Holt knew their tenure at the apex of West Virginia politics could be nearing an end. Holt spent much of 1939 and 1940 as a sort of lame duck, loudly calling on the state legislature to pass austerity measures while surrounded by New Deal Democrats. Most of these Democrats sat on their hands and instead welcomed New Deal funding to the state whenever possible. The 1940 election rapidly approached, and Holt knew his political alliance was in trouble. It was in this political climate that Bruce Crawford was hired to unwittingly become the troubled governor's next political target.

FEDERAL WRITERS' PROJECT

Crawford formally assumed the role of state director of the West Virginia branch of the Federal Writers' Project on October 31, 1938.[26] Such a position—a personnel supervisor and editor of several book projects—was foreign to him as a journalist, but that's not to say he was unprepared. FWP books were generally a mixture of folklore and history, both of which appeared regularly in Crawford's newspaper editorials. Most guidebook projects sought to simply take "facts" from around the state and gussy them up with quality structure and appealing flourish. Crawford was more than capable and possessed the required skills, but he also possessed a grasp on historical writing unlike any of his West Virginia predecessors and uncommon throughout the FWP. Documenting "facts" of the past was important, but more so was representing state history in its fullness. For Crawford, his position as a federal official curating official state history meant an opportunity to represent West Virginia's history in its fullest. If he failed, then portions of West Virginia's past, specifically the state's rich labor history, risked erasure by business-friendly politicians, businessmen, and historians.

Crawford's historical approach reflected a genuine desire to include "good" and "bad" facts, to use his terminology, in all West Virginia FWP products. Such categories were wholly subjective, of course. Pro-coal forces, such as Kump and Holt, considered "bad" facts to be those casting corporate industry in a negative light. To pro-coal politicians, Hawk's Nest Tunnel or the Battle of Blair Mountain were "bad" facts and must be excluded from history, a view that had fallen out of favor with most historians by the 1930s but was still in vogue with many others. The prominent American historian Richard Hofstadter referred to historians uninterested in "bad" facts as "the Brahmins and the satisfied classes." These historians stuck to their version of agreeable "good" facts in an effort to cast their or their client's interests in a positive light. Closely paralleling Crawford's contemporaries who practiced boosterism journalism, such historians focused on economic growth, industry, innovation, technological progress, and heroic figures of the past. History was a celebration of progress, but a type of progress that resulted from the efforts of a few strong men and not the fits and starts of a movement-driven and sometimes violent society. Crawford clearly broke with the "satisfied classes" model described by Hofstadter by representing the past with nuance. Events could be simultaneously both "good" and "bad," with all worthy of inclusion in a state history. What emerged in West Virginia during the late 1930s were two competing models of history writing—a traditional narrative centering industrial growth, and another that included the social history of marginalized people, especially workers and their struggles. To square the two opposites was a much more difficult task than Crawford realized, but off to work he went.[27]

Under Crawford's leadership, the West Virginia FWP initiated a project plan that centralized applied history based in primary source research with a special focus on the state guidebook. Crawford knew someone would challenge the guidebook interpretation no matter the content, so the best protection would be rigorous documentation. In an instructional letter to FWP field workers, he encouraged citing "books, magazine and newspaper articles about the county, county and district records, family histories, old letters and diaries, etc." Oral

histories—or "materials taken from memory"—were to be used only if perti-
nent information was verified from another source. Next, Crawford encouraged
field writers to view the guidebook as a series of interpretive essays organized
chronologically. The motivation here was to create a sense of cohesion and narrative rather than a rote repetition of facts that characterized the few already
existing state histories. Finally, Crawford dispatched over a dozen field workers
to work exclusively as historical researchers. They were to document, gather,
and draft research reports solely based on primary sources while minimizing
their own interpretive voice. Historical writing would be done by Crawford
himself. The guidebook was a work of history, not folklore, he reminded these
field workers. Per Crawford's instructions outlined in a November 1939 memo,

> We are not particularly concerned with the literary excellence of your
> writing. Ordinary statements of fact will be satisfactory in virtually all
> instances, as most of the actual creative work will be done in this office.
> Please note that we are primarily concerned with facts and that the
> following points are important:
>
> 1. On each of the assignments we must have ALL the facts available.
> 2. The statements of fact must be accurate beyond question.
> 3. The sources from which you obtain your material must be given on
>   every possible occasion.[28]

Every publication produced by the FWP required a third-party sponsor to
serve as publishing agent, reviewer, and mediator, a requirement that became
a problem during Crawford's tenure. While most attention was placed on
the guidebook, Crawford also pushed forward a series of smaller folk studies
sponsored by the Braxton County Board of Supervisors. These smaller books
were produced without any notable problems under an agreement pre-dating
Crawford's directorship. Serious problems emerged once Crawford attempted
to find a guidebook sponsor. National FWP officials preferred guidebook sponsors to be state government agencies that could lend the books the authority and expertise of a state government. In practice, sponsors did very little
across the FWP. Most acted as an editorial pass-through and a partner provided
basic manuscript review and liaison services between project and publisher.
Even if disagreements arose, all parties involved negotiated in recognition
that producing quality books was in everyone's best interest. As an example
from another state, the Oklahoma FWP project hired openly radical administrators, most notably the left-wing, pro-labor author William Cunningham
as state project director. Cunningham hired more Oklahoma radicals to round

out his staff, all of whom proved to be excellent editor-writers who easily secured publishing agreements. Senator Thomas Gore, a conservative Oklahoma Democrat, strongly opposed Cunningham's appointment but neither he nor any of his allies ever infringed upon publishing contracts. Cunningham even hired the state secretary of the Communist Party at one point, but conservative Oklahoma politicians never intervened in the federal project. Senator Gore and other conservatives understood that quality books, even those produced by radicals, were good publicity.

The situation Crawford faced was quite different. The guidebook project was in poor condition when Crawford arrived, largely due to ineffective state FWP directors and an obstructive guidebook sponsor. The FWP estimated that as of September 1938, the West Virginia guidebook totaled 207,500 unedited words, almost entirely copied directly from field reports with no citations. Little if any editorial work had been done to synthesize the manuscript, and the guidebook's sponsor was distinctly unhelpful. Crawford's predecessors secured Major Hubbard W. Shawhan, director of the West Virginia Conservation Commission, as the guidebook sponsor, likely at Governor Kump's recommendation. Shawhan's position only existed because of the New Deal. The West Virginia legislature created the state conservation commission in 1933 at Governor Kump's request directly in response to the creation of the federal Civilian Conservation Corps. Kump's belief was that conservation was important to West Virginia tourism and natural resources, so he appointed Shawhan to direct the new agency tasked with developing state parks, hunting and fishing opportunities, and conservation programs. Guidebook sponsorship made sense given the Conservation Commission's mandate.

Major Shawhan, recognizing his lacking writing and editing experience, hired Dr. Roy Bird Cook to fulfill the Conservation Committee's sponsorship duties. Cook was a pharmacist who dabbled in document collection and local history during his spare time, a hobby he partially owed to the influence of his newspaper editor father. A collector more than anything, Cook was instrumental in the early development of West Virginia's early public history institutions and firmly opposed state histories that challenged the status quo. West Virginia University awarded Cook an honorary doctor of laws degree in 1938, the year before Pearl Buck and the year after Homer Holt earned the same honor. Homer Holt, when serving as governor, named Cook's second wife Eleanor Jones Cook as head of the state Department of Archives and History. She would also serve as state historian and archivist from 1946 to 1953. The Cooks used their powerful position to assist in the founding of the West Virginia Historical Society and establish in 1939 the state's official history journal, *West Virginia History: A Quarterly Magazine.* Roy Bird Cook served as the journal's first editor for two years. Without question, Cook was central to the professionalization of West Virginia state history and bringing it under state control. While Crawford worked in the state FWP office, the group of Holt, Shawhan, and the Cooks produced their own version of West Virginia history.

Roy Bird Cook worked as Shawhan's official representative and Holt's unofficial agent throughout Crawford's FWP tenure and was a cantankerous, disagreeable man to anyone who worked within the FWP. "Dirty linen" was how Cook described Crawford's approach, specifically criticizing the inclusion of labor history in the guidebook. He insisted, despite the existence of extensive primary sources, that it impossible to prove coal operators hired private guards or thugs; nor, in his view, could it be proven that companies caused strikes through perpetuating poor working conditions. Some of Crawford's predecessors attempted to include brief passages on such topics, but no amount of primary documentation swayed Cook's stubborn opinion. In the end, Crawford's predecessors bowed to Cook's demands. The national FWP office was aware of Cook's involvement. In February 1938, well before Crawford's hiring, a memo circulated the national and state FWP office alerting staff that the West Virginia guidebook must be reviewed by Cook on behalf of Governor Holt. The memo described Cook as "the foremost amateur historian in the state" and cautioned that citations should be more thorough than normal, especially in the history essay.

An impasse soon developed between Crawford and the national FWP office on one side and Holt, Cook, and Shawhan on the other. At first glance this conflict was just politics, with the Holt camp exerting its power wherever possible. A closer look, though, reveals a debate over state history, the meaning of labor, and the very identity of West Virginia. As already mentioned, previous histories of West Virginia ignored the state's rich labor history. Their authors and consumers came from West Virginia's economic elite, comprising people like Kump, Holt, and Cook. Labor history by its very nature generally interprets conflicts between business owners and workers. In the case of West Virginia, elites knew many such conflicts ended in strikes, violence, and bloodshed. Representing an elite's view of labor was impossible owing to their steadfast opposition to unions, so these historians chose to ignore it altogether in favor of surface-level business history.

Prior to 1940 few publications addressed West Virginia's labor history at all and those that did were intensely pro-business with the most relevant to the FWP guidebook project being writings produced by Phil Conley. The *West*

Virginia Encyclopedia, edited by Conley and published in 1929, was a highly respected resource of West Virginia history during the 1930s. Conley led the state encyclopedia project with Roy Bird Cook serving as one of his associate editors. However, Conley was hardly an unbiased historian; indeed, one might better describe him as a leading coal operator spokesman of the era. Less than a decade before publishing the encyclopedia, Conley served as managing director of the American Constitutional Association (ACA), an organization formed by "prominent business and professional men" and headed by West Virginia governor John J. Cornwell. The ACA wrapped itself in nationalist "respect for law and order" as it mounted major public education campaigns. "Life in a West Virginia Coal Field," a Conley-authored pamphlet published in 1923, was one of the ACA's biggest projects. The pamphlet presented "statements of facts; not expressions of opinions" on allegedly excellent living conditions in southern West Virginia, which they presented favorably compared to average American life. Subchapters such as "Small Mining Town a Better Place to Live Than Ordinary Independent Town" and "Why Miners Do Not Want to Own Their Homes in a Mining Town" depicted striking miners and labor unions as malcontents. Very little of this material was based in reality. Anyone with even passing knowledge of southern West Virginia coal towns would have scoffed at the pamphlet's table of contents, much less the written essays.

Conley's 1923 ACA writings, published just two years after the Battle of Blair Mountain, were a direct response to the Mine Wars in southern West Virginia and aimed to support corporate coal hegemony. As for Conley's 1929 encyclopedia project, the same current of pro-business sentiment appeared throughout. Content focused primarily on the colonial era, the early Republic, and corporate history. The encyclopedia included no entry for the UMW but did include one for the United Daughters of the Confederacy, seventy-odd entries for other civic organizations (including several coal operator associations), and another seventy-odd entries for specific companies based in West Virginia. The twelve-page entry for "Coal"—written by Charles V. Critchfield, vice president of the Domestic Coke Corporation in Fairmont—contained no mention of coal miners. The Mine Wars appeared in Edward Smith's state history entry, in single paragraph:

> In 1919 great disorders occurred in the mine fields of southern West Virginia from the resistance of operators to attempts to unionize the miners in the Logan field. A group of union miners in Kanawha County began an armed march to Logan County, and a clash was averted only by the courageous action of Governor Cornwell in dissuading them. Upon an

investigation which followed, it was shown that mine owners in Logan County had paid the sheriff $32,700 a year for the employment of deputy sheriffs. A continuation of the struggles in Logan and Mingo counties led finally to the introduction of Federal troops and proclamation of martial law.[29]

As can be seen in Smith's short passage, the governor somehow both succeeded in preventing "clashes" and failed to prevent "struggles." Any reader certainly understood there was more to this story, though it would not be found in the state encyclopedia.[30]

Other than Conley's encyclopedia, a few other historical monographs formed the foundational canon of West Virginia history before 1938. Most, such as Virgil Lewis's *History and Government of West Virginia* (1896), John Peter Hale's *Trans-Allegheny Pioneers* (1931), and Oscar D. Lambert's *Pioneer Leaders of Western Virginia* (1935) skirted the question of labor altogether by ignoring industry. James Morton Callahan's *Semi-Centennial History of West Virginia* (1914) portrayed labor organizing as an unwanted, annoying state problem. "Until about 1880 when a labor strike contributed to the decline of the industry, the city was a great mill manufacturing center," Callahan wrote of Wheeling. Strikes at Paint and Cabin Creek—often considered the first battles in the West Virginia Mine Wars—were "difficult problems" faced by Governor John J. Glasscock. The governor "was able to obtain an agreement by which the miners secured important concessions without imposing any unnecessary burden upon the operators." The fate of the miners was left unstated. The conflicts at Paint and Cabin Creek would only grow into a statewide movement after Callahan's publication, an obvious shortcoming in the book's analysis.[31]

The contemporary, widely available state history likely used by Crawford, Holt, Cook, and the rest was Charles Henry Ambler's *A History of West Virginia* (1933). Ambler provided a comprehensive overview of the state's past from prehistory through the present day that was essentially a revision of Callahan's semi-centennial work. Several of Ambler's chapters overlapped with mandated FWP guidebook chapters, such as those on industry, labor, and the arts. Ambler, a West Virginia University history professor, largely grounded his work in other academic writings whenever possible and relied upon state agencies to provide primary sources and illustrations. Since unions and workers were not consulted, social history largely escaped Ambler's attention. He hardly addressed labor unions, strikes, or company towns and when he did so it was in negative terms. In Ambler's West Virginia, there was no John Lewis, no Mother Jones, and no Battle of Blair Mountain.[32] To Ambler, labor unions disrupted West Virginia's industrial development in order to "unionize the state" with no clear final goal. Unions indirectly forced coal companies to hire "special police," otherwise murder and "armed marches" would become the social norm. A dystopian coalfield past existed in Ambler's West Virginia, in which labor unions created effective no-go zones for innocent third parties such as students:

> It was not always safe for disinterested parties to come within range of skirmishes [between organized labor and coal companies]. Even the student canvasser, fresh from his college classes, did not escape suspicion. His paraphernalia was suspicious, and he was sometimes mistaken for a paid organizer. In any event, the consequences were not pleasant. He, with others who shared his fate, was being watched and threatened. In case he were suspected of being an organizer, he heard strange stories of the alleged mysterious disappearance of meddlesome and overzealous persons who had dared to come into the coal fields.[33]

In Ambler's preface, he thanked about a dozen individuals for their help, including State Historian Virgil Lewis, WVU colleague James Morton Callahan, and several students and secretaries. His final thanks were reserved for two men outside of academia who "read the entire manuscript in galley proof and made helpful suggestions"—Charles McCamic and Roy Bird Cook. McCamic was a leading lawyer and businessman who had served in the West Virginia House of Delegates, fought in World War I, and was a member of dozens of clubs and organizations, so Ambler was likely thrilled such a public figure would agree to serve as reviewer.[34]

Cook just seemed to turn up everywhere when West Virginia history was discussed, recognized as a top authority of state history for years before Crawford's arrival in the state.[35] Two governors and his wife allowed Cook to control virtually every published historical work coming out of Charleston. Through his reputation and friendships, Cook further acted as a reviewer of all major state history works published by WVU professors. From this perspective then, it is obvious why Cook would be so hostile to Crawford's work. Ambler published *A History of West Virginia* five years before Crawford's hiring and just two years before the guidebook project was announced. Cook likely believed the history in the planned guidebook was already written and reviewed by West Virginian experts like himself, so why was a new volume being produced using federal resources necessary? Ambler's work settled state history, satisfied business leaders, and suppressed "unsavory" labor history events. A new guidebook—especially one written by a non–West Virginian, nonhistorian like Crawford—would not meet the high standards set by Ambler, Callahan, or Conley.

Further suggesting a division between Crawford's FWP office and Holt's circle, Crawford quickly embraced several somewhat droll FWP folk studies and made them his own. As previously mentioned, when he took up his position, a dozen or so projects primarily short folk studies publications, lingered in a half-finished state. State FWP workers labored hard on these folk studies in the preceding years, it was only that previous directors failed to publish any but the simplest. Those included *Historic Romney* and *Hampshire County Census*, essentially uncontroversial documentaries. Crawford's office finished several other similar folk studies projects, including those on the communities of Burnsville, Flatwoods, Smoke Hole, and Sutton. State Editor Paul Becker wrote most of each book's rough text, with Crawford acting as a strict editor and coauthor. Crawford's characteristic writing imprint appears throughout each of these works. An example may be found in *Smoke Hole and Its People*, an extended essay on a geographically isolated community that, nonetheless, remained connected to modern life via mail service, technological innovation, and politics:

> Still largely isolated from the outside world, the Smoke Holer is little affected by the daily rush of events which command attention from city dwellers. He has access to an occasional newspaper, and the mail is delivered four times each week, weather permitting, bringing in some reading ratter from outside including the customary rural complement of mail order catalogues. There are few radios in the Smoke Hole, as the lack of electric power makes it necessary to use battery sets or to employ home light generating equipment.
>
> Notwithstanding the comparative isolation from daily events, the Smoke Hole resident takes a keen interest in governmental affairs and goes to sore lengths to express his political convictions at the polls. . . . The political situation in the Smoke Hole is certainly unusual; until a few years ago it was said the Smoke Hole had "only one Democrat and lightnin' killed him," but recently there has been some swing of political allegiances.
>
> The mounting interest in the outside world in the Smoke Hole and its people has been reciprocated of late years as young men have gone out of the valley to hold their own with outsiders who had far greater educational advantages. A Smoke Hole man is president of one of the country's leading business colleges. Another is head bookkeeper in one of the large rubber plants in Akron. One has become a prosperous business man in Chicago,

another is a large real estate owner in Kansas City, and still another is a civil engineer of some note in the Southwest. Inside the state, Smoke Hole men have become school teachers, high school principals, and many have held minor public office.[36]

The parallels between this work and "The Mountain White," Crawford's essay from fifteen years earlier, are undeniable. Crawford and Paul Becker represented Smoke Hole as a complex society developing with the times, not an isolated den of hillbillies. Other folk studies of the time, especially those informed by a eugenicist literature, focused on supposed community degeneracy, ignorance, or hapless innocence caused by mountain isolation. These studies' authors conveniently ignored basic truths about the mountains—people went to school, consumed mass-produced goods, emigrated regularly, and were, to put it plainly, part of society. In a simple way, Crawford and Becker recognized the dignity of Smoke Holers; this same style of writing extended to the state guidebook produced through their efforts.

A Guide to the Mountain State

To finish the half-completed guidebook, Crawford took on the familiar role of editor-writer-researcher and directed attention toward lacking sections, most notably a chapter on labor history. To develop new material, Crawford sent letters to trusted experts on the Left, seeking their perspectives on labor topics during the final few weeks of 1938. For instance, he mailed duplicate letters to the editors of *New Republic* and the *Nation*—both of whom knew Crawford from his writing for their respective magazine—asking for more information on the steelworker strikes in Weirton that began in 1933. The letters' purpose, Crawford wrote, was to update the labor chapter by presenting "basic issues without taking sides." At the same time, in writing the labor chapter Crawford and his colleagues consulted little with the national office, seeing no need to do so: a labor chapter was just like the rest, inherently approved by national guidelines.[37]

Crawford knew a chapter on labor history would be controversial with select politicians and business owners within West Virginia. In writing the first draft, he initially distanced himself from unions and recruited other experts to insulate him from criticism. Crawford's predecessors had requested writing contributions from several labor experts outside of the FWP, such as Conley H. Dillon, a political science professor and labor expert at Marshall University, and John Guy Pritchard of the West Virginia Manufacturers Association. Each contributed significant primary source information before and during Crawford's tenure. By the time of first review in October 1939, Crawford drafted a full labor essay, received two sets of revisions from the national FWP office, and responded to each in kind. By all FWP accounts, the essay was Crawford's creation and in quality condition in terms of documentation, historical argument, and writing style.[38]

In his first few months as FWP director, Crawford also targeted other chapter topics. He wrote to university professors, state employees, and celebrities connected to West Virginia (most notably heavyweight boxing champion Jack Dempsey, who lived as a child in Logan County) asking them to share photos and documents.[39] A new chapter on literature, a topic near to Crawford's heart, emerged from this outreach, with former project director John Stender asked to recommend a West Virginia University up for the writing. David Johnson, head of the Department of English, agreed to do the work a week later.[40] Meanwhile, Crawford organized new publicity materials for the guidebook that provided a hint as to its contents. A long list of "the men and women who have made history west of the Alleghenies" became a central component of advertisements. The names listed included, in the order presented, Daniel Boone, Simon Kenton, Jesse Hughes, Betty Zane, Major Sam McCullough, Lewis Wetzel, Stonewall Jackson, Booker T. Washington, David Hunt Strother, Ann Royall, Belle Boyd, William Hope "Coin" Harvey, Henry Gassaway Davis, Stephen B. Elkins, Johnson N. Camden, Collis P. Huntington, and Pearl Buck. These politicians, soldiers, and writers were certainly familiar to potential readers of all backgrounds. Strategically excluded were some of West Virginia's labor history heroes.[41]

The West Virginia FWP also planned other significant titles under Crawford's guidance, largely because Crawford believed the guidebook too long already. However, the FWP's quick decline and closure during the early 1940s meant none of these ideas ever reached publication. Seven additional works were planned; of these four were local histories (*Charleston: A City Builds*, *The Story of Rainelle*, *Pineville: Where Wyoming Trails Cross*, and *West Virginia Factbook*) and one an extended photo-essay (*West Virginia: Profile in Pictures*). The other two manuscripts were *The Negro in West Virginia* and *West Virginia Women*. Surviving contracts suggested *The Negro in West Virginia* was nearly completed but never published. Staff gathered hundreds of stories, newspaper clippings, and archival sources for a comprehensive history of the African American experience in West Virginia, including slavery, abolition, and Jim Crow. Surviving FWP records do not detail what would have appeared in the published work but provide a few hints. Crawford compiled antebellum county court records, articles on the Atlantic and domestic slave trade, materials on John Brown's raid of Harper's Ferry, African Methodist Episcopal church records, segregated Black schools and colleges records, and interviews with prominent African American leaders. This book was, most likely, created in lieu of a full chapter on African Americans in the state guidebook. Some FWP guidebooks, like those produced for Kentucky, Maryland, and Virginia, included a full chapter on African American history. While nothing definitive survived in archival records, it is possible Governor Holt rejected such a chapter considering he regularly demanded photographs of African American miners be removed from guidebook drafts. Other guidebooks' African American history essays critiqued American racism in stark terms, significantly more so than works by contemporary historians published in major academic press, though few carried their narrative beyond 1900. It is also possible that Holt balked at such a critique, instead favoring a history with invisible Black West Virginians.

Crawford believed the state guidebook would be completed by April 1939, but Governor Holt made sure this deadline was far too optimistic.[42] According to Governor Holt, Crawford broke off communication between the state FWP office and Shawhan immediately upon his hiring. There was some truth in Holt's accusation in that Crawford stopped presenting guidebook material to Shawhan the way his predecessors had. Prior directors submitted draft chapters to Shawhan before submission to the national office, a process not recommended by FWP procedures because of how much it slowed down the writing process. Shawhan worked with Cook (and possibly Holt himself) to edit each chapter before returning it to the state FWP office for national delivery. Crawford broke this workflow, most likely because it ran counter to FWP procedure and his office was short on time, though it cannot be discounted that he simply objected to the perceived meddling of Shawhan, Cook, and Holt.

Communication reopened in February 1939, when Crawford informed Shawhan that the guidebook needed to finalize a publishing contract with Viking Press. Viking was a reasonable choice, given the press published several other FWP guidebooks and was liked by national staff. The Viking contract was already in place when Crawford was hired, having existed in draft form since August 1937, though project delays meant the contract lapsed and had to be renegotiated. Communication with Shawhan was all business but cordial enough. The Viking contract negotiation moved forward so far as Crawford was concerned, and staff worked on the guidebook. Suddenly, on April 3, Viking notified Crawford the company was voiding the publication contract due to missed deadlines. However, this was all part of the plan—Crawford had already secured Oxford University Press as a replacement publisher weeks earlier.[43]

The national FWP office was happy with the new Oxford contract but in the end, it nearly killed the guidebook project. At Crawford's request, Oxford mailed Shawhan a publication contract for him to sign. Crawford also reported in May 1939 to all parties that he expected a final guidebook draft in July. Without warning, Shawhan refused to sign the Oxford contract. Acting on Governor Holt's orders, Shawhan informed Oxford he would only sign the contract upon his office's full review and approval of the manuscript. Such an arrangement was, to put it simply, not how the publishing industry operated, not today and not in 1939. Normally, parties signed a contract with the understanding that a final manuscript was in process. The publisher then worked with authors and editors (in this case, including Shawhan) to ensure the book was both high quality and meeting deadlines. Crawford understood all of this, but Shawhan, Cook, and Holt either did not or simply did not care. Oxford, Crawford, and national FWP officials each in turn failed to convince Shawhan to sign the contract even with amended language. In response, Crawford met Shawhan's bullheadedness with his own—he refused to submit drafts to Shawhan altogether. Meanwhile, state FWP staff seemingly ignored the contract debacle. An immense amount of work was completed that summer, most notably resulting in full national office approval for Crawford's Labor essay.[44]

The Oxford contract impasse only solidified as summer moved into early autumn because of the Dies Committee. As already discussed, FWP director Henry Alsberg fared poorly before the committee and FWP funding was, as a result, drastically cut by Congress. The new congressional requirement that FWP projects rely more on state funding crippled negotiating power held by Crawford and Oxford. Shawhan and Holt knew they could simply hold their position, if not press harder. As a result, Crawford now faced a September 30 deadline to find a sponsor willing to fund 25 percent of the state office's budget. Shawhan's Conservation Commission was one of few state agencies that both made sense as a sponsor for the project and could spare the cash. Few other options were available, and everyone involved knew it. National FWP staff grew concerned that with less than two months to the deadline, Crawford had still not secured a sponsor. Shawhan's and Holt's obstruction meant to Crawford that the Conservation Commission was only a last resort. They needed to find stable, responsible sponsorship instead. It was in this context that Crawford made his move.

Changing Guidebook Sponsors

Oxford University Press grew tired of Shawhan's delays during August 1939, so an Oxford publishing agent requested Shawhan return the guidebook contract, signed or unsigned, as soon as possible. Shawhan, still refusing to cooperate at the behest of Governor Holt, dutifully mailed back his unsigned contract. He and Holt both assumed a modified Oxford contract would be returned to meet the congressional sponsorship deadline of September 30. Unbeknownst to Shawhan, Oxford officials subsequently, at Crawford's instruction, mailed that same contract—meaning the same paper document itself—to the guidebook's new sponsor. Crawford had secretly recruited W. W. Trent, superintendent of the State Free Schools, to take over sponsorship responsibilities, including the 25 percent agency funding. Crawford believed Trent to be an honest public educator with genuine interest in West Virginia history; moreover, Trent agreed to personally review the manuscript without Roy Bird Cook's involvement. Perhaps more importantly, Trent was an elected official and thus not beholden to Governor Holt's patronage. The execution of an Oxford contract with Trent's office cut Shawhan, Cook, and Holt completely out of the guidebook process.[45]

Communications with Trent and FWP officials over the next few weeks suggested all was normal since the sponsorship change, though some exchanges hinted at brewing problems between Crawford and Cook. On October 10 Crawford mailed Trent all of Cook's editorial suggestions and specifically noted Cook's good eye for grammar and criticisms of the labor essay. "[Cook] objects to our references to the labor disputes of twenty or more years ago," read Crawford's note. "It was [Cook's] opinion that no mention whatever should be made of strikes, armed marches, and the Weirton controversy. We have tried to treat such matters factually, and if any errors appear in the copy we shall be glad if you or other readers correct them."[46] Cook's insistence of striking out the "Weirton controversy," a union struggle at Weirton Steel Company and home to "the largest company town in America" according to Crawford, was emblematic of the growing problem. In Weirton, CIO-affiliated union workers peacefully agitated for better conditions throughout the 1930s until the mill owner, E. T. Weir, formed an oppositional company employee organization in 1937. The federal government intervened, ruling Wier's company union as illegal under the Wagner Act. Wier's hired police force simply ignored the ruling and physically forced union workers off the job. Governors Kump and Holt ordered police protection for CIO meetings and parades but did nothing to protect workers on the job or help enforce federal rulings. Holt viewed this episode as a potential disaster for his political support among miners and unsuccessfully sought to suppress the story.[47]

Crawford and Trent also discussed Cook's disapproval of the story of Anne Royall, an Antebellum-era writer from Monroe County who was one of the first female journalists in the United States. Cook argued, according to Crawford, that Royall should not be mentioned because she "may have scandalized a president and members of Congress." One of Royall's major accomplishments was the newspaper *Paul Pry*, whose articles targeted Washington, DC, governmental corruption.[48] Unsurprisingly, Crawford disagreed with Cook's assessment. Royall was an example of journalistic excellence, and it was all the better that West Virginia could claim this incredible woman as part of state literary tradition, he argued. Crawford and Cook never came to an agreement about Royall's inclusion. Cook's rejection though just further illustrated his unwillingness to include supposedly controversial history at the expense of the nonpowerful.

Crawford and Trent agreed on history. "I am sure, Dr. Trent, you will agree that the Guide, which treats of historical as well as contemporary affairs," Crawford wrote in an October letter, "would be conspicuously one-sided and the object of criticism by reviewers generally if it contained no mention of issues and incidents which might reflect unfavorable on any persons or interests." Whitewashing history was futile, both Crawford and Trent believed. Crawford's logic was that whitewashed history is boring and cannot scrub the past fully. A curious public seeking information would naturally find other non-state-sanctioned sources, many of which would be flawed and all beyond the state's control. The inclusion of difficult history in the guidebook was West Virginia's opportunity to control the narrative, so to speak.[49] The following week Crawford sent another letter to Trent with three essays for review (on education, industry, and labor), including all material rejected by Cook. Final manuscript submission to Oxford was, at this point, just two weeks away, slated for November 1, 1939.[50]

Within days of the Crawford-Trent-Oxford ploy, Governor Holt learned of the maneuver and erupted into a rage. Letters flew out of the governor's office to anyone even tangentially related to the guidebook. Crawford, Trent, the national FWP office, state and national WPA employees, the White House, and probably still others received Holt's letters. The governor's demand was simple—return all sponsorship agreements to the Conservation Commission immediately. Reasonable responses returned to Holt's desk, but each one was swatted away with increasing degrees of paranoia. Holt accused the federal government, including FDR himself, of a conspiracy against him personally. His smoking gun evidence was "the striking similarity" of letters sent weeks apart by officials in the FWP, WPA, and the White House, which all contained the two-word phrase "careful consideration." In Holt's mind, since this phrase appeared across the letters, then surely their authors were all conspiring against him. Much more likely, "careful consideration" was just common language of a federal bureaucrat in the 1930s.[51]

Holt's outrage centered on a belief that the guidebook was "distinctly discreditable to the State of West Virginia and her people, and, certainly, improper for incorporation in a book designated as a guide to West Virginia"[52] Why the FWP would do such a thing, Holt did not explain. A few pro-Holt editors, like Calvert Estill of *Welch News*, authored newspaper articles detailing the guidebook's supposed liberal bias, an obvious lie given the guidebook remained incomplete.[53] Despite the paranoia, Holt held true to one salient, critically important point: "The reasons for the change [from Shawhan to Trent] are all too obvious . . . those in charge of the FWP were unwilling to go forward with the agreement under which my consent to the sponsoring of this work by the Conservation Commission of West Virginia was procured."[54] Holt was absolutely correct. By mid-1939, every FWP official involved with the West Virginia office believed Shawhan, Holt, and Cook actively obstructed and sometimes sabotaged the guidebook. FWP officials worried the guidebook could be hijacked and transformed into Kump-Holt machine propaganda. Knowing this to be a possibility, the FWP placated Holt by reassuring him the sponsorship change was merely a practicality, but the attempt backfired. "I do not recognize the State superintendent of free schools of West Virginia [W.W. Trent] as a responsible agency," Holt concluded in a letter to federal officials, leaving no question that his demands were an ultimatum.[55]

Seeing no movement from the FWP, Holt escalated his complaints to the White House. FDR received a letter from Holt claiming he had "reason to withhold confidence from a work prepared under the direction of Mr. Bruce H. Crawford," though he did not clarify just what this statement meant.[56] Privately, Shawhan and Holt grew increasingly alarmed. Shawhan disavowed any responsibility for the loss of authority, claiming Cook only made suggestions, not demands, and that Crawford overreacted.[57] WPA officials offered a compromise, with Holt given final editorial review of the manuscript while keeping Trent in place. Holt's reply came quickly—nothing short of a full Conservation Commission reinstatement as guidebook sponsor would be acceptable. "I know full well that [the Trent sponsorship] was affected in an effort to avoid giving any heed to the suggestions made by [Major Shawhan] in the best of faith," wrote Holt, clearing accusing Crawford by this point.[58] The following day Shawhan too wrote FDR that he believed Crawford's actions to be an attempt to circumvent the governor's office and again demanded that the Conservation Commission be reinstated as sponsor. Finally, after weeks of bluster, Holt asked the president himself to directly intervene—"I most earnestly request that you take charge of this matter yourself"—presumably by executive order.[59]

Holt's aggressive behavior baffled federal officials. Nothing required the WPA and FWP to work with the governor's office, much less grant editorial oversight, so many federal employees were simply left confused. From the federal perspective, Crawford simply changed guidebook sponsors because Shawhan refused to sign a publishing contract. J. N. Alderson, WPA administrator for West Virginia, was the first federal official outside of the FWP tasked with handling Holt's complaints. Satisfied with the "factuality and impartiality" of the guidebook's contents, Alderson wrote to Holt, "I am at a loss to understand how you could have gained the impression that any material discreditable to West Virginia or her people would be included in this publication." Alderson later continued, "I certainly have no reason to believe that the book contains any material of this nature, and I am equally sure that the personnel of the WPA engaged in this work are loyal enough to West Virginia to be most careful in the section of material or publication."[60] Trent also wrote Holt that nothing in the guidebook appeared to be "of scurrilous or libelous nature," and that even though he was unwilling to drop the sponsorship, he would personally "take extra precaution because of your warning."[61]

Yet again, Holt rejected all explanations and fired off a terse six-page letter to Alderson outlining Crawford's supposed subversion. Ultimately this letter proved just one thing—Holt was totally clueless regarding the FWP, the guidebook, or book editing. He again demanded the return of the publishing contract to Shawhan and that Cook be reinstated as an official manuscript reviewer. There was, however, now one significant addition to his rhetoric: conservative journalists had just discovered a 1931 *Crawford's Weekly* editorial titled "Harlan: A Study in Futility?" In it, Crawford reflected on his Dreiser Committee work and lambasted Harlan leadership. Conservative journalists and Governor Holt took the essay out of context, using it as evidence of Crawford's radicalism. The key passage—"The only good thing that can come out of Harlan is a scandal, red with sacrificial blood, which will stir workers everywhere to a sacred madness"—was indeed striking. Crawford was now seriously in danger of being labeled a Communist within weeks of the FWP's boss being fired for less.[62]

Meanwhile, Crawford made clear to his allies that all problems, amusing as they were to him, originated with Roy Bird Cook's poor understanding of historical practice.[63] The proposed approach in the guidebook was not radical by the standards of the time, especially considering Crawford's favorable treatment of the state's industrial history and that other FWP guidebooks contained chapters on labor history. "West Virginia has been made by industry," read the industry chapter. "There can be little doubt that the historic separation from the mother State was motivated partly by the difference of opinion natural to an industrial west and an agrarian east." According to the guidebook, West Virginia was a "swift-growing empire of hills," hardly a negative from pro-business viewpoints.[64] Crawford also wrote Dreiser to share the "plots and counterplots—Governor Holt's phrase" and some very real political dangers surrounding the FWP in West Virginia:

> In brief, the Governor, an enemy of organized labor, has tried to stop publication of the West Virginia Guide, which we have about ready for the press. He objects to the labor history treatment in the book. . . . The Anti–New Deal press has scored me. Most of the attacks are lies and wild, malicious guesses as to the contents of the book. One writer—a press agent for the coal association—has quoted from an editorial I wrote back in 1931 about Harlan. Remember Harlan? And how! Well, the coal association secretary has distributed photostat copies of the editorial to all and sundry—also to the Dies Committee! It is a hot, horrendous, hell-may-care editorial, written after I had "escaped" from a sojourn to Bloody Harlan. . . . You can imagine how it is making 'em see red. How they scream "red," "revolutionary," and "libelous"!
>
> I think we are going to suffer somewhat as a Project, but my supervisors here and at Washington fully understand, I am advised. With all this rage about Soviet Russia, the unearthed "red" editorial can't help me, that's certain. However, I have been urged by Washington to write a letter which would set forth my present views, by way of showing "maturity" after eight years! . . . Observe that a lot can be said cautiously in the name of democracy—a most radical thing in reality.[65]

As time passed into October, Holt continued to write federal officials, including the White House, demanding an end to Crawford's "plots" until he finally met success.[66] Holt's increasingly alarming letters accusing the FWP of "double-dealing" caught serious White House attention, so an FDR administration official requested FWP director John D. Newsom, who recently replaced Dies Committee victim Henry Alsberg, travel to Charleston for a meeting with Holt. Newsom made the trip in late October and went straight to Holt's office. According to Newsom, Holt played his hand almost immediately—restore sponsorship of the guidebook to the Conservation Commission or West Virginia would pull support of all WPA projects. States provided between one-tenth and one-quarter of all WPA project funding, so Holt had the power to essentially kill most state WPA projects. Newsom folded: guidebook sponsorship was to be returned to the Conservation Commission, though all other state FWP projects remained under Trent's sponsorship. The FDR administration further placated Holt when Edwin Watson, who effectively served as FDR's chief of staff before such a role was formally created, reassured the governor that "Harry Hopkins said I wasn't a success until he heard three different men 'son-of-a-bitch' me in one day." Amid this conflict, guidebook advertisements began appearing in West Virginia media. In the *West Virginia Review*, then edited by Cook, an FWP advertisement noted that the West Virginia guidebook would include an essay on the state's labor history.[67]

Despite capitulating on the sponsorship issue, Newsom did defend Bruce Crawford against Holt's assaults. Newsom brought with him to the meeting Crawford's statement of his current political values (written at Newsom's urging). Crawford's point was simple: his Harlan editorial was outdated but his accusations of corruption were true and not as radical as they seemed. He pointed to the "dark days of Herbert Hoover" and Republican control when serious discussions of suspending the Constitution took place; in Crawford's view, it would have been un-American not to challenge such ideas. Given that Holt was a Democrat, framing the 1931 Harlan essay as a critique of Republicans was a clever ploy. The statement also identified Crawford as "a loyal government employee" with "a faith in democracy which amounts to fanaticism" who wanted to see "[democracy] extended to our whole economy, with equal opportunities to all and special privileges to none," hardly the words of a Communist as Holt imagined them. Unable to contain himself, Crawford concluded with a less than subtle dig at Holt and the Dies Committee—"I do not believe in penalizing individuals for their opinions. Heresy hunts are contrary to the spirit of democracy." After the Holt meeting, Newsom departed West Virginia confident the Holt troubles were behind them.[68]

If only things were that easy. Multiple newspaper articles, including in the syndicated *Washington Merry-Go-Round* and the *New Republic*, appeared two weeks later reporting on a Crawford-Holt divide. Articles portrayed Holt as a political hack who pointed a figurative gun to the head of the WPA lest he get his way at the expense West Virginia miners. Another common point was that "local historian" Roy Bird Cook recommended "drastic censorship," involving the elimination of labor struggles, specifically strikes, from the guidebook and thus from state history itself. Almost certainly the source of these articles was Crawford, especially the one published in the *New Republic*. Only Crawford and a handful of federal employees even knew of the events described in the articles, much less possessed a motive to expose Holt publicly.

Holt read the articles and retaliated immediately. All state agencies were ordered to terminate all projects involving Trent's office, and Holt demanded Newsom return immediately to Charleston to discuss the guidebook manuscript. A brief conversation between FWP officials, largely driven by Crawford, determined another Holt meeting was pointless. Nonetheless, Newsom again traveled to Charleston in early January 1940. At the meeting, Newsom and Holt primarily discussed guidebook contents, though Newsom did not record details. A bigger meeting issue was that the state Department of Archives and History pulled funding from several WPA projects. Newsom believed the guidebook conflict to be directly related, an accusation Holt flatly denied. The only significant meeting outcome was that Crawford promised to meet with Cook as soon as possible. The two would then discuss Cook's concerns over guidebook contents, though Cook remained skeptical of any mutually acceptable resolution. Yet again, despite all the governor's bluster and candor, the guidebook project remained unsettled.[69]

Just a few days after the second Newsom-Holt meeting, ninety-one miners died in Bartley, West Virginia. An explosion on January 10, 1940, at Pond Creek Number One mine supposedly caused by a methane leakage rocked the mountains and West Virginians. The Bartley disaster was the sixth-deadliest West Virginia mining disaster and the worst in thirteen years.[70] This disaster felt different to left-leaning West Virginians simply because it happened during a Democratic administration both at state and federal levels. Many labor leaders believed New Deal labor protections eliminated the potential for mining disasters, especially as coal production fell in the region. Pound Creek widows received some money and food from the coal company, yet eviction notices went out to company-owned housing in just a few months. Compounding this was community outrage that the Bureau of Mines nearly pinned blame upon a dead miner found with cigarettes in his pocket, though the final report concluded an electric arc was the likely culprit. Crawford took from this that little had changed in the coal industry to safeguard miners, so he drove on to fight for their stories.

With Bartley on Crawford's mind, he worked in February 1940 to prepare the promised guidebook revisions for Holt, Shawhan, and Cook. Most of Cook's suggestions were taken: the photograph of a coal miner taking a bath in a zinc tub was removed, details on the Hatfield-McCoy feud were condensed, and folklore sections that "do not represent our present civilization . . . lest readers too provincial might take offense" were deleted. But Crawford had one more gambit—a final appeal for the labor chapter that Cook wanted so desperately to cut. Crawford, carefully reminding Holt that this was a professional matter, played his hand. The guidebook was, in Crawford's view, a cultural touchstone for West Virginians. Labor defined West Virginia, so it must be included:

> Your most serious objection, we understand, is to the treatment of labor's history, the Armed March, Mother Jones, silicosis fatalities, and Weirton controversy. We quite agree that in the Tour copy there was some needless repetition of labor history that was handled in the essay on labor. So we have cut the duplication and compressed the labor materials. We have tried to remove the connotation that Mother Jones was a heroine. We have deleted the superfluous term "steel baron" before Dr. H. T. Weir's name. . . . We trust you will allow these abridged passages to remain in the book.
>
> We have blacked out the objectionable quotation from the Congressional Committee on the silicosis tragedy at Hawk's Nest, where an undetermined number of workers lost their lives, to the effect that the company "used an antiquated circulation system, no respirators at all, no safeguards against dust concentration, dry drills instead of safer wet drills to save time and labor costs, and bussers to warn workmen of the approach of the inspectors." Etc., Etc. You say that the Committee had no standing, and Dr. Cook compares the tragedy to disasters like "cholera epidemic" or acts of God. Accordingly, we have deleted the quotation and left in a record of the fact that the state passed a law providing for a workmen's compensation silicosis fund and a silicosis medical board.
>
> Dr. Cook, if I am not mistaken, agrees with you that a guidebook of this type is no place for anything more than ordinary tourist information. We had felt, and most of the Guides have demonstrated, that this kind of a book is not merely a guide to what may be encountered when you turn left at Cox's Corner on Route 60, but largely a guide to the state's historical, economic, social, and spiritual whereabouts. To present such information, it has been necessary to give a lot of pertinent detail. However, we have deleted parts which you say might needlessly offend some people.
>
> We sincerely feel that the revised draft will meet with your approval and that of Major H.W. Shawhan and we hope that the manuscript can go on soon to the publishers.[71]

Holt, as his antagonists expected by now, reacted with a mixture of hatred, anger, and political threats. His response to Crawford was also borderline nonsensical as he claimed both ignorance of the guidebook's contents and, just two paragraphs later, detailed the manuscript's shortcomings. He also expressed outrage that Crawford dared to conflate Cook's opinion as Holt's own. "You and I have never discussed the subject matter of this manuscript. Nevertheless, your letter repeatedly refers to criticisms of the previous manuscript made by me," Holt wrote as a pedantic retort given the known relationship between Holt, Shawhan, and Cook. Holt continued.

> While I shall likely review . . . the final draft of the manuscript, I do not feel that I have the knowledge or the time to act as the reviewer in the first instance. . . . I have advised Mr. Newsom that I considered the work anything but complimentary to the State and, when read as a whole, in my opinion, the work is base and crude while such a book on West Virginia could readily be prepared in such a way as to present a broad picture of our State and at the same time embody many of the commendable attainments of the State, thus effecting *[sic]* a work creditable, rather than discreditable, to the State.

Just what was considered "commendable" or "creditable," Holt did not share; nor did he explain how he considered the guidebook "base and crude" without ever having "knowledge or time" to read drafts. From there, the rest of Holt's letter accused Crawford of personal affronts, more paranoia, and further noncooperation:

> In the light of some of the previous occurrences . . . I am led to wonder whether your long letter to me attributing to me many criticisms of which I have not previously heard, was really written for the purpose of facilitating the publication of this work or in an endeavor to make capital at some later time of the fact that I did not consider this work, as it was when originally presented to me, as at all representative of West Virginia. . . . Until such time as the sponsor, and the sponsor's reviewer, and you agree upon the manuscript, I do not believe that a conference between us personally would advance in any way the completion of the manuscript.[72]

Holt's simultaneous intervention and obstruction exhausted Crawford, Newsom, and other federal officials. Yet again, Holt used the Dies Committee, with threats that he had "considerably more information about [Crawford] than you might think" and that "parties other than the WPA and West Virginia government" influenced the guidebook. Crawford's denials of such accusations, which he maintained throughout, ring true in surviving records. No such communications survived, if they ever existed.[73] Even after Holt left office, his allies still accused Crawford of hiring Communists to work in the state FWP office. In late 1941 Crawford's FWP successor blasted the West Virginia state project in the *Fairmont Times*, accusing it to be "infested with Reds." Aiming to stamp out this controversy, a federal investigation found nothing in the claims and forced the accuser to publicly recant. Crawford also made a public statement that such accusations were made "to cover up failure" and "there were not, to my knowledge, any Communist party members on the project while I had charge." Communist accusations were surely hard to kill even as World War II raged in Europe.[74]

This letter was the final straw for the FWP as Crawford bowed to the governor's pressure. Crawford apologized to Holt by explaining one more time that it was believed that "the deletion of certain passages was demanded by you" and that "we were also informed that you had made numerous notes on portions objectionable to you." Through February and March 1940, Crawford edited the guidebook following all of Cook's recommendations. The largest change and biggest concession by far was deleting the labor chapter. Crawford condensed the twenty-page essay into five paragraphs tacked onto the end of the chapter on industry. Gone were Mother Jones, the Mine Wars, Hawk's Nest, and Weirton. In their place, Crawford inserted a few general comments on labor while still supporting the overall story of West Virginia's industrial advancement. A vague note on the "many turbulent struggles" for collective bargaining passed Cook's review, but only because the essay conceded labor struggles had been solved peacefully in recent years. New Deal union protections, specifically the National Industrial Recovery Act, and labor organizations UMW, CIO, AFL, and West Virginia Industrial Council all received mention in name only. As one final act of subversion, Crawford concluded with a reminder of pro-labor state legislation that Holt ignored. Laws governing wage rates, child labor, miners' certification, unemployment compensation, and industrial home-work regulation were all included, likely because the Kump-Holt machine considered them easily achievable and popular agenda items. With that, labor had been excised from the guidebook and a publication date again appeared on the horizon.[75]

Patience

Despite Holt's apparent victory, Crawford and the FWP had yet another card to play—delay the guidebook project until the 1940 election in the hope the Kump-Holt machine would topple from power. The irony was that Holt and Shawhan delayed the guidebook project for months in 1939. Now, Crawford had an opportunity to turn the tables. Given Democratic Party dominance in 1940, it was a foregone conclusion that the winner of the Democratic primary would be the next governor. Most West Virginia political thinkers assumed this candidate would be a handpicked Kump-Holt machine successor. To that end, the machine tapped R. Carl Andrews, a Kanawha County up-and-comer and chair of the West Virginia Democrats, despite his lack of electoral experience. Andrews had never held public office, much less taken on a statewide election, but he was loyal to Kump and Holt.

Meanwhile starting in January 1940, rumors swirled in both Charleston and Washington that West Virginia's senators—Rush Dew Holt and Matthew Neely—both mulled a gubernatorial run. The candidacy of Rush Dew Holt, a conservative Democrat and distant cousin to Homer Holt, made sense as his term expired in 1940 and he was generally popular in the state. However, Senator Holt avoided the pull of the Kump-Holt machine, owing to his staunchly individualist political style and quick political ascent (he had been elected to the Senate at just twenty-nine years old). Rather than buck the loosely allied machine, Rush Dew Holt instead ran for Senate reelection, only to lose in the Democratic primary to Judge Harley Kilgore. Senator Neely, on the other hand, received endorsements from many New Deal Democrats, the CIO, and other large unions. With the support of coal country, Neely easily won the gubernatorial nomination against the Kump-Holt-backed Andrews, with 57 percent of the vote. Throughout 1940 Governor Holt campaigned against Neely, fueling a disjointed, hostile political environment. From Crawford's point of view, Neely was a shoo-in, meaning the next governor would be friendlier to federal agencies, labor, and Crawford personally. FWP employees believed that if Crawford could only delay the publication of the guidebook until Neely's likely inauguration—January 20, 1941—then Neely would allow the readmission of labor history into the volume.[76]

Guidebook editing took a few months, but the FWP ran out of editorial delays and sent the final manuscript to Oxford in June 1940, seemingly ensuring a 1940 release. However, this submission was likely part of the plan. For no stated reason beyond "backlog," Oxford did not touch the manuscript until about six months later. "We really don't see how, with our present heavy production schedule, we can get to the West Virginia guidebook before the end of the year," wrote an Oxford representative to the FWP. "We are, of course, as anxious as anyone to get it into production and out, but we are still struggling with four Guides simultaneously, not to say a rather heavy list of other books." For the six months that Oxford sat on the manuscript, Crawford remained unusually quiet, possibly due to his personal life. Kate Crawford had major surgery during the summer of 1940 that required an eighteen-day hospital stay, so it's likely that Bruce's attention was far from the state guidebook. It is also possible that his FWP absence further delayed the process, though there was no evidence of this.[77]

Governor Holt and Shawhan both harassed Oxford about the delay, but an Oxford employee placated them each time with a benign, legitimate excuse. While Shawhan grew increasingly irritated at Oxford this time, Holt just assumed it was Crawford's doing. Apparently with nothing better to do, Shawhan personally typed and submitted Cook's manuscript revisions to Oxford in the spring. Oxford employees took a disliking for Shawhan, describing him as someone who communicated with them "with a peremptory tone" and "placed the State Seal on every page of the manuscript," making it difficult to make copies and use the papers at all.[78] Ironically, Shawhan's actions were the biggest cause of the guidebook's delay. National FWP officials reported that Oxford intentionally shelved the West Virginia guidebook for months out of contempt for Shawhan's behavior.[79] Had Shawhan simply delegated the work and been cordial, then the guidebook may have gone to press months sooner. Regardless, Holt accepted Oxford's excuses and, apparently satisfied the guidebook was on the way, ended his office's direct involvement. Cook was dismissed from his duties and paid $500 "as a modest honorarium and a thank you."[80]

In November 1940 Matthew Neely easily won the race for governor. Governor Holt, sitting in his soon-to-be-vacated Charleston office, received a letter notifying him that Oxford had delayed guidebook publication yet again. He knew by then that he had been bested, so he wrote what he had to know to be his final letter on the guidebook while still in office. He complained to Shawhan that "the original scurrilous manuscript" might just return because of these delays. Crawford escaped blame this time, however, as he no longer controlled of the state FWP office. Once Neely officially entered the governor's mansion in January, Crawford accepted an appointment as secretary of the West Virginia Publicity Commission. The state FWP continued to function for a few more months, primarily to steer a few manuscripts toward publication with Crawford assisting in the shadows.[81]

In early April 1941, as the guidebook inched toward publication, the national FWP office received an eleventh-hour letter from West Virginia FWP administrators requesting a major guidebook change—the labor chapter was back in. State FWP officials instructed, per a request from Crawford by way of Governor Neely's office, that the final five paragraphs of the industry chapter be cut and replaced by a twelve-page section on labor. This new essay was the original seventeen-page chapter that had, according to the state officials, been "compressed . . . in anticipation of some public discussion of the inclusion of this material." Oxford further delayed printing the volume a few more weeks to accommodate the change. Galleys were sent to Crawford and Neely, which they both approved within a day. And that was that—Crawford won, the labor essay was in, and the guidebook was officially off to the printers.[82]

A few days later, Newsom wrote to Crawford acknowledging the West Virginia guidebook saga was finally over. Both men were thrilled Oxford agreed to insert the labor chapter. Newsom also inserted a few jokes at the expense of the now former governor Holt. Recalling Holt's paranoia over the phrase "careful consideration," Newsom spelled out just how valuable he understood Crawford had been to the FWP:

> I want to thank you for the revised Labor essay which was sent us by the West Virginia Writers' Project for use in the West Virginia guidebook. We are glad to have it, for the few paragraphs tacked on at the end of the Industry essay were wholly inadequate. The Labor essay is, if anything, too highly condensed and, after giving the matter careful consideration (I hope those two words have not lost their savor), we have added a few transitional paragraphs which we feel tie the whole thing together. . . . I am planning to visit West Virginia and look forward to seeing you again. It will be a singularly pleasant experience to see you sitting behind your new desk.[83]

Only after the guidebook was physically printed did Crawford put the truth in writing—he was personally responsible for all publishing delays, and Holt had every reason to be paranoid. Writing to Dreiser in May 1941, he cut loose the bombshell, spilling a secret that he had only told to federal allies for the preceding three years. The only thing left to speculation is just how he convinced Oxford to go along with the plan:

> By the way, the West Virginia Guide, which the outgoing governor made us purge of all important labor history, is coming out soon. I purposely had its publication deferred in anticipation of a change in the state government. Governor Neely approved the restoration of the labor material! There's a real story—a WPA literary outfit having to conspire for the overthrow of a state regime before being able to get its book out.[84]

Crawford won his duel with Governor Holt and, in some small way, helped accelerate the capitulation of the Kump-Holt machine. Though the two never directly interacted again, they remained enemies for life. Crawford's new Publicity Commission appointment assuredly irked the former governor, as the agency was actually founded by then-Governor Holt to protect the state's image from the stain (as Holt viewed it) of labor union politics. Holt had no say any longer, of course. He returned to the protected corporate life from which he came, working as a private lawyer from 1941 to 1947. A cushy corporate job came next, as general counsel for Union Carbide, the company responsible for the Hawk's Nest Tunnel silicosis disaster that Holt had so desperately attempted to purge from the guidebook. During his tenure as governor, union leaders in fact argued Holt could not be trusted because he intended to return to a pro-corporate law career post-governorship. In Holt's 1939 "A Message to the Miners of West Virginia," he rejected such accusations, writing that "neither Mr. Bittner [UMW] nor Mr. Easton [CIO] has any information of what work I may do upon the expiration of my official term I do not have such information myself." Holt continued, "They merely made these assertions in a malicious effort to seek to create the impression that I am subject to influences not compatible with the interests of all the people of the state." As it turned out, union leaders were entirely correct about Homer Holt.[85]

HISTORIAN

The tug-of-war between Crawford and Holt was a fight for West Virginian identity. The federal government marketed the American Guide Series as a map to America—not just its landscapes, but its very soul. The guidebooks were, according to historian Christine Bold, "at once more modest and more persuasive as arbiters of public culture" that welcomed the public to "discover" the varied American cultures all around them.[86] A politician like Holt, who was also a native West Virginian, understood this clearly and sought to harness the power of identity for his and his political machine's gain. In contrast, Crawford publicly downplayed the cultural importance of the guidebook at the time. In a short description of the project appearing in *West Virginia History*, Crawford identified the guidebook project as, primarily, "employment for persons whose talents, education, and experience might otherwise be wasted," and secondarily as a "factually sound and lucidly written guide to tourists" that simultaneously would "afford West Virginians themselves a better picture of life within their state." Of course, Crawford played politics here. He absolutely understood the importance of the state's labor past, as was articulated by the *New Republic:* "Any book on West Virginia that failed to mention Mother Jones, the Logan Armed March, and the Weirton strikes would not be a guide, but a fairy story."[87] Still, Crawford likely did not understand just how important his work was for its time or for the historical profession.[88]

Over twenty years separated the FWP guidebook from subsequent West Virginian labor history publications. Writing in 1977, Appalachian historian Ron Eller wrote in reference to early Appalachian color writers, "The effect of this static perspective has been seriously to impede the development of Appalachian historiography." Eller's argument was that Appalachian history was built upon a flawed foundation and that only his generation, many of whom came of academic age around 1970, began correcting the written record. On labor history, Eller cited Winthrop Lane's 1921 work on the Civil War in West Virginia alongside *Harlan Miners Speak* as "older classics." Nothing else published before 1969 caught his attention.[89] A cynic might say then that Crawford's work had no impact. If labor history failed to develop shortly after the guidebook's publication, not to mention Eller's apparent disregard for the work, then it is fair to question its lasting resonance. On the contrary, Crawford had laid a foundation just as local color writers had done decades before him. It just took some time for others to build, and some of them chose to build upon Crawford the historical actor as opposed to Crawford the historian.

Historian John Alexander Williams, writing in 1976, was the first to specifically interpret the Crawford-Holt encounter, which he described as a skirmish within a larger national conflict between "local representatives of rival metropolitan elites." While Holt represented "leaders of big business and organized labor," Crawford stood in for "officials of the federal bureaucracy" in a "major war for control of West Virginia's future as well as its past." To describe Holt as representing organized labor and Crawford as a bureaucrat in service of elites was hardly fair. By the time of Crawford's arrival in Charleston, Holt was organized labor's top enemy in the state. True, Crawford collected a federal paycheck, but he was largely independent in his writing. If anything, Crawford recruited political elites, including Neely and FWP officials in Washington, DC, to his radical perspective rather than quietly serving as a good bureaucrat.[90]

Writing nearly two decades after Williams, Jerry Bruce Thomas, another vaunted West Virginia historian, revisited the guidebook drama in depth with a drastically different conclusion. In Thomas's view, Crawford's successful publication of the labor chapter "legitimized and authenticated the history of workers and unions." Thomas concluded his essay with a sweeping approbation of how the guidebook changed historical writing in West Virginia: "Henceforth, histories of West Virginia had to include not only the frontier pioneers, Civil War heroes, state makers and business leaders but also workers, their unions and accounts of those days when, as Bruce Crawford said, the pistol rather than the conference table prevailed in settling disputes among employers and employees."[91] In Thomas's view, Crawford entered labor into state history, thus forcing successive historians to include labor stories into their own narratives as well.

The problem with Thomas's conclusions is the same as the one outlined above—histories of West Virginia printed by mainstream publishers continued to neglect, if not outright ignore, labor history well into the 1960s. West Virginia's major historical power centers, such as the WVU History Department, the journal *West Virginia History*, and the state archives, were all controlled by the same conservative, pro-business forces who opposed Crawford. Roy Bird Cook continued his work until his death in 1961. Festus Summers, a student of Charles Ambler, chaired the WVU History Department from 1947 to 1962. In 1958 the pair produced a second edition of Ambler's *West Virginia: The Mountain State*. This edition did not differ much from Ambler's original text, though it included brief notes on Mother Jones, reported positively about labor union actions, and offered a sympathetic view of the Battle of Blair Mountain. However, even the second edition excluded Hawks Nest and Weirton, among other conflicts. In other words, Summers may have been more favorable toward labor history, but he was still not ready to embrace Bruce Crawford's version thereof, assuming he and Ambler were even aware of it. Later works, such as *The Thirty Fifth-State* (1966) edited by Elizabeth Cornetti and Festus Summers and Howard Burton Lee's *Bloodletting in Appalachia* (1969) included significant details of the Mine Wars, entries that were followed by an avalanche of West Virginia labor history writings. John Alexander Williams included significant labor history in his works, largely built on the radical peoples' history and the burgeoning Appalachian studies movement. Writers like Robert Coles, Suzanne Crowell, Brit Hume, and Tom Nugent all published detailed labor history accounts in the late 1960s and early 1970s. Historical actors themselves, such as Fred Mooney, published firsthand accounts, radical academics like the Peoples' Appalachian Research Collection generated immense quantities of labor research, and the National Endowment for the Humanities funded oral history projects to document central Appalachian coal fields. This era truly saw an explosion of historical interest in Appalachian labor.[92]

What is left then is a legacy unknown, both to historians today and the nebulous "people" in Crawford's own time. Crawford helped dismantle the Kump-Holt machine and entered major labor events into the official state history. If historians of West Virginia outright missed or ignored his writings until Jerry Bruce Thomas's 1993 article, then so be it. But another way to view Crawford's FWP work is as a sort of top-down victory. FWP guidelines mandated projects give voice to regular folks so they could tell their own story.

By writing the labor essay himself, Crawford changed the character of the guidebook from being written by the people to one that was written *for* the people. In presenting the state's labor history, he relied on his own experiences as an activist, state officials, and editors for radical publications. There is no evidence Crawford ever consulted his own field writers or, for example, local miners or labor leaders, even though he had those connections at his disposal.[93] Crawford's goal with the labor chapter was to elevate the lives of working people, but it remained a significant missed opportunity to not include their stories directly, as with other sections of the guidebook or a work like *Harlan Miners Speak*, with which Crawford was highly familiar.[94]

West Virginia: A Guide to the Mountain State was the legacy of many hands and Crawford's last book-length project. Its political and historical impact was deep, though not necessarily understood at the time. Crawford's politicking ensured labor history's victory and the decline of the Kump-Holt machine, but a staff of dozens created this peoples' history of the state. The West Virginia FWP office, from top to bottom, laid crucial groundwork in the coming decades for labor, social, and cultural histories set in the state, essentially advancing the cause of labor in the historical record nearly three decades before academics. Despite this importance, the state FWP office effectively closed with America's entry into World War II. Federal funding originally allocated to social projects were redirected to the war effort, so all FWP projects were functioning on a skeleton crew by February 1942 and ended the following year. This did not matter to Crawford, though—Matthew Neely's entry to the governor's mansion resulted in a new chapter in Crawford's life as a state employee and later as a political consultant. Though a change of pace from small-town newspaper life, a career as a politico was one for which Crawford had long been planning and one for which he was well prepared.

CHAPTER 5

AN INABILITY TO ADAPT

Bruce Crawford never again worked as a journalist after 1938 or as a writer after 1942. He loved writing, editorializing, and occasionally lecturing, so this career change was a surprise to his friends. On the surface, Crawford's move was practical. Being a Democratic Party operative meant government appointments and contracts plus a far more stable income than he ever enjoyed with *Crawford's Weekly*. Even considering such an obvious financial motivation, his support of West Virginia Democrats appeared to be genuine. Gone was the viciously aggressive socialist of the early 1930s who harshly criticized Senator Harry Byrd, replaced by a progressive Democrat who, later in his active career, praised the value of hard work and distrusted modern science. In the end, Crawford's career with the Democrats lasted about twenty-five years, from 1935 to about 1960. This was a longer time than his stint as a newspaper editor, yet his work within West Virginia politics had far less impact on the world than he may have hoped. *Crawford's Weekly* was a magnet for controversy, and Crawford regularly found himself the center of Wise County conversation. His West Virginia career could not have been more different. Crawford retreated to the political shadows, only occasionally sharing ad hoc thoughts in regional newspapers. His interest was truly keeping quiet publicly while working to get Democrats elected. Such a career paid the bills, but it also dulled his once sharp editorial edge and pulled him away from the label of public intellectual he once craved.

So how does an avowed Communist with open disdain for many Democrats come to be a West Virginia Democratic Party appointee and operative? During the 1930s, this seemed an impossible future as Crawford harshly criticized Democrats, Republicans, and seemingly democracy itself. Publicly and privately, Crawford supported the idea of an open popular revolt against

American capitalism and democracy. "I should like to see this country social-ized. . . . Eventually it will be, even capitalists admit," Crawford wrote. "But any thorough-going socialization will be brought about only by a revolt of the masses . . . [against] the anti-social and arrogant rich."[1] Privately, in his let-ters to Theodore Dreiser he often suggested that popular Democratic actions, such as poor relief in the form of "Red Cross flour, cotton cloth, 'relief work', and everything but bona fide opportunity," were opiates meant to placate the masses just enough to prevent revolution.[2]

Further complicating Crawford's views on Democrats was his rapid souring on the New Deal. At first, he argued the 1932 election was a choice between Republican barbarism or Democratic socialism. "[Socialist leaders] may favor public ownership and democratic control, but they assume that change can be brought about by 'evolution'—by means of public consent in a capitalist soci-ety," he wrote, concluding that "when the tight squeeze comes, capital and state will fuse completely—unless the masses, aided by liberal and radical thinkers, prevent it." To many, it appeared that Crawford saw a fascist specter behind every elected official, for instance writing in *Crawford's Weekly* that Louisiana governor Huey Long—a champion, if controversial, for progressivism—was a fraud for championing a "program not honestly and soundly radical."[3] The New Deal became Crawford's boogeyman, as he saw it as a missed opportunity for socialist change. For all its potential, in his view the Democratic Party agenda protected the economic status quo. He argued both publicly and privately that economic hardships were only temporarily softened and would return once Roosevelt left office. *Crawford's Weekly* declared in 1934 that the New Deal was a failure that would need to "go altogether one way or the other soon—to the Right or to the Left" in order to be perceived as a success.[4]

Crawford's time with the Federal Writers' Project seems to have been the turning point in his political evolution. It was accompanied by the affirmation of his belief in radical labor politics, a shunning of past Communist sensibili-ties, and an opportunity to both stick it to Republicans and find new progres-sive Democratic allies. He walked a fine line when in the political spotlight. For instance, he carefully denounced his Communist past without denouncing socialism and fought hard for labor strikes to be included in the state guide-book. In doing so, Crawford fell into the good graces of liberal Democratic politicians like Matthew Neely and dozens of Roosevelt appointees within the Works Progress Administration. Most likely, Crawford learned that lightly fib-bing about his radical past benefited his career, although this will never be known for sure.

After Crawford left the FWP in 1941 for an appointment in the West

Virginia government, his life suddenly became poorly documented and would remain so for the next few decades. His publications nearly dried up, and most of his work came in the form of political consultation and advertisement production, the type of work that did not generate a paper trail bearing his name. He left behind no business papers. Most work generated in these years was without credit. At times, it was difficult to know just what he was up to. His public writing increased after he retired in about 1960, as after which he featured as a semiregular opinion writer for the *Roanoke Times*. The socialist writings of Crawford's youth disappeared in favor of a more socially conservative approach. In total, Crawford wrote around a hundred *Roanoke Times* columns, with most being weekly "one-off" commentaries on whatever struck Crawford that week as being of interest. No overarching campaign linked his thoughts as had been the case decades earlier. Instead, Crawford lauded the benefits of hard work, dismissed concerns over racist Virginian and West Virginian laws, and heavily criticized feminist and Black Power activists. While the tacit supporter of liberal politicians, the elder Crawford was hardly an ally and more accurately could be described as a white moderate demanding civility.

This seemingly strange evolution—from socialist to West Virginia Democrat to conservative—is worth following for the insight it can provide into Crawford's generation of socialist activists and scholars as well as those who would follow in younger generations. Appalachian studies developed as a rigorous field of study by the 1960s with a spectrum of perspectives. "Culture of poverty" theorists blamed poor people for their own problems, while class-conscious writers argued capitalism was the root of Appalachia's economic downfall. Appalachian historiography and college syllabuses essentially trace the field's origin to the "culture of poverty" historical moment, usually identified with Harry Caudill's 1963 book *Night Comes to the Cumberlands*. By choosing this starting point, academics recognize Caudill as the originator of an Appalachian academic movement, which is true to a point. However, as Ron Eller pointed out in the 1980s, Caudill was by no means the first or the best historian writing in this field, just the synthesizer of new theory for a popular audience. This point is reiterated by historian Bruce Tucker, who later argued that Appalachian historians use Harry Caudill's work as a "master narrative of the Appalachian Past which, despite its flaws, still has currency outside of the region" while outright ignoring other academic writers of the 1950s and 1960s. As Tuck details, beginning a historiography with a "master narrative" has a host of problems. Perhaps the largest problem is that any history of Appalachia preceding Caudill's is automatically assumed to be obsolete, insufficient, or nonscholarly. This is not to suggest that Caudill's primacy should be dismissed entirely, but *Night Comes to the Cumberlands* must not be discussed at the expense of writers like Bruce Crawford. Crawford's work had academic merit even if it only rarely appeared in university syllabuses and must be included in an Appalachian canon.[5]

Thinking beyond Crawford, it is similarly worth considering activist-scholars like Theodore Dreiser and Sherwood Anderson within the Appalachian canon. Neither of these writers wrote about Appalachia explicitly, but both thought deeply about rural poverty in the mountain South. Both considered the problems facing coal miners to be the same as those facing, for example, impoverished southerners, yet slightly different from those in northern factories. The difference was that the northern poor generally, in their view, possessed the ability to quit a job and find another. Southern farmers and Appalachian coal miners had no such option in their respective mono-economies, which allowed for few land and business owners. However, the fact is that neither Dreiser nor Anderson published on the history of the region, remaining firmly within the world of fiction and political commentary. Certainly, history played a role in their arguments, but neither came anywhere near the historical thinking about Appalachia like Bruce Crawford or generations of historians to come.

Any blame for Crawford's exclusion from Appalachian historiography narratives must fall upon him as well. The Crawford of 1930 dreamed of becoming a public intellectual. He had his opportunities. Theodore Dreiser brought him into New York and Chicago author communities; Crawford himself wrote articles for *Harlan Miners Speak* and *Challenge to the New Deal* and edited the West Virginia FWP guidebook, a genuinely groundbreaking text for labor history. Other FWP employees, such as Richard Wright and Zora Neale Hurston, went on to be recognized as some of the most important writers of the twentieth century. Crawford had the added benefit of fifteen years' worth of editorials from which to pull inspiration or to self-plagiarize if he felt like it. The path seemed clear—Crawford was ready in 1941 to bust out as an Appalachian public intellectual. All he needed to do was write, but he instead worked an office job for nearly two decades. By the time he returned to print postretirement, his perspectives came across as outdated humbuggery. Bruce Crawford's Appalachia deserved better. For that reason, it is worth exploring these last few writings of his career because, if nothing else, they highlight the brilliance of the first twenty years of his work.

WEST VIRGINIA DEMOCRAT

Theodore Dreiser continued to mentor Crawford throughout the latter's time with the FWP, regularly providing advice and encouraging him to write more often. A common refrain from Dreiser was that he believed Crawford could be an excellent state-level politician. He urged Crawford to run for a seat in Charleston or back home in Norton, hinting that he should nurture long-term ambitions for Congress, but Crawford always resisted, claiming he relished the attention brought to him by a campaign but loathed the day-to-day dullness of politics. On this, Crawford was disingenuous. He loved politics, the scheming, the backstabbing, and the chess-like maneuvers.

The FWP gig also brought Crawford into contact with New Deal Democrats in West Virginia. Progressives like Matthew Neely and his allies had an affinity with Crawford in that they both supported and challenged the New Deal and heavily supported unions and labor rights. Essentially, Neely was what Crawford once hoped to be minus the revolutionary rhetoric. Despite having little positive to say about Democrats just a few years earlier, Crawford sang the praises of the Neely administration publicly and privately. For instance, he asserted that Neely was the first governor who refused to dispatch troops to put down coal strikes. Though this was an unpopular move with the press, Neely held strong because of his CIO membership base and other pro-union allies.[6] Crawford, sensing a career opportunity he could stomach, hitched his political fortunes to Neely.[7] Knowing the Neely Democrats would look out for them, Bruce and Kate Crawford made Charleston their permanent home in 1942 after three years of uncertain FWP work. The Crawford couple bought a small riverside home on the appropriately named Virginia Avenue about two miles from the capitol.[8]

Crawford's new job, as of Neely's ascendency to the governor's mansion, was as secretary of the West Virginia Publicity Commission. The post brought Crawford, for the first time, into a position of power without a singular deliverable like a weekly newspaper or state guidebook. The five-person Publicity Commission's task was to plan and conduct "a campaign of information, advertising, and publicity" related to state programs, especially tourism and economic development. Since the Publicity Commission did not have its own media outlets, one of Crawford's core responsibilities was to maintain friendly relationships with newspapers, magazines, and radio stations in the state and beyond.[9] A few media outlets took notice of Crawford's appointment; for example, the Associated Negro Press Charleston News Service announced Crawford's appointment, noting he was "known as a liberal." Crawford's appointment was unanimously supported by Charleston's Black journalists due to his past anti-Klan and anti-lynching campaigns and because Crawford "never overlooks an opportunity to advertise the general advancement of the colored citizens of West Virginia." This same report also noted Crawford was "surprised and pleased" when an African American band greeted him with patriotic music when he delivered a speech in Pocahontas County not long before his appointment.[10]

Crawford's understanding of his role in the Neely administration was, according to him, the decidedly "non-partisan task of boosting tourist trade." The agency produced advertisements for West Virginia tourist destinations in varied media formats distributed throughout the country. The majority were simple brochures and posters, most of which have not survived in archives, but the work did allow Crawford's team to demonstrate some creativity. An example of such work was a 1942 series of dramatized radio programs in celebration of the two hundredth anniversary of the discovery of coal, a program that "portrayed not only the discovery of coal by Peter Salley in 1742 but also the fuel's role in the development of the state and its importance in the war effort."[11] Another was new vacation literature for bus and train travelers designed to capitalize on captive mass transit travelers who could not travel by car as they normally would due to wartime gasoline rationing. One such piece of vacation writing was an article titled "Know Your West Virginia," published in *American Motorist* in 1942, which encouraged "sightseeing and exploring at home" within the wartime context.[12]

Crawford also dabbled in songwriting, using the West Virginia Publicity Commission to encourage the writing of songs about the state. To Crawford, "our mountain grandeur" was the most likely topic for any such song, but lyrics should also prioritize "the greatness and variety and significance of what we are doing in these hills." Timber, iron, steel, coal, oil, gas, vitrolite, chromium, plastics, neon, rayon, nylon, stained glass, electricity—each of these booming industries could inspire. So too should the "deeds and events of deathless renown" inspire state music, with Crawford suggesting songwriters explore the state's diversity in all ways:

> Sing . . . of Morgan Morgan and his first white settlement at Bunker Hill; of James Rumsey and his steamboat on the Potomac; of C&O's epic completion across the State in '73 to the tune of legendary John Henry's steel-driving ballad in Big Bend tunnel; of turnpikes, taverns, and toll houses long abandoned; of civic-minded men and women of service clubs today working as quietly, as surely, and as beautifully as grass growing; of our leaders, Negro and white, in business, industry, labor, education, religion, and government, whose vision, social comprehension, and courage helped to bring a new day for all.[13]

Crawford's own songwriting effort was published and distributed in 1943. Esther Eugenia Davis, a Charleston-based soprano and poet active in promoting state folkways, was recruited to partner with Crawford and the West Virginia Publicity Commission to write "In West Virginia." Davis produced music to go along with Crawford's words, which followed his own recommendations by evoking natural wonders, such as the "blue sky over Berkeley Springs" and "A Blue Ridge Eagle's golden wings," before concluding with the stanza "A lusty song the miner sings / And ballads heard when nights are still; / And with noteworthy other things / A freeman standing on a hill." Disappointing to Crawford surely, "In West Virginia" did not become a state song and seems to have had little impact in its time.[14]

As the agency's work developed, Crawford and Neely drew closer, brought together by a mutual disdain for the conservative Charleston press. Neely resented accusations of Communism made against Crawford; Crawford resented unfair criticisms lobbed at Neely that he sought to become a West Virginia populist demagogue molded after Huey Long. By all outward appearances, Crawford was a Democratic Party man.[15] At the same time, he hired William C. Blizzard, son of the famed UMW labor organizer and veteran of the Battle of Blair Mountain William H. "Bill" Blizzard, as part of his small staff. The younger Blizzard was certainly qualified, having recently graduated from both West Virginia University and the Columbia School of Journalism, but Crawford's willingness to seek out and hire Blizzard indicated a continued attachment to radicalism despite his liberal Democratic patronage.[16]

In 1943, after Crawford completed two successful and uncontroversial years with the Publicity Commission, Neely reassigned him to the Highway Safety Bureau as its new director. The Publicity Commission was not given a replacement for Crawford and, instead, Neely converted the agency into a committee consisting of himself and a few public officials, effectively dissolving the commission. This was not unexpected: Crawford's staff had shrunk from four to two the previous year, with William Blizzard taking a position with the National Youth Administration in April 1942, and neither the assistant secretary or receptionist positions were renewed later that year.[17]

Crawford worked as director of the Highway Safety Bureau for a little over three years under both Neely and briefly his successor, Democrat Clarence Watson Meadows. His primary duties in this office were to produce public literature on state highways, such as scenic routes, driver safety, and explaining construction plans.[18] By the end of 1945, Crawford openly told his friends that he was an operative in the Democratic Party of West Virginia working behind the scenes on labor rights. For instance, that year Crawford claimed to Dreiser that he worked with the party in developing national and state unemployment and anti-trust legislation aimed at Charleston chemical corporations. He also claimed that Neely, Meadows, and Senator Harley M. Kilgore, Neely's replacement, all invited him to contribute to various projects, though he was always short on details in letters to friends. Beyond such happenings, Crawford's Highway Safety Bureau employment was quiet. He and Kate seemingly enjoyed their calmer life.[19]

While Crawford left little documentation of his time within state government, hints of his political work came through scattered newspaper articles and private letters. The only political cause he discussed at length with Dreiser was what he generally called the "railroad proposition." In his view, the Pullman Company, a major railcar manufacturer, had charged exorbitant fees for its services for the previous fifty years, thus pricing most regular working people out of affordable transportation. Crawford proposed to, at a minimum, work with Governor Neely to create a state cabinet position to oversee transportation issues with the goal of making Pullman service "available to more and more people in this age of mass production for mass consumption." Crawford shared these ideas with Dreiser as he entered his first state job, but five years later there was no indication he was able to follow up on these ambitious ideas.[20] Freelance writing also occupied some of Crawford's time alongside government work. Some was serious political commentary, but most of what he produced at this time was simple local history articles probably inspired by his time with the FWP. For instance, the *Coalfield Progress* published a series of Crawford's brief historical overviews of old Appalachian settlements like Rankin's Ferry near Chattanooga, Tennessee.[21]

For all his bragging about political connections, Crawford resigned from the Highway Safety Bureau on December 31, 1946, to join the West Virginia Advertising Agency as a partner. This new venture also emerged through Democratic connections: Don F. Freeman, who himself worked in the state purchasing office and was a Democratic Party mover and shaker, sold Crawford part of his managing interest.[22] The move was somewhat prescient. Four years in the statehouse opened to Crawford the world of political advertising, an industry about to enter a boom period with the continued development of radio, the advent of television, and the postwar mass consumption economy.[23] For the next two decades, Charleston was Crawford's home and political advertising was his domain. Neither Crawford nor his company left behind significant records from this venture, so it is difficult to know just what he accomplished.

Given his connections, it can be assumed the company had a hand in West Virginia Democrat advertisements from 1946 to about 1970.[24]

We can with certainty identify Crawford's participation in the gubernatorial campaign of Fairmont Democrat Robert H. "Bob" Mollohan. Mollohan hired Crawford as his publicity director for a 1956 gubernatorial run, a fact only known because Crawford was hired individually as opposed to the company. Fresh from two terms in the U.S. House of Representatives, Mollohan had a real chance of winning, especially with the public backing of his mentor Matthew Neely. Few in the West Virginia press noted Crawford's hiring, but the Black press generally reported favorably. The *Chicago Defender* informed readers that Crawford was the same activist editor who, nearly three decades earlier, had strongly opposed lynching and the KKK, so voters should take note of Mollohan. Despite Crawford's best efforts, Mollohan lost his bid to Republican Cecil Underwood. He ran again for the House of Representatives in 1958 but lost that race too, to Republican Arch Moore Jr. It is unclear just what advertisements, if any, Crawford created for these campaigns, but he was a core decision maker in both losing ventures.[25]

Crawford then met success as part of the team managing the victorious Democratic senatorial campaign of Jennings Randolph in 1958. Matthew Neely, Crawford's old friend whom he affectionately called "our old political warhorse," died in January 1958 while in office, at age eighty-three. Republican governor Cecil Underwood appointed fellow Republican John Hoblitzell Jr. to the open seat despite Neely's Democratic Party affiliation for the next ten months pending an election later that year for the final two years of Neely's term. Jennings Randolph, a highly popular fourteen-year veteran of the House, was next in line within the state party apparatus. Perhaps Randolph's most notable action in the House was annually sponsoring a constitutional amendment annually from 1942 onward to lower the voting age from twenty-one to eighteen, a change that would not be made until 1971. He also sponsored the Randolph-Sheppard Act providing job opportunities for blind people.[26]

Crawford would finally come to the aid of the Democrats in August 1958. Randolph successfully campaigned throughout 1958 for the Democratic nomination, winning in early August, and with that the campaign truly began with mass advertising and a barrage of public events. The Randolph campaign retained Bruce Crawford's West Virginia Advertising Agency and entrusted him with most, if not all, campaign billboard, newspaper advertisements, and placement in local event flyers. Crawford also managed another campaign employee, Earl Vickers, who handled television and radio ads.[27]

Randolph won the 1958 election against the electorally untested John Hoblitzell Jr. in a landslide (59 percent to 40 percent), so he decided to run again in 1960 on essentially the same platform. This 1960 campaign faced steeper opposition in the form of West Virginia Governor Cecil Underwood, but no matter. The national popularity of Democrats, namely John F. Kennedy, certainly aided Randolph. Crawford's West Virginia Advertising Agency again got to work during the campaign season, starting in August. Operating primarily out of Bluefield, Crawford purchased hundreds of billboards, thousands of brochures, and placed advertising in dozens of event programs from Morgantown to Mingo County, focusing particularly on events associated with Labor Day. When Election Day came, Randolph carried the day, much like in 1958.[28]

With these successful senatorial campaigns under his belt, Crawford moved on to the 1960 gubernatorial campaign of William Wallace "Wally" Barron, likely his last. This campaign was successful too, based on Barron's platform of clean government and civil rights reforms, though he would ironically be convicted of corruption charges less than a decade later. The extent of Crawford's participation in this campaign was not known, but it certainly was one of his last. Crawford retired from Democratic campaign, advertising, and communications work in 1960 or 1961. He may have experienced some rough patches with unsuccessful campaigns like Bob Mollohan's, but it was worth it in the end, as he helped place someone like Jennings Randolph in a position of power.[29]

RETIREMENT AND ROANOKE

After a two-decade career in the political machine, Crawford retired in the early 1960s. He and Kate left Charleston for a sunnier, warmer climate, first to California and then Florida after they found that neither of them enjoyed the West Coast. They moved to St. Petersburg, living there year-round except for a few weeks annually when Bruce visited Virginia and West Virginia for business. The Crawfords had considered the move away from Appalachia long before Bruce's retirement; for example, in 1936 he floated the idea to Dreiser that he would consider an editorial job in New York City. Crawford later claimed that he nearly accepted a job offer from the *Philadelphia Record* in 1938, but he turned it down to stay in the mountains.[30] Even though Crawford referred to his "retirement" in the early 1960s, he spent a few years chasing leads just in case another big-time political campaign manifested. Having found nothing of the sort, he essentially quit all political advertising work by about 1965. He never explained why he quit, probably just because he was ready to retire, and never explained why he and his wife chose Florida. Then again, who wouldn't enjoy the warm weather and fresh start after a lifetime of Appalachian politics? A cozy retirement was well earned.

In Florida, Crawford continued to write about his Virginia home, clearly missing home and angered by what he saw as the continued exploitation of working people. Essays appeared here and there in regional magazines and newspapers carrying his familiar political edge. In 1965, for instance, the *Appalachian South* published a Crawford essay proposing the expansion of the Tennessee Valley Authority into other states. National overdependence on coal was the root cause of Appalachian poverty, Crawford argued, as it led directly to "Congo-like control by outsiders" and "colonial-like rule." Capitalist corporations chased profits, suppressed development, and overall harmed the people living in coal country. An "Appalachian Authority" could help modernize utility infrastructure and drive away exploitive systems, especially in southern West Virginia and southwest Virginia. His solution was radical—federal purchase of all energy companies in the Appalachian region to form an "Appalachian Authority" modeled on the TVA.[31]

A few of Crawford's articles from this time were significantly advanced in their thinking. The "Appalachian Authority" article itself advanced the concept of an Appalachian "internal colony" years before its primacy in Appalachian activist and academic thinking. Academics studying Appalachian poverty developed the idea that Appalachia was an "internal colony" of the United States during the late 1960s at about the same time as Crawford's essay. Harry Caudill, famous for his much-criticized *Night Comes to the Cumberlands*, first used the concept in 1965, but it took several years for other writers to develop the term within a broad academic framework. The model caught on by the 1970s, especially among the younger generation of activist-scholars like Helen Lewis, Ron Eller, and Si Kahn. It was entirely possible Crawford pulled the term "internal colony" from these writers, but there simply was no such academic framework when he wrote the piece. Other notable Crawford essays reported on studies connecting massive floods to strip mining and called for greater social program investment in West Virginia.[32] In 1968 he reported on a black lung symposium at Clinch Valley College, one of the first of its kind. "Both participants and observers came away with a feeling of optimism," he wrote, noting that "concerned leaders from six states seemed determined to prove that pneumoconiosis is no longer to be a byproduct of our aspirations!"[33]

Such radical writings were few compared to Crawford's primary retirement activity as a regular editorial columnist for the *Roanoke Times*. The Roanoke paper published about forty Crawford articles during the 1960s and early

1970s. These ran the gamut of quality—from investigative journalism, to sensationalism, to out-of-touch editorials crossing into bigotry. An example of a light-hearted Crawford article was a 1966 dispatch on the far-fetched idea of converting abandoned coal seams into edible protein. Coal companies would, in theory, apply coal-eating microbes to abandoned mines, which would over time convert coal into edible foodstuffs. Americans could then be sold the product or, more likely, it could be exported as emergency sustenance to famine-stricken nations. This idea, no matter how ludicrous it sounded, appeared in mainstream science journals like *Nature*. Crawford reported that scientists from several West Virginia corporations, including Union Carbide, claimed to have developed microbes that "thrive on coal chemicals to such an extent they produce protein 2,500 times faster than domestic meat animals." Crawford, after first questioning the carcinogenic possibilities, disapproved of such a project unless it first benefited Appalachian communities. If the food would not go toward Appalachians, then "obviously a severance tax would be necessary," he wrote, in classic Crawford fashion.[34]

Pro-socialist sentiment faded from Crawford's writings by the 1960s. Many articles bore no resemblance whatsoever to his radical writings just two decades earlier. An emphasis on personal industriousness pervaded his work, exemplified by an *American Mercury* essay sounding like a self-help book and titled "Don't Hate Your Job—Do it Better!" "'Go the second mile' with your effort," Crawford wrote, "not simply to please your employer, indispensable as that is, but to prevent atrophy of your earning power and deterioration of your personality." The article's bulk shared three similar anecdotes on the work ethic. A few individuals who hated their jobs shared stories in which they applied creativity to their work, resulting in better mental health and, more importantly, a fatter paycheck. Such an argument would never have appeared in *Crawford's Weekly*. It is confounding how Crawford arrived at this woefully contradictory position in the 1960s.[35]

More troubling were Crawford's *Roanoke Times* essays on race and civil rights. *Crawford's Weekly* writings on race from decades earlier were largely driven by ignorance of white supremacist movements and a belief that white America was not ready for integration. By the 1960s, the growing civil rights movement clearly incensed the old Appalachian radical for whatever reason. In 1966 Crawford wrote about a hypothetical conversation between himself and a "middle-aged Baltimore professor" he happened to encounter on an airplane. Both had read an article about a recent "race riot." To avoid being overheard, the professor whispered to Crawford "the 'obvious' solution" to such a problem—"the homogenization of the races." The professor predicted a future America of interracial marriage, procreation licenses instead of marriage licenses, and the eventual integration of African Americans, all of which he roundly approved. Crawford reacted in disturbed shock. He made clear that segregation was wrong, yet he had no qualms about using terms like "miscegenation" and joking about Georgia governor Lester Maddox intimidating Black voters. The editorial reads as an academic exercise, something meant to be a fun debate about Black life in America. The closest Crawford came to clarifying his personal view, and not that of the doomsaying professor, was stating he was for "civil rights and human progress," though he failed to qualify just what that meant.[36]

About a year later, Crawford wrote about "miscegenation" and interracial marriage. The U.S. Supreme Court had just unanimously ruled on *Loving v. Virginia*, making anti-miscegenation laws unconstitutional and effectively legalizing interracial marriage nationally. The core of Crawford's essay on this occasion praised political leaders and residents of both Virginia and West Virginia for embracing the Supreme Court verdict without "extremists." Evidence provided included two anecdotes of Charleston churches, one white and one Black, which had recently hired spiritual leaders of the opposite race, both of which were completely accepted by their respective congregation. A "now let's get on with life attitude" was how Crawford described public sentiment, in effect declaring the civil rights movement should come to an end. The conclusion included a dig at "Cassius Clay," who had changed his name three years earlier to Muhammad Ali, and at Stokely Carmichael for "embarrassing Dr. King" by supposedly causing riots throughout the South and Midwest. Never fear, Crawford argued, because "Virginians and West Virginians, though traditionally conservative on some racial matters, may be setting truly civilized examples for laggard states, in the North as well as the South, to follow."

In reality, most white Americans, including those in Virginia and West Virginia, resisted the *Loving v. Virginia* ruling. Gallup polls suggested less than 20 percent of Americans approved of marriage between Black and white people in the late 1960s, and a majority disapproved well into the 1990s. Virginia, despite being party to the *Loving* case, did not remove all laws governing race and marriage until eight years after the ruling.[37] Crawford referred to Virginia and West Virginia as having been "traditionally conservative on racial matters," without providing detail. Surely, he referred to brutally enforced segregation, Jim Crow laws, and lynching, so why provide a vague sugar coating? Virginia was among the worst state governments during the civil rights era in employing so-called Massive Resistance, the practice of simply closing public schools rather than integrating them after *Brown v. Board*. The tactic was endorsed by politicians of both parties, not least among them Democratic senator Harry Byrd. Massive Resistance began in 1956 and continued until about 1968, a full two years after the *Roanoke Times* published Crawford's essay. Ignorance was no excuse. This essay in particular was an unabashed attack on Black civil rights.[38]

Crawford's *Roanoke Times* essays also criticized second-wave feminism. On May 16, 1970, the *Times* published a short, Crawford-authored profile of Glenn T. Foust, a retired doctor whose career spanned decades in and around Norton. Crawford's opening paragraph, meant as a joke, posed a question to Foust—"What do you, a long-time family physician, think about a switch to the test-tube for baby production, as advocated by some members of the current feminist movement?" Foust responded, "Well now, I don't believe most men would want to marry a test-tube!" After describing Foust's career of delivering babies between rounds of golf, Crawford again took sexist aim—"We cannot believe [Dr. Faust] will be very concerned about the rebellious feminists and their ideas of rendering men practically obsolete!" In the end, this article contributed little to discourse about feminism, serving instead as a cruel punching-down against ideas he did not understand.[39]

What is to be made of articles like these that broke sharply with Crawford's earlier compassion for progressives, radicals, and rights advocates? Was this really the same man who championed the working class, denigrated the Klan, and chastised elites from his small Virginia home? Something changed in Crawford after his departure from public life, but the exact cause is elusive. One possibility was the 1946 death of Theodore Dreiser, but Crawford rarely wrote about his loss of such a friend and mentor. Similarly, it is possible that Crawford's politics adapted those of postwar West Virginia Democrats, even though he was never one to cling to static ideology.[40]

Bruce Crawford, a man who so valued rationality and intelligence, succumbed to the basest of logical fallacies in accepting the worst ideas on offer in America. "Miscegenation" was an invented right-wing eugenicist idea designed to stoke racial fears in white Americans that allowing just one interracial marriage would lead to the collapse of Western society. Any such "slippery slope" argument dismantled itself given that American had been a multiracial, multiethnic society since the day the Virginia Company landed colonists in 1607. Regardless, the civil rights movement changed significantly between 1920 and 1967 by adapting to political party shifts and radicalizing somewhat after World War II. Crawford, for his part, failed to adapt. Considering Crawford was once a labor radical the fact that he failed to sympathize with, or even understand, fellow radicals like Stokely Carmichael or Malcolm X was all the more disappointing. As for feminism, the term "test-tube babies" had been in use as a derogatory term for several decades by the time Crawford wrote on the topic. In vitro fertilization was viewed by scientists, feminists, and most Americans as a celebrated scientific achievement, yet Crawford held it up as an anti-feminism straw man. In no way did most women, feminists, or academics call upon the "test-tube" to totally replace conception and pregnancy as he claimed. *Roanoke Times* arguments such as these were misinformed, at best, and outright anti–civil rights, anti-woman propaganda at worst. In the end, Crawford's essays were too often in the genre of the bitter, "punching-down" editorialist he so despised in the 1930s.[41]

Crawford was but one of several formerly left-leaning radicals who seemed to abandon radicalism in their later years. Acknowledging this is by no means making excuses but shows Crawford was part of a trend. John Dos Passos, a Crawford compatriot in Dreiser Committee work, was perhaps the most famous individual to make such a shift. From the publication of Dos Passos's first novel in 1920, he was a vigorously antiwar, pro-union supporter of Communism. Yet, Dos Passos changed his political views after visiting Spain with Ernest Hemingway during the Spanish Civil War. His good friend and the Spanish translator of his books, José Robles, was arrested and executed, accused of being a Nationalist spy. The circumstances around Robles's death were never fully explained but the execution was carried out by communist secret police, likely because they perceived Robles to be too loose with military plans, not because he was a fascist spy. Dos Passos upended his political life because of Robles's execution after about 1940. He wrote often, sometimes in the *National Review*, in opposition to Communism, in support of Barry Goldwater, or attacking New Left intellectuals for their ignorance to the world around them.[42]

Another such example was Max Eastman, once an editor of the radical serials the *Masses* and the *Liberator*. Eastman traveled to Soviet Russia and remained there about two years in the early 1920s. Unlike Theodore Dreiser, who admired much of the young Communist system, Eastman's temporary residence precipitated a total rejection of Joseph Stalin, Communism, and socialist policies more broadly. These views did not fully coalesce until the 1940s, when Eastman, like Dos Passos, began writing regularly for the *National Review*. For the next thirty years until his death, Eastman remained a stalwart conservative writer, if unconventionally dovish on war and skeptical of Christianity.[43]

Dos Passos and Eastman recognized each other as ex-Communists turned conservatives. Though the pair disagreed on many things—Dos Passos was militant and a defender of brutalities like poison gas in the name of war—they felt mutual respect as honest thinkers proven by a willingness to abandon left-wing friendships for new ideas.[44] Several other *National Review* writers during the 1950s and 1960s were self-proclaimed former Marxists or Communists, namely Will Herberg, James Burnham, and Whittaker Chambers. What each of these writers had generally in common was representing themselves as apostates who only "found" conservatism after a long journey with the Left, thus lending more credence to their current beliefs. Each saw themselves as wiser, world-traveled, and more practical than their past, idealist selves.[45]

Unlike these other men who went on to join the conservative intellectual elite, Crawford never explicitly rejected his left-leaning politics despite his unsavory writings. An explanation for this seemingly strange position may be found in his Democratic Party experiences. Turning the calendar back to mid-1942, Crawford was a brand-new appointee of the Governor Matthew Neely administration as director of the West Virginia Publicity Commission. He now had to tow a party line for the first time in his life as part of his job responsibilities, which likely weighed on Crawford's mind as he submitted an essay to *West Virginia History*, the state's preeminent academic history journal.

Crawford's published article was a transcript of his address delivered on September 6, 1942, to the Tri-State McGuffey Clubs Conference, a small gathering held in the home of Jean Thomas in Ashland, Kentucky. The conference subject matter squarely focused upon a series of nineteenth-century texts for schoolchildren commonly known as McGuffey's Readers. William Holmes McGuffey and Alexander Hamilton McGuffey, brothers who split labor on the reader series, were educators who emphasized that schools should instruct students, especially those in grades one through six, in spelling, phonics, speaking, logical thinking, and morality based on the McGuffeys' Calvinist beliefs. The Readers were also financially successful beyond belief. An estimated 120 million copies sold between the first publishing date in 1836 and 1960. Considering few other books came anywhere close to these sales numbers and the near universal presence of McGuffey's Readers in schools nationwide, it is safe to conclude the McGuffeys' conservative version of morality, patriotism, and Christianity helped shape America's youth for nearly a century.[46]

Starting in the 1920s, many white Americans experienced a revival of interest in McGuffey's Readers as the books began to fade from American classrooms. McGuffey clubs and magazines cropped up primarily in Indiana, Ohio, Tennessee, Virginia, and West Virginia as a form of collective nostalgia for an old style of education. Club attendees would read passages from Readers, the older the better typically, and show off their prized McGuffey artifacts. The movement peaked in 1941, the year before Crawford's *West Virginia History* article, with the unveiling of a McGuffey memorial on the campus of Miami

University in Oxford, Ohio, where William McGuffey taught, by the Federal Association of McGuffey Societies.[47]

Central to McGuffey's Readers—and Crawford's understanding of the books as presented in his talk—was the value of work, hard work to be specific. Without hard work, the rest of the Readers' principles, namely faith, morality, peace, goodness, happiness, and so on, would collapse into lazy idleness. Crawford's speech opened with a greeting from Governor Neely's West Virginia, asserting that Neely, who quoted often from the Readers, "often bejewels his speeches with gems of truth and beauty from the peerless readers." Clearly, Crawford identified himself as an agent of the state, possibly even acting on Neely's orders. Further underscoring Crawford's presentation as a Democrat, as opposed to a socialist who did not believe in God, was his point that only "the deathless parables of Holy Writ" were remembered so well as McGuffey's oeuvre. To make such a public statement contradicted his own politics from less than a decade earlier, clearly marking a professional transformation for the former newspaperman.

What was Crawford's true goals in this essay, which was written just months after America's entry into World War II? On one hand, Crawford called for a return to the McGuffeys' conservative educational values. "Can we be sure that the children of our day know the lessons our country learned in its youth?" asked Crawford rhetorically, not quite calling for a return to McGuffey education but certainly a return to the McGuffey values of goodness, hard work, and humility. On the other hand, Crawford insisted that without McGuffey fables, especially those emphasizing the value of solidarity, all would be lost to the fascist menace rampaging across Europe. Maybe it was a bit naive to think McGuffey could fight Hitler, yet that was one of Crawford's points. Hard work, antifascism, and McGuffey nostalgia—clearly Crawford in 1942 wrestled to reconcile his socialist values with his Democratic Party career. This essay demonstrates a man unsure of his place in the world, though unfortunately Crawford's two-decade retreat from public writing does not provide an entrée into his further evolution. All that was left was the series of *Roanoke Times* editorials and other scant writings.[48]

The *Roanoke Times* editorials were too folksy and nostalgic to be considered serious conservative think-pieces but make sense when viewed through the lens of McGuffey nostalgia. Crawford's final *Roanoke Times* essays were published from December 1967 to December 1970. In many of them, he spun tales about "early pioneers," evoked the image of a "granny doctor," and documented recent economic changes in Wise County. But in others, hints of his old radicalism shone through, just with an added dosage of the elder cynic yelling at the next generation to shape up fast. First, he bemoaned the declining interest in electoral politics despite the growing threat of nuclear annihilation. Next, he called upon the West Virginia state legislature to allocate matching funds to provide all state residents with clean water and highway access. Only then could West Virginia become a leading force in Appalachian programs, such as the recently formed Appalachian Regional Commission. Crawford's concluding essay in this series focused on black lung. He covered a symposium on the topic held at Clinch Valley College, now UVA-Wise, which documented the utter failure to prevent the disease in the preceding thirty years. The meeting was described as "optimistic" that something could be done to help suffering miners; Crawford implied he supported regular X-ray examinations for miners and including measures for black lung prevention in union contracts. While none of these writings included a deep political argument, they were unlikely to have appeared in the pages of the *National Review*.[49]

LEGACY

Legacy mattered greatly to Crawford and was something he considered as early as the 1930s. As a young editor, he hoped that *Crawford's Weekly* would be remembered as a launching pad for his grandest ideas and adventures. He never discussed legacy-building in his newspaper though, instead reserving that for his public lectures. For instance, a lecture he delivered several times in 1935 outright stated he hoped later generations would remember him for "the Harlan adventure, the shot in the leg, the investigation by [the Dreiser] committee, the slander suit which was abandoned, my war on lynching, and many other tilts and tempests."[50] He must have understood the importance of his work, both in his own time and the future, as he tried to preserve his written output. After selling *Crawford's Weekly* in 1935, Crawford arranged for the press's business papers to be acquired by the University of Virginia. A local newspaper article indicated as much, but according to both the University of Virginia and UVA-Wise, *Crawford's Weekly* business papers never entered either university's collection. Some of Crawford's work did land in UVA-Wise archives due to his own efforts. In the mid-1970s, Crawford donated two boxes of his papers, magazines, and books to Clinch Valley College (now UVA-Wise) and some copies of those same materials to Charleston public libraries.

Crawford's donation to Clinch Valley College was possibly his last work in Appalachia. After nearly seventy years of labor, Crawford left the region permanently behind in the early 1970s. With no fanfare, farewell, or a proper send off, he simply stopped writing. From the early 1970s until his death in 1993, he lived full time in Florida and seems to have written absolutely nothing. Kate Crawford, who had been living in Florida year-round since Bruce's retirement, died on September 28, 1979. Unfortunately, nothing survived in Crawford's papers detailing what she had been up to for most of the couple's life.

Few journalists sought out Crawford for interviews in his old age. One key exception came in 1984 when Arthur Prichard, a writer who was working on a book about Mannington, visited Crawford in Florida to talk about the Federal Writers' Project. This was the only documented time that Crawford went on record about his feud with Governor Homer Holt. The *Goldenseal* article written by Prichard after the interview was sparse on detail, but it was clear that Crawford enjoyed rehashing his victory of Holt forty years later.[51] For the last few decades of Bruce's life, he received letters from writers asking about his time in Harlan, thoughts on Wise County, and a host of other issues. He usually responded with copies of some of his old newspaper clippings with a few lines of explanation. For example, in 1972 he sent a correspondent a batch of clippings along with a nostalgic note reading, "I thought you might see from them what sort of berserk editor I was back then! Really, I'm rather proud of my *Crawford's Weekly* days, in spite of any haymakers. Of course, as I grew older and elder, I lost sensitivity and response, I guess. But I don't regret those days. Maybe if I had kept the Weekly and tried a hunger strike of some sort until I could have achieved national support (subscriptions, more checks for articles, books, etc.) I might have 'kept in character' until old age." But other than these few highlights, Crawford seems to have quietly lived out his days in sunny Florida enjoying a well-deserved retirement.[52]

Even though Crawford did not receive any glowing farewells for his retirement, he had already received plenty when he first walked away from publishing in 1935. Crawford believed that upon selling *Crawford's Weekly* he would likely never write again, at least for a popular audience, so his peers treated the sale as an opportunity to deliver a professional eulogy of sorts. Sherwood Anderson wrote that "the country needs more weekly newspapers edited by men like Bruce Crawford." Similar plaudits for Crawford's talents poured into newsprint from across the state no matter the author's political persuasion.

> Virginius Dabney, editor of the *Richmond Times-Dispatch*: "If we should be asked to name the qualities which have won for Bruce Crawford the respect of his journalistic leagues, we should say that they are courage and intellectual honesty. He is one newspaper man in whose integrity one can repose absolute faith."

Richmond News Leader: "He has been one of the few men of prominence who have openly espoused the cause of the coal miners in his section, and he has never hesitated to assail political plundering anywhere or in any guise."

Middlesboro Daily News: "Bruce Crawford, quiet, mild, even-tempered, has a mean twist with his words, which scintillate fire when he lights into the deadwood of the established order and assaults the citadels of capitalism."

Charlottesville Daily Progress: "Bruce Crawford's writings are so militant that people are usually surprised at his manner when they meet him. Expecting an ogre, they find him mild-mannered, gentle, considerate, and not at all egotistical."

Radford News-Journal: "Bruce Crawford has been a valiant campaigner for social justice, for a better standard of living and for the rights of the small man. Certainly, the best interests of the public are served by the writings and crusades of a man like Crawford. He has been an invaluable stimulant to thinking."

Other editors wrote shorter farewells, including descriptions such as "militant and virile," showing "sincerity, courage, and humanity," "a singularly outspoken critic of his fellow Southerners," "brilliant," one who "maddens or gladdens," "picturesque," and a fighter for "truth and righteousness."[53] Nothing of the sort appear later on when he retired from the advertising world or when he died in 1993. His legacy had essentially faded away. His body is buried in St. Petersburg near his final home, a far cry from Dooley, West Virginia. But even though he was largely forgotten by many in 1993, his legacy refused to die.

Bruce Crawford's name reappeared in 2019 within, of all places, Norton city council meetings. In the late 2010s, spurred forward by the election of Donald Trump, the rising popularity of Black Lives Matter, and the murder of George Floyd, communities large and small began to reassess racial equity and justice. Many Americans had been lulled into believing the nation's worst racism was behind us, so a reassessment of local racial histories was in order. Race massacres such as 1898 Wilmington and 1921 Tulsa became major points in public discourse, as did acknowledgments of the evils of segregation, discrimination, and lynching violence. Monuments, statues, and building names were removed (either by popular vote or popular force) throughout the country as seemingly every community assessed its own past. Crawford's original home of Wise County, and more specifically Norton, was one such community that began to explore its own history.

The city of Norton unanimously passed a resolution acknowledging Bruce Crawford's role in resisting lynching in Wise County. Most important were his 1923 anti-Klan writings, reporting on the Leonard Wood lynching, and campaign for anti-lynching laws that were ultimately signed into law by Governor Byrd in 1928. Crawford's death went unacknowledged in 1993, yet here he was being recognized as a local hero twenty-six years later for actions nearly a century old. As to why this happened when it happened, local leaders identified the largest cause as the 2017 Unite the Right terrorist attacks in Charlottesville, located about three hundred miles away. Charlottesville and Albemarle County residents reacted to these horrific events by exploring their own racist past to understand what precipitated them, ultimately culminating in an Alabama pilgrimage to the National Memorial for Peace and Justice. The pilgrims donated soil from the site where locals murdered John Henry James in 1898 and returned to install a historic marker explaining this history. Wise County residents hoped to emulate the Charlottesville-Albemarle pilgrimage and thus initiated their own investigation into local lynching history. Early research uncovered Bruce Crawford, who quickly became the county's touchstone for the past. Local leadership held Crawford up as a worthy ancestor in sharp contrast with other ancestors' sins. If Crawford could see the wrongness of his peers' actions and, more importantly, speak out publicly for justice, then it should be easy for those in the present day to continue his legacy and do the same.[54]

But at a time when one aspect of Crawford's legacy resurfaced, so too did another fall. The *Coalfield Progress*, Crawford's old rival that bought *Crawford's Weekly* in 1935, was still active into the twenty-first century, though its economic fortunes lagged. The newspaper changed ownership a few times over the years yet its family legacy stayed intact until recently. Jenay Tate perpetuated this legacy as the granddaughter of Pres Atkins, former *Coalfield Progress* editor and personal rival to Bruce Crawford. Tate worked for forty years as a jack-of-all-trades for the paper, serving at various times as a writer, editor, publisher, manager, and other roles. In 2019 Lewis County Press, a Missouri-based "rural weeklies" newspaper company, made a large offer to purchase the *Coalfield Progress* along with two other nearby newspapers, the *Dickenson Star* and the Big Stone Gap *Post*. The offer was accepted and as expected by those in the know, Lewis County Press initiated austerity measures to cut costs. Just two months later, Lewis County Press unceremoniously fired Jenay Tate. Since 1945, the *Coalfield Progress* had occupied a downtown Norton office building constructed under the leadership of Pres Atkins. As of 2019, Lewis County

Press rents a much smaller space across from Atkins's building. This lease agreement was secured by the newspaper's long-time general manager just days before he himself was forced by Lewis County Press into an early retirement. A modern viewer will never know for certain how the 1930s Crawford would have reacted, but it's safe to say he would not have ignored the 2019 gutting of the *Coalfield Progress*.[55]

Crawford's most widely known legacy so far in the twenty-first century has been, by far, the West Virginia FWP guidebook. Yet, only rarely does Crawford receive credit for the guidebook, despite being its most important editor (it was a book-by-committee, after all) with his name inscribed on the first page. Such nonrecognition could be expected, though, as most guidebook interest came from renewed attention given to the full FWP American Guide Series and not just West Virginia's entry. Dozens of books and academic articles analyze guidebook production, but it took a documentary, Spark Media's *Soul of a People*, to generate popular attention when it aired in 2009 on the Smithsonian Channel. This documentary was one major reason for an increase in calls to create a new Federal Writers' Project, especially in response to economic crises stemming from 2009 Great Recession and the COVID-19 pandemic. One such FWP-inspired example at a small scale launched in West Virginia—*Traveling 219*, a digital multimedia project that documented oral stories along one of the FWP guidebook's tour routes. *Traveling 219* proved, among other things, that there will always be a social need for such cultural projects blending folklore, sociology, and history. It remains to be seen if a new FWP forms in the twenty-first century, but projects like *Traveling 219* at least prove efficacy at a small scale.

Most of Crawford's peers are largely forgotten today, but a few retain prominent legacies for their writings, politics, or both. However, those with similar politics to Crawford during the prewar era are rarely remembered for their political activism. One would have to investigate niche historical scholarship to find, for instance, leftists who challenged the New Deal or Communists who advocated for civil rights in the 1930s. The most famous writers—Dreiser, Sherwood Anderson, and Dos Passos—rarely appear in high school or college literature courses outside of their popular novels, much less public discourse, but their books are still read and republished broadly. Politicians like Homer Holt and Matthew Neely are rarely remembered beyond gubernatorial lists. Crawford villain Harry Byrd does retain a legacy in today's Virginia, though it is rapidly turning negative. The General Assembly voted to remove Byrd's statue from the state's Capitol Square in June 2021 largely due to his central role in Virginia's Massive Resistance.

Legacy is at least in part defined by the magnitude of one's success. But which success of a person's life should be measured and thus remembered as representative of their life? Was Bruce Crawford the thirty-year-old socialist firebrand? The forty-year-old guidebook editor? The seventy-year-old crotchety editorialist for the *Roanoke Times*? Or the man he was at his death, a ninety-eight-year-old Free Methodist who largely kept to himself? He was obviously all these things and more despite falling short so often in his career. Bruce Crawford failed to achieve most of his life's major goals. He was never elected to any political office, his personal newspaper likely went bankrupt, and the left-leaning policies he championed in the 1930s were an utter pipe dream by the time he retreated from public life in the 1970s.

Yet, Bruce Crawford at his peak captured what it meant to be a radical editor, public historian, and defender of working people in Appalachian Virginia. The capitalist world scoffed at him as a hayseed, then became astonished at his grasp of Communist theory, socialism, and Appalachia's economic problems. He was smart and world-wise from a young age. He bravely fought for the rights of those who had none. And he put his life on the line multiple times in the faint hope the economic inequalities in the mountains might even out in his lifetime. At the very worst, Crawford was willing to take up arms, or at least a typewriter, when the time came. At his very best, he successfully battled powerful men who challenged his worldview and, in doing so, reshaped the politics and historical narrative of a region. He faltered in post–World War II America, seemingly abandoning his political philosophy, writing aspirations, and historical understanding for party politics. Crawford may have been one of the best examples of Appalachian Communists and of early West Virginian applied historians, but he did not move forward in those roles and Appalachia moved on without him. By the time of Crawford's 1960s *Roanoke Times* editorials, a new generation of scholars, activists, historians, and editors had firmly taken his place. He must have felt like a footnote as President Lyndon Johnson's War on Poverty and the Appalachian Regional Commission attempted to address the very problems he addressed four decades earlier.

When Crawford sold his newspaper in 1935, one of his final published lines was "On to a new and meaningful freedom." Of what meaningful freedom did he speak? Practically, Crawford meant the freedom to sell his labor for the first time in fifteen years. He and Kate could go wherever they wished for a decent income and meaningful work, so they left Norton forever for Bluefield, Charleston, California, and Florida. Freedom also meant the ability to challenge—or integrate within—the system without worrying about alienating newspaper subscribers. If there was a benefit to Crawford's abandonment of radical life, it was that he and Kate were able to live peacefully for the remainder of their years after 1942, Crawford's last year writing for the public as his primary income. There were no governors or Harlan police threatening them any longer. But there are also plenty of "what ifs." Could Crawford have won a congressional seat in Virginia or West Virginia with Democratic Party backing? Would an older, wiser Crawford been able to reignite *Crawford's Weekly* after World War II? Perhaps most interesting, if Crawford had simply written more often, could he have properly received a socialist baton from Theodore Dreiser or Sherwood Anderson? Of course, the answers to such questions are impossible because Crawford chose another direction.

Rather than focus on where Crawford failed, instead we—as people living today with agency—should focus on the example he provided. In the end, electoral politics at the state and federal level failed Crawford and the places he called home. The Virginia and West Virginia Democratic Party absorbed Crawford's radicalism and pulled him toward the center. In another world Crawford may have been elected to a local office in Norton or Wise County, climbed the ranks of a radical national organization, or formed his own Appalachian regional organization. Challenging every election is important, of course, but not at the expense of our towns and counties. Radicals must continue to embracing the hard work of small-scale local change. No amount of peaceful protest will ever change the hearts and minds of national GOP leadership, but a little bit of local politicking can save local libraries, build infrastructure, and secure conservation funding.

Except for the brief hope of the War on Poverty, there has been no large-scale assistance provided to Appalachia since World War II. The Appalachian Regional Commission continues to function with funding far too low to even dent the issues facing the region. A few small-scale political efforts emerge periodically to challenge two-party, capitalist hegemony in the region, but there has yet to be a singular force to bring people together across state lines to engender change. While unlikely, it was possible that Bruce Crawford or *Crawford's Weekly* could have coalesced power around a left-wing platform after World War II, but of course this is a counterfactual. His failure in radicalism, if one wishes to call it that, precluded the slower yet similar failure of union politics in Appalachia. There is no statue of Crawford in Norton. *Crawford's Weekly* is no more; all we have are preserved images on microfilm and on archival servers. Appalachia needed (and still needs) heroes under the crush of capitalism. No doubt an aged Crawford had regrets about not doing more for his home. Present observers cannot fault him for choosing a peaceful retirement, but now more than ever, we can fault ourselves for refusing to take up the radical baton some eighty years later.

NOTES

INTRODUCTION

1. Crawford, "Why I Quit Liberalism," *New Masses*, April 16, 1935.
2. Emily Clark, *Innocence Abroad*, quoted in Scott, "Experiment in Southern Letters," 69.
3. "Crawford Retires," *Smyth County News*, reprinted in *Richmond Times-Dispatch*, February 24, 1935.
4. Richard Nelson, "A Virginia Editor Who Is Different," *Country Editor* (Staten Island, NY), July 1927, reprinted in "Moonlighting with the Muse," *West Virginia Hillbilly*, July 26, 1969.
5. Crawford, "A Prophet Drops In," *Crawford's Weekly*, June 27, 1934.
6. "On the Editor's Mind," *Crawford's Weekly*, April 10, 1926.
7. "Heads I Win, Tails You Lose," *Crawford's Weekly*, July 12, 1924.
8. "Always Jobs," *Crawford's Weekly*, August 2, 1929.
9. The *Richmond Times-Dispatch* recognized Crawford in 1929 as penning one of the best two editorial pages in the Commonwealth. *Crawford's Weekly* also received plaudits from the University of Missouri School of Journalism as the seventh best editorial page as determined by the National Editorial Association in 1926. "Best Editorial Pages," *Richmond Times-Dispatch*, February 10, 1929; John H. Casey to Crawford, May 8, 1924, Crawford Papers, box 1.
10. "Editor of Crawford's Is Wearing a Cane," *Richmond Times-Dispatch*, January 15, 1925; "Bruce Crawford Keeps Up War on Lynchings," *Afro-American*, January 21, 1928; "Virginia Editor Finds Readers Mob Advocates," *Chicago Defender*, January 21, 1928.
11. A National Bureau of Economic Research study estimated that in 1920 about 40 percent of all urban newspapers claimed independence with an additional 22 percent claiming both independence and specific party support. Gentzkow, Glaeser, and Goldin, "Rise of the Fourth Estate," 2.
12. "Bruce Crawford Says," undated [1935], Dreiser Papers.
13. A proclivity for literature's finer things dates back to Crawford's earliest newspaper days, for instance seen in his review of the play "Lost Paradise" by H. B. Warner in 1915. Crawford, "H. B. Warner," *Crawford's Weekly*, December 30, 1915.
14. Ball, "Mountain Scribes," 14–19. Beverly published a poem anthology titled *Echoes from the Cumberlands* in 1928.
15. Crawford, *Nuggets*, 4.
16. "Women on Council?," January 21, 1923; "For Birth Control," June 21, 1929 (both in *Crawford's Weekly*).

17. "The Democracy of the Dead," *Crawford's Weekly*, April 18, 1931.
18. About a dozen small newspapers affiliated with the Socialist Party existed in Appalachia, primarily concentrated in northern West Virginia and the Pittsburgh area. Very few continued beyond about 1920, and all in West Virginia closed by the end of the 1920s. For more, see *Mapping American Social Movements Project*; and Barkey, *Working Class Radicals*.

CHAPTER I

1. Bruce Crawford's siblings were James W. (b. 1895), Mary E. (b. 1898), and Virginia L. (b. 1909).
2. The other coeditor who worked with Crawford was Walter F. Beverly.
3. John Fox Jr. to Crawford, March 21, 1914, Bruce Crawford Papers.
4. West Virginia University records listed him as a "subfreshman," meaning Crawford was technically enrolled in classes but needed to meet university entrance requirements to become a fully admitted student.
5. Crawford volunteered for the coming war effort in 1917 and was assigned to the 215th Engineers in the U.S. Army, a logistics unit, located at Camp Humphreys in Fairfax County, VA. By his own accounts, World War I service greatly affected his politics, especially inspiring him to campaign for veterans' rights and participate in antiwar movements, but he never shared specifics about this time of his life.
6. J. W. Palmer served as editor while Crawford was serving his country. Only two issues of the *Norton Reporter* survive in archival collections. *N. W. Ayer and Son's American Newspaper Annual and Directory* (1916), 988; *N. W. Ayer and Son's American Newspaper Annual and Directory* (1917), 993; *N .W. Ayer and Son's American Newspaper Annual and Directory* (1918), 1011; *N. W. Ayer and Son's American Newspaper Annual and Directory* (1917), 990.
7. Addington, *Story of Wise County*, 281; *N. W. Ayer and Son's American Newspaper Annual and Directory* (1920), 984; *N. W. Ayer and Son's American Newspaper Annual and Directory* (1922), 1017.
8. Crawford referred to his father's trade as a "carpenter, contractor, and merchant." Crawford also noted that his father and uncle (Robert R. Crawford) formed the Lansing Telephone Company to service small communities in Fayette County, West Virginia. The company operated its switchboard from the family's home and store, which young Bruce often operated. Around 1912 the Crawford brothers sold to a local cooperate that was most likely absorbed by Bell. Crawford, "When the Telephone Came to Possum Creek," *Crawford's Weekly*, April 16, 1927; Crawford, "Buggy Riding on Possum Creek," *Crawford's Weekly*, March 3, 1928.
9. The Department of the Interior established new county seats, Enid and Pond Creek, in two new Oklahoman counties. Cherokee Nations citizens then exercised their right by treaty to obtain plots of land within the newly created county seats. In response, the Department of the Interior, believing the Cherokee Nation conspired with railroad companies to profit immensely, simply moved the designated county seat locations, thus making two versions of Enid and Pond Creek. One seat was formally recognized by the U.S. government and the other by the railroad company. Settlers, workers, and speculators quickly occupied four towns with the Rock Island Railroad escalating its duel with the government. Rock Island simply refused to provide service to the two government-backed towns. Making matters even more confusing, Congress split on the issue; the House supported the rights of the government town citizens, while the Senate supported Rock Island Railroad. A tense stalemate settled upon the area.
10. Miller, "Cultivating Capital," 1–3.
11. Locals first attempted to disrupt Rock Island trains through less invasive means—placing dummies on the tracks, leaving derelict wagons in the way, and attempting to flag down railroad engineers. In the end, U.S. Marshals were sent to restore order, though locals continued to dynamite and burn bridges. Congress bowed to protests by passing a bill

requiring railroads to build and maintain both passenger stations and freight depots within a quarter mile of all town sites in the area established prior to August 8, 1894, meaning all four in this particular dispute. Crawford, "Recollections of a Common Man," *Appalachian South*, Summer 1965, 34; Crawford to Dreiser, January 4, 1933, Dreiser Papers.

12. In using the term "mountain white," Crawford meant a common Appalachian stereotype of uneducated, gruff, inbred, drunk, and violent carried forth in local color writing. Crawford, "They're All Wrong," *Crawford's Weekly Industrial Supplement*, October 1920; Isenberg, *White Trash*, 187.

13. Crawford, "The Mountain White," *Crawford's Weekly Industrial Supplement*, October 1920.

14. John Fox Jr., himself a local color writer, did not upset Crawford though, likely because Fox actually lived in the area and was known personally. Plein, "Portraits of Appalachia."

15. Crawford, "'Youth's Sweet-Scented Manuscript,'" in *Nuggets*, 27–28.

16. Crawford, "'Youth's Sweet-Scented Manuscript,'" in *Nuggets*, 27–28.

17. "Appalachia!," *Crawford's Weekly*, November 21, 1925.

18. Firstenberger, *In Rare Form*, 29–30; McLoughlin, *Billy Sunday Was His Real Name*, 274–76; Hofstadter, *Anti-Intellectualism in American Life*, 132; Sirgiovanni, *Undercurrent of Suspicion*, 27.

19. Marow, "George Bellows and Religious Art," 121; "[Untitled]," *Crawford's Weekly*, January 19, 1923.

20. "Some Day an Editor Will Do It," *Crawford's Weekly*, January 28, 1922.

21. Moore, *Citizen Klansman*, 94–102.

22. Crawford, "Recollections of a Common Man," 35.

23. Crawford, "[Untitled]," *Crawford's Weekly*, January 19, 1923.

24. "[Untitled]," November 17, 1923; "[Untitled]," November 24, 1923; "Just a Minute!," December 8, 1923; "Nuts and Notions," December 29, 1923 (all in *Crawford's Weekly*).

25. "[Untitled]," November 17, 1923; "[Untitled]," November 24, 1923; "Just a Minute!," December 8, 1923; "Nuts and Notions," December 29, 1923 (all in *Crawford's Weekly*).

26. "[Untitled]," January 24, 1924; "[Untitled]," February 23, 1924; "[Untitled]," September 29, 1923 (all in *Crawford's Weekly*).

27. "A Test at Hand," *Crawford's Weekly*, December 22, 1923.

28. "Klan Asks to Parade Here," May 2, 1924; "Announsemint," May 17, 1924 (both in *Crawford's Weekly*).

29. "Norton Klan Divided," *Crawford's Weekly*, June 28, 1924; "New Banks Organizing," *Financier*, 79 (1902), 1075; "Huettel Coal & Coke Co.," *Coal Field Directory* (Pittsburgh, PA: Keystone Consolidated, 1915), 509. Edith Ould was the widow of E. H. Ould, a descendant of one of Norton's wealthiest early families. "Appalachia!," *Crawford's Weekly* November 21, 1925.

30. "A Hitler Possible Here," *Crawford's Weekly*, April 19, 1933.

31. "[Untitled]," *Crawford's Weekly*, December 8, 1923.

32. "Best Editorial Pages," *Richmond Times-Dispatch*, February 10, 1929.

33. No copies of Crawford's writings from 1920 survive, so Crawford's response to the murder of David Hunt is unknown.

34. "Will Governor Byrd Take a Hand?," *Crawford's Weekly*, August 23, 1926.

35. Beers, "Wythe County Lynching of Raymond Bird."

36. "License to Lynch," *Crawford's Weekly*, September 11, 1926.

37. "50 Murderers," *Crawford's Weekly*, October 16, 1926.

38. Beers, "Wythe County Lynching of Raymond Bird"; "Gov. Byrd Makes Good," *Staunton Tribune*, January 22, 1927; "Lyncher Is Free," *Richmond Planet*, July 23, 1927; "'Unfinished Business,'" *Crawford's Weekly*, July 23, 1927.

39. "The Mob," *Crawford's Weekly*, December 3, 1927.

40. "The Mob," *Crawford's Weekly*, December 3, 1927.

174 / Notes to Pages 26–32

41. "Hypocrites," *New York Amsterdam News*, January 4, 1928; "Nice Virginia People Favor Lynchings," *Afro-American*, December 31, 1927; "Where It Requires Courage to Speak," *New Journal and Guide*, December 24, 1927; "Virginia Editor Finds Readers Mob Advocates," *Chicago Defender*, January 21, 1928; "Va. White Man Makes Scottsboro Protest," *Afro-American*, January 30, 1932; "Are Virginia Editors Superficial?," *New Journal and Guide*, February 4, 1928; "Mob Sympathizers Criticize Editor Who Flayed Lynchings," *New Journal and Guide*, December 24, 1927.

42. "Hypocrites," *New York Amsterdam News*, January 4, 1928; "Nice Virginia People Favor Lynchings," *Afro-American*, December 31, 1927; "Where It Requires Courage to Speak," *New Journal and Guide*, December 24, 1927; "Virginia Editor Finds Readers Mob Advocates," *Chicago Defender*, January 21, 1928; "Va. White Man Makes Scottsboro Protest," *Afro-American*, January 30, 1932; Crawford, "Are Virginia Editors Superficial?," *New Journal and Guide*, February 4, 1928; "Mob Sympathizers Criticize Editor Who Flayed Lynchings," *New Journal and Guide*, December 24, 1927.

43. "Courts vs. Mobs," *Crawford's Weekly*, December 17, 1927.

44. Crawford, "After Two Weeks," *New Journal and Guide* [reprinted from *Crawford's Weekly*], December 17, 1927.

45. Crawford, "From West Virginia," *Afro-American*, August 13, 1938; Crawford, "Bruce Crawford Tells of Hostile Reaction to His Efforts in South," *Pittsburgh Courier*, January 7, 1927.

46. Other Virginia newspapers writing anti-lynching editorials included the *Richmond News Leader* and *Richmond Times-Dispatch*. See Schaikewitz and Lisby, "Harry F. Byrd and Louis I. Jaffe." The final official lynching in Virginia was the murder of Shedrick Thompson in Fauquier County on September 15, 1932.

47. Crawford, "From West Virginia," *Afro-American*, August 13, 1938; Crawford, "Bruce Crawford Tells of Hostile Reaction to His Efforts in South," *Pittsburgh Courier*, January 7, 1927.

48. Leidholdt, "Never Thot This Could Happen," 198–232.

49. "[Untitled]," March 21, 1931, *Crawford's Weekly*; "Two Innocent Persons Were Lynched Last Year," *Crawford's Weekly*, November 21, 1931; "Lynchings in Nation Must Be Abolished," *Crawford's Weekly*, January 11, 1933; "Local Editor Is Threatened," *Crawford's Weekly*, November 8, 1933; "A Warning from Sherwood Anderson," November 22, 1930; Sherwood Anderson, "Look Out, Brown Man!," *Nation*, November 26, 1930.

50. "Abolish the Lash," *Crawford's Weekly*, October 17, 1925.

51. "That Report on Whippings," *Crawford's Weekly*, November 21, 1925.

52. "Virginia Does Whip," *Crawford's Weekly*, November 28, 1925; Leep, "First Seeds," 143; Shepherd, *Avenues of Faith*, 171–72.

53. "Whipping in Virginia Penitentiary," *Crawford's Weekly*, November 12, 1927.

54. "His Legal Deserts," *Crawford's Weekly*, February 11, 1928.

55. "Prison Reform," *Crawford's Weekly*, May 4, 1929.

56. "Prison Reform Imperative," *Crawford's Weekly*, March 21, 1931.

57. "The Poll Tax Injustice," *Crawford's Weekly*, May 2, 1934.

58. "Poverty Disenfranchises," *Crawford's Weekly*, August 17, 1934.

59. "Virginia's Political Aristocracy," *Crawford's Weekly*, November 16, 1934; "Too Poor to Vote," *Crawford's Weekly*, September 21, 1934.

60. "The Poll Tax Discussion," December 14, 1934.

61. As of 2018, the U.S. Census Bureau estimated that Wise County had 38,012 residents with 5.9 percent identifying as African American. Comparatively, Wise County in 1930 had 51,167 residents, of whom 6.2 percent were African American. The overall population had risen sharply during Crawford's life, having more than doubled since 1900, but by 1930 it had essentially leveled.

62. "And America Condemns Christian Anglo-Saxon," June 25, 1927; "Stuart Eulogizes Beauty of Southwest," June 11, 1927; "Let's Grow, But," January 14, 1928 (all in *Crawford's Weekly*).

63. "Anglo-Saxon Ancestry," *Crawford's Weekly*, June 3, 1921.
64. In 1930 Buchanan and Craig counties were 99.1 percent and 99.5 percent native white, according to the U.S. Census. "Dickenson Asks State to Give More to Schools," *Crawford's Weekly*, September 5, 1925.
65. "Color Line Is Fast Fading in Old Dominion," *Crawford's Weekly*, March 1, 1924.
66. "John Powell Helps Form Anglo-Saxon Club," *Collegian* (Richmond, VA), February 16, 1923; Smith, *Managing White Supremacy*, 84.
67. Note that the Racial Integrity Act of 1924 remained law until the U.S. Supreme Court ruled on *Loving v. Virginia* in 1967. Also, Radford University stripped John Powell's name from the school's arts and music building by unanimous vote in 2010. Tonia Moxley, "White Supremacist's Name Removed from Radford U. Building," *Roanoke Times*, September 16, 2010; Paul Lombardo, "Eugenic Laws against Race Mixing," Image Archive of the American Eugenics Movement, Dolan DNA Learning Center, Cold Springs Harbor Laboratory, http://www.eugenicsarchive.org/html/eugenics/essay7text.html; Whisnant, *All That Is Native and Fine*.
68. "After 64 Years," *Crawford's Weekly*, January 19, 1929.
69. "Tribute to a Negro," *Richmond Times-Dispatch*, reprinted in *Crawford's Weekly*, June 6, 1925.
70. "South's Peerless Leader," *Crawford's Weekly*, October 3, 1925; Crawford, "Freeman—Modern and Unmaudlin," *Scribner's Magazine*, January 1926, 7.
71. The bill pushed by Coolidge authorized up to five million coins to be struck. Around one million were actually sold of the 2.31 million created. "1925 Stone Mountain," NGC Coin, accessed June 14, 2019, https://www.ngccoin.com/coin-explorer/silver-commemoratives-1892-1954-pscid-71/1925-stone-mountain-50c-ms-coinid-19378.
72. "Why American Is Great," *Crawford's Weekly*, April 10, 1926.
73. "The Last Reunion," *Crawford's Weekly*, May 9, 1931.
74. "Historic—And Human!," *Crawford's Weekly*, May 23, 1925.
75. "Our Anglo-Saxons," *Crawford's Weekly*, March 12, 1927; Crawford, "Piney Ridge, Virginia," *Virginia Quarterly Review* 8, no. 3 (July 1932): 371.
76. Isenberg, *White Trash*, 218–19; Baldwin, *Poverty and Politics*, chap. 4.
77. "[Untitled]," *Crawford's Weekly*, August 9, 1924; "The Racial Rumpus," *Crawford's Weekly*, June 28, 1924.
78. Clarence Darrow, "Untitled Speech, 10 Feb. 1927," reprinted in *Crawford's Weekly*; "The Black Citizen," *Crawford's Weekly*, April 30, 1927.
79. "Slavery in Alabama," *Crawford's Weekly*, July 25, 1932.
80. "From Bruce Crawford," Papers of the Institute of Public Affairs, 1927–1953, University of Virginia.
81. "The Racial Rumpus," *Crawford's Weekly*, June 28, 1924; "[Untitled]," *Crawford's Weekly*, August 30, 1924.
82. Sherman and Henry, *Hollow Folk*; Catte, *What You Are Getting Wrong about Appalachia*; Stoll, *Ramp Hollow*, 241.
83. Crawford, "Piney Ridge, Virginia," 372.
84. "What Is Left?," *Crawford's Weekly*, September 10, 1932.
85. "The Future of Coal," *Crawford's Weekly*, November 24, 1928.
86. "Unfair Taxing," August 2, 1930; "Virginia's Defective Mine Laws," August 10, 1934; "Tears of a Crocodile," August 31, 1934 (all in *Crawford's Weekly*).
87. "What Are the Facts?," *Crawford's Weekly*, March 25, 1922.
88. "Put Them Out," *Crawford's Weekly*, September 3, 1921.
89. "The Merchant and the Miner," *Crawford's Weekly*, September 6, 1933.
90. "Industrial War Begins," April 6, 1929; "A Mob Attitude," May 11, 1929; "The Epileptic South," September 21, 1929; "More Violence," October 26, 1929; "After 64 Years," January 19, 1929 (all in *Crawford's Weekly*).

91. "Appalled at Our Poverty," *Crawford's Weekly*, July 26, 1933.
92. "Work, But Know Your Rights," November 26, 1939; "Are Depressions Necessary?," December 5, 1931; "The 'Your Own Boss' Myth," April 9, 1932 (all in *Crawford's Weekly*).
93. "Don't Be a Mud-Dauber," *Crawford's Weekly*, November 17, 1928.
94. Crawford, "Prohibition in the Small Town," *Outlook and Independent*, March 26, 1930, 488–89.
95. "How About It?," *Crawford's Weekly*, December 13, 1930.
96. "[Untitled]," *Crawford's Weekly*, February 7, 1931; "Troops Called Out in Virginia Strike," *New York Times*, November 27, 1930; "Communist Leader Arrested in Strike," October 5, 1930, *New York Times*; Smith, *Mill on the Dan*.
97. "The State Takes Sides," *Crawford's Weekly*, November 30, 1930.
98. Workplaces were grouped into four union-based categories: closed shops mandated union membership for all employees; union shops allowed hiring of nonunion workers on the condition they join the union by a set time; agency shops required payment of union dues but not necessarily membership; and open shops could not compel union membership.
99. "The Right to Work," *Crawford's Weekly*, July 13, 1934.
100. Crawford, "The South versus the CIO," *New Masses*, September 7, 1937; Fry, "Rayon, Riot, and Repression," 6–12; "Union Wins Covington, Va., Vote," *New York Times*, July 18, 1937; "[Untitled]," *Roanoke Times*, July 8, 1937.
101. "[Untitled]," July 2, 1932; "Work, but Not Servility," May 24, 1933; "The Last of the Covered Wagons," September 22, 1928; "Wealth Concentration Increases," August 10, 1934; "Politician Roosevelt's 'Relief,'" September 24, 1932; "In Terror of Technocracy," January 18, 1933; "National Pirates," August 13, 1921; "Out of Gear," October 8, 1932; "They're Talking Technocracy," December 31, 1932 (all in *Crawford's Weekly*).
102. ODP still exists as of 2020 as part of the Kentucky Utilities Company and is not the same as the larger energy company Dominion Energy.
103. "An Ironical Lesson," August 6, 1932; "Beware of This," September 19, 1931; "If One, Why Not More?," December 13, 1930 (all in *Crawford's Weekly*).
104. "The Inescapable Answer," *Crawford's Weekly*, July 20, 1934.
105. "The Worm May Turn," *Crawford's Weekly*, April 18, 1934.
106. "Mere Reform Is Futile," January 18, 1933; "The Quick and the Dead," September 17, 1932 (both in *Crawford's Weekly*).
107. "Mr. Ford's Eyesight," *Crawford's Weekly*, March 21, 1931.
108. "Economic Fatheadism," *Crawford's Weekly*, February 7, 1931.
109. "Our 'Nightmare,'" *Crawford's Weekly*, January 3, 1931.
110. "It Won't Soft-Pedal," *Crawford's Weekly*, May 28, 1932.
111. "Investigate," *Crawford's Weekly*, October 19, 1929.

CHAPTER 2

1. "A Day with Theodore Dreiser," *Real America* 6 (November 1935): 49, 68–69.
2. "A Day with Theodore Dreiser," *Real America* 6 (November 1935): 49, 68–69.
3. Anderson moved to a farm in Marion, Virginia, in 1926 and bought two newspapers, one in Marion and another in Smyth County. He wrote for them often, though not always on political topics. Over the next decade and as Anderson's stature grew as a novelist, his newspaper work drifted toward critique, especially of southwest Virginia labor conditions, always from a progressive or socialist point of view. Robert Dunne, "Sherwood Anderson (1876–1941)," *Encyclopedia Virginia*, Virginia Foundation for the Humanities, October 28, 2015; Bassett, *Sherwood Anderson*, 24.
4. "Parable of the Potato," *Crawford's Weekly*, May 16, 1931.
5. "Industrial War Begins," April 6, 1929; "Consider Elizabethton," March 23, 1929; "Aspects of the Strike," April 27, 1929 (all in *Crawford's Weekly*).

6. Institute of Public Affairs, "Statement of Purpose," accessed June 15, 2019, https://ead.lib.virginia.edu/vivaxtf/view?docId=uva-sc/viu03880.xml.
7. Crawford to Charles Maphis, July 4, 1929, Crawford Papers, box 1.
8. Crawford, "Labor Situation in the South," paper delivered at the Institute of Public Affairs Open Forum, Charlottesville, VA, August 5, 1929, http://ead.lib.virginia.edu/vivaxtf/view?docId=uva-sc/viu03880.xml; Crawford, "Discussing the South's Labor Policy," *New Journal and Guide*, August 17, 1929.
9. Sherwood Anderson to Crawford, August 26, 1929; Crawford to Anderson, August 31, 1929; Anderson to Crawford, December 16, 1930 (all found in Sherwood Anderson Papers).
10. Bruce Crawford, "Labor Situation in the South."
11. Virginius Dabney, "South's Labor Condition Held by Crawford to be Archaic," *Richmond Times-Dispatch*, August 7, 1929. Other newspapers reporting on Crawford's speech included the *New York Times*, *New York World*, the *Nation*, *Time*, *Philadelphia Record*, and the *Norfolk Virginian-Pilot*. Charles Maphis to Crawford, August 23, 1929, Crawford Papers, box 1; John W. Edelman to Crawford, August 12, 1929, Crawford Papers, box 1.
12. Shifflett, *Coal Towns*, xii–xiii; Buckley, *Extracting Appalachia*, 37; Eller, *Miners, Millhands, and Mountaineers*, 157–58.
13. "Harlan: A Study in Futility?," *Crawford's Weekly*, May 16, 1931.
14. "Comparing Records," *Crawford's Weekly*, May 17, 1924; Crawford, "Tyranny and Terrorism Reign in Harlan County," *Crawford's Weekly*, August 1, 1931; Tess Huff, "Coal War in Kentucky," *Labor Age*, June 1931, 9–11.
15. "Tyranny and Terrorism Reign in Harlan County," *Crawford's Weekly*, August 1, 1931; *Harlan Miners Speak*, 122–23.
16. *Harlan Miners Speak*, 124–25; "Tyranny and Terrorism Reign in Harlan County," *Crawford's Weekly*, August 1, 1931.
17. "Tyranny and Terrorism Reign in Harlan County," *Crawford's Weekly*, August 1, 1931.
18. *Harlan Miners Speak*, 127.
19. "[Untitled]," *Crawford's Weekly*, August 8, 1931.
20. Louis Jaffe, "Norfolk Newspaper Says Bruce Crawford Winged but Not Squelched," *Crawford's Weekly*, August 15, 1931.
21. Dreiser, *Dreiser Looks at Russia*.
22. Lingeman, *Theodore Dreiser*, 347–51.
23. "Va. White Man Makes Scottsboro Protest," *Afro-American*, January 30, 1932; "Four Lynchings in Tuscaloosa Being Probed," *New Journal and Guide*, November 11, 1933; "Lynch Investigators Get Scant Courtesy from Alabama Officials," *Afro-American*, November 18, 1933.
24. Duke, *Writers and Miners*, 28–29; Lester Cohen, "Harlan," in Pizer, *Theodore Dreiser Recalled*, 177–78; Lingeman, *Theodore Dreiser*, 347–51; Howard, *Forgotten Radicals*, 63–126; Miller, *Remembering Scottsboro*, 17–30; "Lynch Investigators Get Scant Courtesy from Alabama Officials," *Afro-American*, November 18, 1933; "Knight Refuses to Cooperate in Lynching Quiz," *New Journal and Guide*, November 18, 1933.
25. Cohen, "Harlan," 179; Lingeman, *Theodore Dreiser*, 355–56.
26. Rochester, *Labor and Coal*.
27. Walker and Walker, *Modern Technology and Civilization*; Walker and Walker, *Technology, Industry, and Man*; Charles Rumford Walker, *Our Gods Are Not Born*; Charles Rumford Walker, *Bread and Fire*; Adelaide Walker, "Pioneer's Return."
28. In 1952 Levy appeared before the House Un-American Activities Committee and testified against several of his colleagues. Cohen, "Of Human Bondage: A Play"; Levy, *The Last Pioneers*; Levy, *Wedding*; "Lester Cohen, 61, Novelist Is Dead," *New York Times*, July 19, 1963.
29. Stanton, *Red, Black, White*, 56; "Congressional Record: Appendix, Vol. 87, Part 11, March 17, 1941 to May 20, 1941," A1353.

30. "Guide to the Arnold Johnson Papers TAM 137," Tamiment Library and Robert F. Wagner Labor Archives, http://dlib.nyu.edu/findingaids/html/tamwag/tam_137/bioghist.html; Joan Cook, "Arnold Johnson Is Dead at 84," *New York Times*, September 28, 1989.

31. Duke, *Writers and Miners*, 31–32; Stanton, *Red, Black, White*, 55.

32. Lee, *Comrades and Partners*; John Dos Passos, "Harlan: Working under the Gun," *New Republic*, December 2, 1931; Allen, *Organizing in the Depression South*, 52.

33. Dreiser, "Judges Jones, the Harlan Miners, and Myself," Dreiser Papers.

34. *Harlan Miners Speak*, 92–96; "Tells Story of Mistreatment by KY Officers," *Crawford's Weekly*, September 26, 1931.

35. *Harlan Miners Speak*, 206.

36. *Harlan Miners Speak*, 225–26.

37. Also factoring into Powers's decision was his knowledge that a miner was murdered by hanging with barbed wire the previous year. *Harlan Miners Speak*, 146–48.

38. Dreiser, "Judges Jones, the Harlan Miners, and Myself."

39. National Committee for the Defense of Political Prisoners to Judge Jones, December 7, 1931, Dreiser Papers.

40. Crawford, in *Harlan Miners Speak*, 80; Crawford to Dreiser, November 12, 1931, Dreiser Papers; "Indictment Sought of Dreiser and Girl," *Washington Post*, November 10, 1931.

41. *Harlan Miners Speak*, 256.

42. Dreiser, undated telegram, Dreiser Papers.

43. Crawford to Dreiser, December 2, 1931; Dreiser to Crawford, December 14, 1931 (both in Dreiser Papers).

44. Crawford to Dreiser, November 12, 1931; Crawford to Dreiser, November 17, 1931 (both in Dreiser Papers).

45. "A Sojourn in Kentucky," *Crawford's Weekly*, May 28, 1932.

46. Crawford to Dreiser, October 7, 1932; Crawford to Dreiser, October 20, 1932; Crawford to Dreiser, October 21, 1932 (all in Dreiser Papers).

47. Crawford to Dreiser, March 29, 1932, Dreiser Papers.

48. Crawford to Dreiser, May 14, 1934, Dreiser Papers; "John H. Blair, Harlan's Famed Former Sheriff, Dies," *Knoxville News-Sentinel*, May 11, 1934.

49. Crawford to Dreiser, December 2, 1931, Dreiser Papers.

50. Dreiser to Anderson, December 4, 1931, Anderson Papers.

51. Crawford, "What Have We to Lose?," *Labor Age*, December 1931, 7–8.

52. For more, see Copple, *Harlan County USA*; and Portelli, *They Say in Harlan County*.

53. Waldo Frank was a Communist and writer who participated in coal country activism. He visited Harlan County three months after the Dreiser Committee as the chair of an Independent Miners Relief Committee group with the intent of bringing supplies to striking miners there and elsewhere in Tennessee and Kentucky. Frank's Harlan County trip was cut short when unknown assailants, likely coal operator thugs, drove the group from the area. He recovered briefly in a Knoxville hospital before joining the NCDPP in their next campaign in favor of the Bonus Army, which included an ultimately unsuccessful meeting with President Hoover. "Conditions in Coal Fields in Harlan and Bell Counties, Kentucky," U.S. Congress, Senate, Committee on Manufacturers, May 1932; "Writers Are Escorted Out of Pineville," *Crawford's Weekly*, February 13, 1932; "Keeping the White House Informed," *Crawford's Weekly*, August 27, 1932.

54. *Harlan Miners Speak*, 18; Legnini, "Radicals, Reunion, and Repatriation," 485–86.

55. *Harlan Miners Speak*, 20–21.

56. Duke, *Writers and Miners*, 32–33.

57. Crawford, in *Harlan Miners Speak*, 80.

58. Crawford to Dreiser, March 29, 1932, Dreiser Papers.

59. "Writers Are Escorted Out of Pineville," *Crawford's Weekly*, February 13, 1932; "Stupid

Kentucky," *Crawford's Weekly*, February 13, 1932; "Now We See," *Crawford's Weekly*, March 19, 1932; Hevener, *Which Side Are You On?*, 77–82.

60. Anderson to Dreiser, undated [ca. 1934], Sherwood Anderson Papers.

61. Titler, *Hell in Harlan*, 26.

62. Dreiser to Crawford, December 29, 1931, Dreiser Papers; Dreiser to Crawford, January 7, 1932, Dreiser Papers; Bush, "Faith, Power, and Conflict"; Titler, *Hell in Harlan*.

63. Crawford to Anderson, May 16, 1933, Sherwood Anderson Papers.

64. An appeals court overturned Herndon's conviction in December 1935; it was then upheld by the Georgia Supreme Court. The U.S. Supreme Court struck down Georgia's insurrection law as unconstitutional on April 26, 1937, clearing Herndon permanently. Moore, "Angelo Herndon Case"; Edward A. Hatfield, "Angelo Herndon Case," New Georgia Encyclopedia, December 3, 2013; Gilmore, *Defying Dixie*; Herndon, *Let Me Live*.

65. Crawford to Anderson, May 16, 1933, Anderson Papers.

66. Stone and other leaders supported African American and Communist leader James Ford, an individual considered unsavory by many white Southern liberals. UNC professor E. E. Erickson dined with James Ford, leading to UNC's attempts to fire Erickson. The Southern Committee for People's Rights, as it was known at the time, came to Erickson's defense. Membership went down shortly thereafter for unknown reasons, although the most likely culprit was a combination of racism, respectability politics, and red-baiting. Uhlmann, "Communist Civil Rights Movement," 231; "Interview with Olive Stone, August 13, 1975," Southern Oral History Program Collection, Documenting the American South, University of North Carolina Library, https://docsouth.unc.edu/sohp/playback .html?base_file=G-0059-4; Kelley, *Hammer and Hoe*, 178.

67. Dreiser to Crawford, April 6, 1932, Dreiser Papers.

68. Dreiser to Crawford, April 6, 1932, Dreiser Papers.

69. Crawford to Dreiser, April 15, 1932, Dreiser Papers.

70. Crawford to Dreiser, April 15, 1932, Dreiser Papers.

71. Crawford to Dreiser, April 15, 1932, Dreiser Papers. See also Crawford, "Fascist Efforts to Save Capitalism," May 17, 1933; "Dictatorship Ahead," December 20, 1930; "A Disquieting Victory?," November 16, 1934 (all in *Crawford's Weekly*).

72. "We Recognize the Reds," *Crawford's Weekly*, November 22, 1933; Dreiser to Crawford, January 15, 1935, Dreiser Papers.

CHAPTER 3

1. "Impelled by Necessity," July 26, 1933; "The Fascist Menace," February 21, 1934 (both in *Crawford's Weekly*).

2. Barkey, *Working Class Radicals*, xiv.

3. Crawford, "The Small Town and the Depression," *Common Sense*, December 1932; Bingham and Rodman, *Challenge to the New Deal*.

4. "Wanted: A Vision and a Plan," *Crawford's Weekly*, November 26, 1932.

5. "Fascism or Communist—Which?," *Crawford's Weekly*, November 21, 1931.

6. "The Roosevelt Plan," *Crawford's Weekly*, February 8, 1933.

7. "Roosevelt a Dictator?," *Crawford's Weekly*, February 22, 1933.

8. "Inauguration Note," *Crawford's Weekly*, March 1, 1933.

9. "Give NRA a Chance," August 23, 1933; "NRA for Whom?," September 6, 1933; "O Ye White-Eying Democrats!," September 20, 1933; "Relaxing the NRA?," May 16, 1934; "Does the NRA Mean Monopoly?," May 16, 1934 (all in *Crawford's Weekly*).

10. "Babson Predicts the Obvious," October 4, 1933; "Those Ten Percenters," October 11, 1933; "A Permanent NRA," November 8, 1933; "The Corporate State," December 6, 1933; "Whither NRA?," January 10, 1934 (all in *Crawford's Weekly*).

11. "A Civilian Army," *Crawford's Weekly*, April 19, 1933; Maher, *Nature's New Deal*, 107.

12. "The 'Buy American' Lunacy," *Crawford's Weekly*, January 7, 1933.
13. "The Recovery Bill," June 14, 1933; "Is History Repeating Itself?," June 21, 1933 (both in *Crawford's Weekly*).
14. "[Untitled]," *Crawford's Weekly*, January 31, 1934.
15. "New Relief Work for Votes?," April 25, 1934; "Whither Relief," March 2, 1934 (both in *Crawford's Weekly*).
16. "Demand Corrections," May 2, 1934; "Beware of Baruch," September 21, 1934; "AAA Helps Big Farmers First," September 28, 1934 (all in *Crawford's Weekly*). See also Ohl, *Hugh S. Johnson*, 225, 284.
17. "Shunting the Victims," *Crawford's Weekly*, January 21, 1935.
18. "That's What We've Been Saying," *Crawford's Weekly*, November 23, 1934.
19. "The Why," *Crawford's Weekly*, October 16, 1924.
20. "Poltroonery?," *Crawford's Weekly*, February 9, 1929.
21. "Don't Do It, Democrats," *Crawford's Weekly*, March 15, 1930.
22. "I am a 'Red,'" *Crawford's Weekly*, August 22, 1931.
23. "The Late John W. Flannagan," Congressional Record: Proceedings and Debates of the 84th Congress, First Session, vol. 101, part 4 (April 4, 1955, to May 4, 1955), 5247–48. "[Untitled]," *Smithfield Times*, September 25, 1930. The *Virginia Farm Bureau News* was a heavy supporter of Flannagan for his championing of farmer revenues during the Depression and World War II war effort. See issues dated October 15, 1942; May 1, 1945; November 1, 1945; June 1, 1949.
24. "Flannagan Hits GOP Failures," September 13, 1930; "Railroad Men Make Statement," October 25, 1930; "Reasons for Supporting," November 1, 1930; "Flannagan and Chase to Wage Hot Campaign," March 19, 1932; "How 'Foolish' Is Flannagan?," June 14, 1933; "Flannagan Horns Away Opposition," March 21, 1934; "Byrd and Flannagan," June 13, 1934; "Notes," June 27, 1934; "Coalition for Whom?," July 2, 1932 (all in *Crawford's Weekly*).
25. "Am I a Candidate?," May 3, 1934; "Crawford Announces for Congress," June 27, 1934 (both in *Crawford's Weekly*).
26. "Crawford Announces for Congress," *Crawford's Weekly*, June 27, 1934; Hunter, "Virginia and the New Deal," 117.
27. "Crawford Announces for Congress."
28. "Editors in the Ninth View Crawford's Race," *Crawford's Weekly*, July 13 1934; George Engeman, "Riding Roads through Old Virginia—III," *Baltimore Sun*, September 2, 1934.
29. "Gang Government," October 6, 1928; "Am I A Candidate?," May 3, 1934 (both in *Crawford's Weekly*).
30. Crawford to Dreiser, May 14, 1934, Dreiser Papers.
31. "Does Crawford Want to Be the Goat," *Clinch Valley News*, June 15, 1934.
32. A few years earlier, *Crawford's Weekly* lambasted Ruth Hanna McCormick's expenditure of $252,000 on the Illinois 1930 Senate Republican nomination only to lose in the General Election. That McCormick would have been the first female senator had she won was apparently lost on Crawford. See "A Sordid Commentary," May 3, 1930.
33. "The Fixers Are Frantic," June 27, 1934; "Editors in the Ninth View Crawford's Race," July 13, 1934 (both in *Crawford's Weekly*).
34. "How J. W. Flannagan's Own Coal Mine Treats Labor," *Crawford's Weekly*, August 24, 1934.
35. "Thousands Hear Labor Day Speaking in Norton," *Crawford's Weekly*, September 7, 1934.
36. "Thousands Hear Labor Day Speaking in Norton," *Crawford's Weekly*, September 7, 1934.
37. "Thousands Hear Labor Day Speaking in Norton," *Crawford's Weekly*, September 7, 1934.
38. "Miners Okay Crawford's Platform," *Crawford's Weekly*, September 14, 1934.
39. "Where the Apathy Is," *Crawford's Weekly*, October 26, 1934.
40. A few years earlier, Crawford questioned the New York Bar's inclusion of a question

asking about applicants' military service, including draft status. "Evidently pacifists are not desired as lawyers in New York," he wrote. "All the new lawyers must march in goose step with military medals on their chests carrying banners." *Crawford's Weekly 1934 Supplement*, November 2, 1934.

41. "Flannagan Is Easy Winner for Congress," *Crawford's Weekly*, November 9, 1934; *Crawford's Weekly 1934 Supplement*, November 2, 1934.

42. *Crawford's Weekly 1934 Supplement*, November 2, 1934.

43. Crawford to Dreiser, September 6, 1934; Dreiser to Crawford, September 24, 1934; Crawford to Dreiser, September 26, 1934; Crawford to Dreiser, January 21, 1935 (all in Dreiser Papers).

44. Dreiser to Crawford, January 15, 1935, Dreiser Papers.

45. "He Kept His Integrity," *Richmond Times-Dispatch*, November 13, 1934.

46. "They Win Either Way," *Crawford's Weekly*, November 9, 1934.

47. For more on such third-party arguments, see essays by John Dewey, J. B. S. Hardman, Wisconsin Progressive Party congressman Thomas R. Amlie, and Floyd B. Olson in Bingham and Rodman, *Challenge to the New Deal*. Crawford's "15 percent" statistic was likely accurate. Wise County, for instance, had 5,182 ballots cast. The county population was 51,167 in 1930 and 52,458 in 1940, so it stands to reason the population in 1934 was about the same. Based on 2018 Virginia voting data, approximately two-thirds of the population would be expected to be registered to vote, or about thirty-four thousand in 1934 Wise County. Based on this approximation, just 15 percent of individuals who would be expected to vote actually voted. Crawford to Dreiser, January 21, 1935, Dreiser Papers.

48. "The Future Weekly," *Crawford's Weekly*, November 28, 1931.

49. "Boarding among the scholars" was an educational practice in societies without formal schools. Teachers signed agreements with patrons whereby the individual would teach pupils for an agreed period of time in exchange for room and board. Sometimes financial compensation was also included in the agreement, but traditionally this was not the case. Generally, the lodging rotated between the patrons of the teacher in turn one week at a time, though occasionally a single patron housed the teacher at a reduced fee. This practice continued in America until the early twentieth century as a way for teachers in rural areas to make money during summer vacation. Addington, *Story of Wise County*, 165–66; Hamelle, *Standard History of White County, Indiana*, 121–22; Crawford to Dreiser, March 29, 1932, Dreiser Papers.

50. Crawford to Dreiser, September 5, 1932, Dreiser Papers.

51. Virginia Tech was then officially known as the Virginia Agricultural and Mechanical College and Polytechnic Institute but informally known as Virginia Polytechnic Institute.

52. Crawford to Dreiser, September 2, 1936; Crawford to Dreiser, November 21, 1932; Crawford to Dreiser, January 21, 1935; Crawford to Dreiser, August 7, 1933; Dreiser to Crawford, February 25, 1935, Dreiser Papers; "Bruce Crawford Talks," undated, Dreiser Papers; "Local Publications to Take Part in VIPA Meeting," *Rotunda* (Farmville, VA), October 24, 1934; "Students to Hear Two Noted Editors," *Washington Post*, October 25, 1934; "Bruce Crawford Talks on Small Town Life and the Country Editorship," Management Ernest Briggs, 1935, Dreiser Papers.

53. The choice of the phrase "native Americans" was likely an attempt to draw parallels between Kentucky miners and Native Americans, as Crawford knew full well that readers would note the genuine tragedy America's abuse of Natives.

54. Ferris, "Deepest Reality of Life," 11–12; Crawford, "Coal Miner," 361–73.

55. Gardner, *Reviewing the South*, 239–47.

56. *N. W. Ayer and Son's American Newspaper Annual and Directory* (1934); *N. W. Ayer and Son's American Newspaper Annual and Directory* (1931), 996; *N. W. Ayer & Son's American Newspaper Annual and Directory* (1930), 1020; *N. W. Ayer and Son's American Newspaper Annual*

and Directory (1928), 1108; *N. W. Ayer and Son's American Newspaper Annual and Directory* (1927), 1090.

57. John Dos Passos to Bruce Crawford, undated letter [ca. 1934–35], Crawford Papers, box 1.

58. "University to Preserve Crawford's Weekly Files," *Richmond Times-Dispatch*, March 19, 1935.

59. Crawford to Dreiser, January 21, 1935, Dreiser Papers; "Crawford Sells Virginia Paper," *Washington Post*, February 12, 1935.

60. *N. W. Ayer and Son's American Newspaper Annual and Directory* (1934); *N. W. Ayer and Son's American Newspaper Annual and Directory* (1937), 935.

61. "Bruce Crawford Says," undated [ca. 1935], Dreiser Papers.

62. Crawford to Dreiser, February 23, 1935, Dreiser Papers.

63. "Fascism Here Next," *Crawford's Weekly*, August 8, 1931. The AFL received plenty of scorn from Crawford: "The AFL seems pretty much like a lawyer who doesn't care whether he wins for his client or not," Crawford wrote after a series of failed strikes throughout the South, further arguing the organization had grown lazier with no plan while acting "as bad as the usual politicians" themselves. Crawford concluded with a swipe at Samuel Gompers, the AFL's founder, as "a Grand Old Man, good for nothing but to mislead his followers." "[Untitled]," October 18, 1930; "Fascist Efforts to Save Capitalism," May 17, 1933; "How Roosevelt Goes Radical," August 2, 1933; "Armed Revolutions," September 20, 1930 (all in *Crawford's Weekly*).

64. Crawford, "Why I Quit Liberalism," *New Masses*, April 16, 1935.

65. For more on Graves, see Feldman, *Politics, Society, and the Klan in Alabama*.

66. Other members of the group included writer Jack Conroy, writer Emmett Gowen, leftist fundraiser Shirley Hopkins, and National Committee for the Defense of Political Prisoners lawyer Alfred Hirsch. Leidholdt, "Never Thot This Could Happen," 224; Prichard, "In West Virginia I Had More Freedom," 35; Crawford, "Bullets Fell on Alabama," *Nation*, September 18, 1935, 319–20; Wixson, *Worker-Writer in America*, 410–11; "No Further Proof Needed," *Richmond Times-Dispatch*, September 15, 1935; "4 Writers Defy Threats to Probe Ga. Insurrection Law," *Afro-American*, August 3, 1935; Kelley, *Hammer and Hoe*, 128–29, 273.

67. Dreiser to Crawford, August 28, 1936; Crawford to Dreiser, September 2, 1936; Crawford to Dreiser, April 29, 1938; Crawford to Dreiser, September 28, 1938, Dreiser Papers; *Sunset News and Times Leader*, April 29, 1936.

68. "[Untitled]," *Bluefield Daily Telegraph*, June 14, 1936.

69. Crawford, "Ere the Sun Sets," *Bluefield Sunset News*, June 13, 1936; Charles R. Armentrout, "Bruce Crawford Takes New Post," *Bluefield Sunset News*, October 31, 1938.

70. Crawford to Dreiser, April 29, 1938; Crawford to Dreiser, September 28, 1938, Dreiser Papers.

71. Crawford to Dreiser, November 10, 1938, Dreiser Papers; Crawford, "Ere the Sun Sets."

72. Armentrout, "Bruce Crawford Takes New Post."

73. Crawford to Dreiser, November 10, 1938, Dreiser Papers.

CHAPTER 4

1. Crawford to Holt, February 9, 1940, WVWP Papers, box 104.

2. Becker, "Everyman His Own Historian."

3. See also Conard, *Benjamin Shambaugh*; and Bohan, *Go to the Sources*.

4. Kammen, "What Is the Good of History?," 86; Becker, "Everyman His Own Historian," 234–35, 248.

5. Crawford to Alsberg, October 20, 1938; Crawford to Alsberg, October 31, 1938, WPA Records.

6. Crawford, "A Guide to West Virginia," *West Virginia Review*, October 1939, 10.

7. McConkey to Alsberg, March 15, 1936; McConkey to Alsberg, March 1, 1936; McConkey to Alsberg, December 29, 1936, WPA Records, box 6.

8. The Dies Committee's infamous legacy was further cemented after Pearl Harbor with the production of the "Yellow Report," a justification for interning Japanese Americans based in exaggerations and fabrications. After the war, the Dies Committee explicitly chose not to investigate the Ku Klux Klan by arguing the Klan was an "old" group in America and thus not dangerous to the nation. Myer, *Uprooted Americans*, 19.

9. Mangione, *Dream and the Deal*, 315–22.

10. Mangione, *Dream and the Deal*, 323–26; DeMasi, *Henry Alsberg*, 214–16; Hirsch, *Portrait of America*, 215–16; Griswold, *American Guides*, 127.

11. Mangione, *Dream and the Deal*, 329–30; Griswold, *American Guides*, 127.

12. Crawford, "The Right to Read," *Bookplate*, December 1939, 3–4, Crawford Papers.

13. Alsberg to Puckett, October 6, 1938; Crawford to Alsberg, October 31, 1938; Stewart to Crawford, November 19, 1938; Stewart to Crawford, December 2, 1938; Stewart to Crawford, December 9, 1938; Crawford to Wilkinson, December 10, 1938; Miller to Woodward, December 10, 1938; Crawford to Wilkinson, December 20, 1938; Alsberg to Crawford, December 23, 1938; Crawford to Alsberg, December 27, 1938; Alsberg to Crawford, December 30, 1938, WPA Records, Box 48.

14. Thomas, *Appalachian New Deal*, 138–41.

15. The state-federal dispute revolved around licensing of the overall Hawk's Nest project. Union Carbide affiliates filed project intentions in 1927 but did not secure a federal license as was mandated, according to the U.S. government's argument, by the Federal Water Power Act. The U.S. government sued to stay the project, but the case was ultimately dismissed on jurisdictional grounds. More lawsuits would be filed in subsequent decades with the federal government finally mandating licensing in 1964. Williams, *West Virginia*, 161; United States v. West Virginia, 295 U.S. 463 (1935); Catherine Venable Moore, "Introduction," in Rukeyser, *Book of the Dead*, 6–9; Shriver, "Opinion No. 442."

16. Patterson, *New Deal and the States*, 196.

17. Thomas, *Appalachian New Deal*, 224–31; Homer A. Holt, "A Message to the Miners of West Virginia," December 15, 1939, in Hughes, *State Papers*, 403–4; Hughes, *State Papers*, 449.

18. Hughes, *State Papers*, 430–31, 435.

19. Hughes, *State Papers*, 441.

20. Holt, "A Message to the Miners of West Virginia," in Hughes, *State Papers*; "Holt's Stand on Labor," *Sunday Gazette Mail* (Charleston, WV), February 14, 1960; "Governor Homer A. Holt Hits Back at CIO Leaders," *Cumberland News*, December 18, 1939.

21. "The Bonus March: Herbert Hoover's View," *American History* 39, no. 2 (June 2004): 36–37.

22. Holt, "Labor Must Choose," in Hughes, *State Papers*.

23. Harris, *State Papers*, 15; Myers, "Coal Mechanization," 58.

24. Alderson to Rush D. Holt, December 13, 1935, Rush D. Holt Papers, box 178; "Governor Says Some Who Speak for Labor Want Laws Applied to Everyone Except Themselves," *Raleigh Register* (Beckley, WV), August 8, 1939; Elizabeth Gurley Flynn, "The Miners Knew What They Wanted," *New Masses* May 23, 1939, 5–6.

25. "Kump-Holt Political Combine Accused," *Mannington Times*, December 1, 1939.

26. Crawford drew a salary of $266.66 per month. "WPA Payrolls: Kanawha County," Rush D. Holt Papers, box 236; "Bluefield Editor to Head WPA Project," *Washington Post*, November 11, 1938.

27. Fitzpatrick, *History's Memory*; Hofstadter, *Progressive Historians*.

28. Crawford, "Office Letter: Assignments," November 18, 1939, WVWP Papers.

29. Edward Smith, in Conley, *West Virginia Encyclopedia*, 405–6.

30. Marshall Buckalew, "Phil Conley," *e-WV: The West Virginia Encyclopedia*, October 5, 2012;

Conley, "Life in a West Virginia Coal Field"; Hennen, *Americanization of West Virginia*, 123–26.

31. Callahan, *Semi-Centennial History of West Virginia*, 247–48. Other works that contain little to no mention of labor history include Lewis, *History and Government of West Virginia*; Hale, *Trans-Allegheny Pioneers*; and Lambert, *Pioneer Leaders of Western Virginia*.
32. Ambler and Summers, *West Virginia, the Mountain State*.
33. Ambler, *History of West Virginia*, vii–viii.
34. Ambler, *History of West Virginia*, vii.
35. Ambler and Summers, *West Virginia, the Mountain State*, 495.
36. West Virginia Writers' Project, *Smoke Hole and Its People*, 25–27.
37. Crawford to the *Nation*, WVWP Records, box 104; Crawford to *New Republic*, December 5, 1938, WVWP Records, box 104; Crawford to McConkey, November 9, 1938, WVWP Records, box 104.
38. Crawford to Trent, October 17, 1939, WVWP Records, box 104; Crawford to Newsom, December 29, 1939, Homer Holt Papers, box 1.
39. Crawford to Jack Dempsey, November 26, 1938, WVWP Records, box 104.
40. Crawford to Stender, November 26, 1938, WVWP Records, box 104; Johnson to Crawford, December 2, 1938, WVWP Records, box 104.
41. Crawford, "A Guide to West Virginia," *West Virginia Review* (October 1939): 11.
42. Crawford to Alsberg, March 10, 1939, WVWP Records, box 104.
43. Holt to Alderson, October 12, 1939, Hughes, *State Papers*, 623–24; Alsberg to Guinzberg, August 28, 1937; Alsberg to Guinzberg, March 23, 1939; Alsberg to Guinzberg, February 16, 1939; Guinzberg to Alsberg, February 14, 1939, WPA Records.
44. Holt to Alderson, October 12, 1939, in Hughes, *State Papers*, 625; Alsberg to Crawford, July 19, 1939, WPA Records.
45. Vaudrin to Crawford, September 13, 1939, WVWP, box 104.
46. Crawford to Trent, October 17, 1939, WVWP, box 104.
47. Hughes, *State Papers*, 591–604.
48. Cynthia Earman, "An Uncommon Scold," *Library of Congress Information Bulletin* (January 2000), https://www.loc.gov/loc/lcib/0001/royall.html.
49. Crawford to Trent, October 10, 1939, WVWP, box 104.
50. Crawford to Trent, October 17, 1939, WVWP, box 104.
51. Holt to Alderson, October 12, 1939, in Hughes, *State Papers*, 626.
52. Holt to F. C. Harrington, September 21, 1939, in Hughes, *State Papers*, 615.
53. Thomas, *Appalachian New Deal*, 96; Calvert Estill, *Welch News*, August 28, 1939, Holt Papers, box 1.
54. Holt to Alderson, October 12, 1939, in Hughes, *State Papers*, 626.
55. Holt to F. C. Harrington, September 21, 1939, in Hughes, *State Papers*, 615.
56. Holt to Franklin Roosevelt, September 21, 1939, in Hughes, *State Papers*, 616–17.
57. Shawhan to Holt, September 21, 1939, Holt Papers, box 1.
58. Harrington to Holt, September 28, 1939, Holt Papers, box 1; Holt to Harrington, October 3, 1939, Holt Papers, box 1.
59. Holt to Edwin Watson, October 4, 1939, in Hughes, *State Papers*.
60. Alderson to Holt, October 7, 1939, in Hughes, *State Papers*; Crawford to Alderson, October 11, 1939, WVWP Papers, box 105.
61. Trent to Holt, October 13, 1939, WVWP, box 104.
62. "Harlan: A Study in Futility?," *Crawford's Weekly*, May 16, 1931, copy in Dreiser Papers.
63. Crawford to Trent, September 10, 1939, Holt Papers, box 1.
64. West Virginia Writers' Project, *West Virginia*, 86.
65. Crawford to Dreiser, October 26, 1939, Dreiser Papers.
66. Holt to Watson, October 12, 1939, in Hughes, *State Papers*, 628.
67. Crawford, "A Guide to West Virginia," *West Virginia Review* (October 1939): 10.

68. Franklin Roosevelt to Holt, October 18, 1939, in Hughes, *State Papers*, 630; Holt to Newsom, October 26, 1939, in Hughes, *State Papers*, 631; Holt to Newsom, November 17, 1939, Holt Papers, box 1; Watson to Holt, November 20, 1939, Holt Papers, box 1; Crawford to Alderson, October 26, 1939, Dreiser Papers.

69. Drew Pearson and Robert S. Allen, "Watching Waiting," *Washington Merry-Go-Round*, November 17, 1939; Alderson to Holt, December 14, 1939, Holt Papers, box 1; Holt to Alderson, December 15, 1939, Holt Papers, box 1; "The Nearly Perfect State," *New Republic*, November 29, 1939.

70. "Mine Disaster Entombs Nearly 100 Miners," *Mannington Times*, January 12, 1940; "Where 91 Miners Were Killed," *Mannington Times*, January 19, 1940; Dolores Riggs David, "A Time to Weep—Bartley 1940," *Logan, WV History and Nostalgia* (blog), accessed June 10, 2019, https://loganwv.us/a-time-to-weep/.

71. Crawford to Holt, February 9, 1940, WVWP Records, box 104.

72. Holt to Crawford, February 10, 1940, WVWP Records, box 104.

73. Holt to Newsom, March 1, 1940, Holt Papers, box 1.

74. Crawford to Newsom, October 10, 1941; "[Untitled]," *Fairmont Times*, October 7, 1941; unknown newspaper clipping, October 6, 1941, WVWP Records.

75. Crawford to Holt, February 15, 1940; Newsom to Holt, February 29, 1940; Kerr to Holt, February 19, 1940; Holt to Newsom, February 22, 1930 (all in Holt Papers, box 1). See also "Industries" draft essay, pp. 15–18, WVWP, box 104.

76. "Holt May Run for Governor," *Evening Star*, January 21, 1940; "West Virginia Peace," *Wilmington Morning Star*, February 27, 1940; "Two New Senators to be Sent Here by West Virginia, *Evening Star*, November 6, 1940.

77. Newsom to Alderson, October 10, 1940, WPA Records; Crawford to Dreiser, February 9, 1940; Crawford to Dreiser, July 14, 1940, Dreiser Papers; Rice and Brown, *West Virginia*, 271.

78. Crawford to Kerr, July 22, 1940, WPA Records; Crawford to Oxford, April 30, 1940, WVWP Papers, box 104.

79. Newsom to Alderson, July 16, 1940, WPA Records.

80. Holt to Cook, June 29, 1940, Homer Holt Papers, box 1.

81. Holt to Shawhan, December 9, 1940, Homer Holt Papers, box 1.

82. Becker and Harmon to Kerr, April 11, 1941, WVWP Records, box 105; Newsom to Alderson, April 10, 1941, WVWP Records, box 105; Crawford to Harmon, April 23, 1941, WVWP Papers, box 105; "Final Manuscript," WVWP Records, box 105.

83. Newsom to Crawford, April 19, 1941, WPA Records.

84. Crawford to Dreiser, May 12, 1941, Dreiser Papers.

85. Rice and Brown, *West Virginia*, 270; Homer A. Holt, "A Message to the Miners of West Virginia," December 15, 1939, in Hughes, *State Papers*, 403–4; "Governor Homer A. Holt Hits Back at C.I.O. Leaders," *Cumberland News*, December 18, 1939.

86. Bold, *WPA Guides*, xiii.

87. Clipping from *New Republic* 101 (November 29, 1939), 153, Homer Holt Papers, box 1.

88. Crawford, "A Guide to West Virginia," *West Virginia Review* (October 1939): 10.

89. Eller, "Toward a New History of the Appalachian South," 75–78.

90. Williams, *West Virginia*, 163.

91. Thomas, *Appalachian New Deal*, 108.

92. Keith Dix was kind enough to share with me his collection of Peoples' Appalachia publications, most of which concerned anti-strip-mining activism and were printed 1968–1973. Fred Mooney, *Struggle in the Coal Fields*; Summers and Cornetti, *Documentary History of West Virginia*, 522–44; Coles, *Children of Crisis*; Hume, *Death and the Mines*; Nugent, *Death at Buffalo Creek*; Lawrence, *On Dark and Bloody Ground*; Crowell, *Appalachian People's History Book*.

93. Thomas, "Nearly Perfect State" and Prichard, "In West Virginia I Had More Freedom,"

34–37. Crawford referred to the author of the labor chapter as "Mr. Morse" less than a month after his hiring and revised "Morse's" work significantly in the following years. Crawford to McConkey, November 10, 1938, WPA Records; and Crawford to Paul Becker, April 11, 1941, WVWP Papers, box 105.

94. Howard, "Edith Lett Papers," 122–23.

CHAPTER 5

1. "Eliminate the Extremes," *Crawford's Weekly*, November 5, 1932.
2. Crawford to Dreiser, September 5, 1932, Dreiser Papers.
3. "Huey the Demagogue," *Crawford's Weekly*, April 12, 1934.
4. "Concessions to Critics," *Crawford's Weekly*, October 12, 1934.
5. Tucker, "Harry Caudill and the Problem of the Past," 114, 126.
6. Crawford to Dreiser, May 21, 1941, Dreiser Papers.
7. Dreiser to Crawford, January 11, 1939; Crawford to Dreiser, February 14, 1939, Dreiser Papers.
8. Crawford to Dreiser, July 1, 1942, Dreiser Papers.
9. Watkins, *West Virginia Blue Book* (1941), 65; Watkins, *West Virginia Blue Book* (1942), 46.
10. "West Virginia's Publicity Director Known as Liberal," *Afro-American*, April 4, 1942.
11. "[Untitled]," *Charleston Gazette*, September 18, 1942.
12. "Mountains of West Virginia Attractive to Visitors," *Washington Post*, June 13, 1943; "Know Your West Virginia," *American Motorist*, 15, no. 6 (June 1942).
13. "Sing of West Virginia!," undated (ca. 1942), Vertical Files, West Virginia Archives & History.
14. "Scrapbook of Helen Keller and the Blind, Book XIV," Helen Keller Archive, American Foundation for the Blind; "[Untitled]," *Charleston Gazette*, May 17, 1942.
15. Crawford to Dreiser, July 1, 1942, Dreiser Papers.
16. Watkins, *West Virginia Blue Book* (1941), 65; William C. Blizzard Photography Collection, accessed June 5, 2023, https://mozart.radford.edu/archives/findingaids/BlizzardPhotographyCollection.html.
17. Watkins, *West Virginia Blue Book* (1941, 1942, 1943); "[Untitled]," *Beckley Post-Herald*, April 17, 1942.
18. "[Untitled]," *Charleston Daily-Mail*, December 23, 1946; Watkins, *WV Blue Book* (1943), 64; Watkins, *WV Blue Book* (1944), 43; Myers, *WV Blue Book* (1945), 66; Myers, *WV Blue Book* (1946), 46.
19. Crawford to Dreiser, August 28, 1945, Dreiser Papers.
20. Dreiser to Crawford, January 11, 1939, Dreiser Papers; Crawford to Dreiser, February 14 1939, Dreiser Papers.
21. Ball, *Melungeons*, 65; "[Untitled]," *Charleston Daily-Mail*, November 16, 1943; "[Untitled]," *Charleston Daily-Mail*, December 23, 1946.
22. "[Untitled]," *Charleston Daily-Mail*, November 16, 1943; "[Untitled]," *Charleston Daily-Mail*, December 23, 1946.
23. Crawford to Helen Dreiser, February 6, 1946, Dreiser Papers; Crawford to Helen Dreiser, February 28, 1948, Dreiser Papers.
24. Few documents from the West Virginia Advertising Company appear in any documents left behind by Crawford. To my knowledge, no archival repository holds any other documents related to the company not presented in this book.
25. "Candidate Gets Liberal as Aide," *Chicago Defender*, March 10, 1956; McCormick, *This Nest of Vipers*, 164.
26. "No Charges Filed," *Morgantown Dominion News*, March 20, 1958; "Should Voters Permit a Ruthless Push to Power?," *Beckley Post-Herald*, October 10, 1958; Victoria Myers, "The Unusual Senate Race of 1958 in West Virginia," Robert C. Byrd Center blog, July 2020,

https://www.byrdcenter.org/draft-blog/the-unusual-senate-race-of-1958-in-west
-virginia.
27. Randolph Collection, box 137 and 367.
28. Randolph Collection, box 137 and 367.
29. Randolph Collection, box 137 and 367; "Ex Governor of West Virginia Pleads Guilty to
    Bribing Foreman of His Jury," *New York Times*, March 30, 1971.
30. Crawford to Dreiser, September 2, 1936, Dreiser Papers; Crawford to Dreiser, September
    28, 1938, Dreiser Papers.
31. Crawford, "A King-Size TVA," *Appalachian South* 1, no. 2 (1965): 40.
32. Crawford, "Effects of Stripmining on Floods Needs Study," *Roanoke Times*, April 7, 1963;
    Crawford, "Economy, Environment Get Attention," *Roanoke Times*, November 27, 1970.
33. Crawford, "Black Lung Battle Planned," *Roanoke Times*, November 16, 1968.
34. Crawford, "Protein from Black Diamonds," *Roanoke Times*, reprinted in *Appalachian South*
    (Spring/Summer 1966): 55; Crawford, "Coal Seen as Food Source in Future," *Charleston
    Gazette*, June 8, 1963, 11; Silverman, Gordon, and Wender, "Food from Coal-Derived
    Materials."
35. Crawford, "Don't Hate Your Job, Do it Better," *American Mercury* (January 1959), 40–42.
36. Maddox had recently become a folk hero to racists and segregationists for closing his
    restaurant rather than desegregate and lying about an interaction with three African
    American Georgia Tech students wherein he claimed to have chased off a mob of twelve
    Black men with nothing by a bare pickaxe handle. Crawford, "Racial Homogenization:
    One Man's View," *Roanoke Times*, October 20, 1966.
37. Crawford, "Va., W.Va. Set Example in Tolerance," *Roanoke Times*, June 30, 1967; Newbeck,
    Virginia Hasn't Always Been for Lovers, 193; Justin McCarthy, "U.S. Approval of Interracial
    Marriage at New High of 94%," *Gallup News*, September 2021, https://news.gallup.com
    /poll/354638/approval-interracial-marriage-new-high.aspx.
38. Newbeck, *Virginia Hasn't Always Been for Lovers*, 215.
39. Crawford, "Virginia 'Granny' Doctor and Hillsman Patients," *Roanoke Times*, May 16,
    1970.
40. Bruce and Kate wrote Dreiser's widow, Helen, regularly to maintain a friendly connec-
    tion. Crawford to Helen Dreiser, February 6, 1946, Dreiser Papers; Crawford to Helen
    Dreiser, February 28, 1948, Dreiser Papers.
41. Le Blanc, *Marx, Lenin*, 91; Eastman, *Reflections on the Failure of Socialism*; Diggins, "Vi-
    sions of Order," in *Up From Communism*," 233–68.
42. Carr, *Dos Passos*; Koch, *Breaking Point*.
43. Irmscher, *Max Eastman*.
44. O'Neill, *Last Romantic*.
45. Diggins, *Up from Communism*; Oppenheimer, *Exit Right*.
46. "William Holmes McGuffey and His Readers," *Museum Gazette*, Jefferson National Ex-
    pansion Memorial, National Park Service, undated.
47. Wiley, "Education of a Backwoods Hoosier"; "Memorial Is Planned for Reader's Author,"
    Manchester Evening Herald, March 25, 1941.
48. McHenry, "Silent, No More."
49. Crawford, "Virginia 'Granny' Doctor' and Hillsman Patients," *Roanoke Times*, May 16,
    1970; "Charlie Bowers, a Modern Pioneer," *Roanoke Times*, February 23, 1970; "Wise
    County Revisited," *Roanoke Times*, September 30, 1970; "Better Shape Up Fast, World,"
    Roanoke Times, December 30, 1967; "Has Appalachia Been Forgotten All Over Again?,"
    Roanoke Times, February 7, 1968; "Black Lung Battle Planned," *Roanoke Times*, November
    16, 1968.
50. Crawford to Dreiser, January 23, 1935, Dreiser Papers.
51. Prichard, "In West Virginia I Had More Freedom."

52. Crawford to "Earl," October 5, 1972, Crawford Papers (ASU).

53. "Bruce Crawford Says," undated [ca. 1935], Dreiser Papers.

54. Mike Still, "Students Take Part in Study of 20th Century Lynchings in Wise," *Times-News*, August 5, 2019; Mike Still, "Norton Council Passes Gun Rights Sanctuary Resolution," *Times-News*, December 3, 2019; City of Norton, "City Council Meeting Packet," December 3, 2019, https://www.nortonva.gov/ArchiveCenter/ViewFile/Item/2706.

55. "Newspaper Offices to Relocate," *Coalfield Progress*, November 22, 2019; "Newspapers Will See Leadership Changes," *Coalfield Progress*, November 26, 2019; "Southwest Virginia Coalfield Papers Sold," *Rural Blog*, September 12, 2019, http://irjci.blogspot.com/2019 /09/southwest-virginia-weeklies-sold-to.html.

BIBLIOGRAPHY

BRUCE CRAWFORD'S WRITINGS

NEWSPAPERS
Bluefield Sunset News (Bluefield, WV, 1935–1939)
Crawford's Weekly (Norton, VA, 1920–1935)
Daily Progress (Norton, 1912–1920)
Norton Reporter (Norton, 1915–1917)
Norton Reporter and Miners' Enterprise (Norton, 1917–1920)
Virginia Digest (Norton, 1926–1927)

PUBLISHED WORKS
Nuggets (Norton, VA: n. p., 1924)

WORKS PRODUCED BY THE WEST VIRGINIA WRITERS' PROJECT
Bulltown Country (1940)
Burnsville-on-the-Kanawha (1941)
Flatwoods-Heaters Communities (1942)
Gilmer: The Birth of a County (1940)
Hampshire County Census (1938)
Historic Romney (1938)
Mountain State Tintypes (1940)
My Memory Book (1940)
Oceana and the Cook Family (1940)
Of Stars and Bars (1940)
Plant Life in Braxton County (1940)
Smoke Hole and Its People (1940)
Sutton-on-the-Elk (1941)
West Virginia: A Guide to the Mountain State (1941)

SERIALS PUBLISHING CRAWFORD'S ARTICLES
American Mercury
Appalachian South
Bookplate

Commonwealth
Kiwanis Magazine
Labor Ace
Literary Digest
Nation
New Masses
New Republic
New York Times Magazine
Outlook and Independent
Plain Talk
Real America
Scribner's Magazine
South Atlantic Quarterly
Southern Literary Messenger
Spectator
Virginia Quarterly Weekly
West Virginia History
Writer

ARCHIVAL COLLECTIONS

Appalachian State University, Special Collections, W. L. Eury Appalachian Collection
Bruce Crawford Papers, 1971
Library of Virginia
National Archives and Records Administration, College Park, MD
Works Projects Administration (WPA) Records, RG 69
    Records of the Federal Writers' Project (FWP)
The Newberry, Chicago, IL
Sherwood Anderson Papers
Pine Mountain Settlement School Archive, Harlan, KY (pinemountainsettlement.net)
Mary Rockwell Hook Correspondence
Radford University, McConnell Library, Appalachian Collection, Radford, VA
William C. Blizzard Photography Collection
University of Pennsylvania, University Archives and Records Center, Philadelphia, PA
Theodore Dreiser Papers
University of Virginia, Charlottesville, VA
Papers of the Institute of Public Affairs, 1927–1953
Papers of the Virginia Quarterly Review, 1925–1954
Virginius Dabney Papers, 1944–1971
University of Virginia at Wise, Wise, VA
Bruce Crawford Collection
West Virginia State Archives, Charleston, WV
Jennings Randolph Collection
State Documents
Vertical Files
West Virginia and Regional History Center, West Virginia University, Morgantown, WV
Herman G. Kump Papers
Homer A. Holt Papers
Newspaper Collection
Roy Bird Cook Papers
Rush D. Holt Papers
West Virginia University, WPA Writers Project, Records
Works Progress Administration, West Virginia Publications

Writers' Program in West Virginia Records
Writers' Program in West Virginia, Records Regarding Mineral and Hampshire Counties and
    Other Material

NEWSPAPERS

Afro-American (Baltimore, MD)
Appalachian Independent (Appalachia, VA)
Chicago Defender
Clinch Valley News (Tazewell, VA)
Coalfield Progress
Collegian (Richmond, VA)
Cumberland News
Mannington Times
New Journal and Guide (Norfolk, VA)
New York Amsterdam News
New York Times
Pittsburgh Courier
Richmond News Leader
Richmond Times-Dispatch
Roanoke Times
Sunday Gazette Mail (Charleston, WV)
Washington Post

OTHER PUBLISHED SOURCES

Addington, Luther Foster. *The Story of Wise County*. Johnson City, TN: Overmountain Press,
    1988 [1956].
Akin, William. *Technocracy and the American Dream*. Berkeley: University of California Press,
    1977.
Allen, James S. *Organizing in the Depression South*. Minneapolis: MEP Publications, 2001.
Ambler, Charles H. *A History of West Virginia*. New York: Prentice Hall, 1933.
Ambler, Charles H., and Festus P. Summers. *West Virginia, the Mountain State*. New York:
    Prentice Hall, 1958 [1940].
Baldwin, Sidney. *Poverty and Politics: The Rise and Decline of the Farm Security Administration*.
    Chapel Hill: University of North Carolina Press, 1968.
Ball, Bonnie S. *Melungeons*. Johnson City, TN: Overmountain Press, 1992.
———. "Mountain Scribes," in *Historical Sketches of Southwest Virginia*, 14–19. Historical
    Society of Southwest Virginia, 1981.
Barkey, Frederick A. *Working Class Radicals*. Morgantown: West Virginia University Press,
    2012.
Bassett, John Earl. *Sherwood Anderson*. Selinsgrove, PA: Susquehanna University Press, 2006.
Becker, Carl. "Everyman His Own Historian." *American Historical Review* 37, no. 2 (1931):
    221–36.
Beers, Paul. "The Wythe County Lynching of Raymond Bird: Progressivism vs. Mob Violence
    in the '20s." *Appalachian Journal* 22 no. 1 (1994): 34–59.
Beverly, Frank Monroe. *Echoes from the Cumberlands*. Strasburg, VA: Shenandoah Publishing
    House, 1928.
Bingham, Alfred, and Selden Rodman, eds. *Challenge to the New Deal*. New York: Falcon Press,
    1934.
Bodnar, John. *Remaking America: Public Memory, Commemoration, and Patriotism in the
    Twentieth Century*. Princeton, NJ: Princeton University Press, 1992.
Bohan, Chara Haeussler. *Go to the Sources: Lucy Maynard Salmon and the Teaching of History*.
    New York: Peter Lang, 2004.

Bold, Christine. *The WPA Guides: Mapping America*. Jackson: University Press of Mississippi, 1999.

Buckley, Geoffrey L. *Extracting Appalachia*. Athens: Ohio University Press, 2004.

Bush, Carletta. "Faith, Power, and Conflict: Miner Preachers and the United Mine Workers of America in the Harlan County Mine Wars, 1931–1939." MA thesis, West Virginia University, 2006.

Callahan, James. *Semi-Centennial History of West Virginia*. Charleston, WV: Semi-Centennial Commission of West Virginia, 1913.

Carr, Virginia Spencer. *Dos Passos: A Life*. Garden City, NY: Doubleday, 1984.

Catte, Elizabeth. *What You Are Getting Wrong about Appalachia*. Cleveland, OH: Belt, 2018.

Caudill, Harry. *Night Comes to the Cumberlands*. Boston: Little, Brown, 1963.

Cohen, Leonard. *Of Human Bondage*. Directed by John Cromwell. Los Angeles, CA: RKO Studios, 1934.

Coles, Robert. *Children of Crisis: Selections from the Pulitzer Prize-Winning Five-Volume Children of Crisis Series*. Boston: Little, Brown, 2003 [1967–1977].

Conard, Rebecca. *Benjamin Shambaugh and the Intellectual Foundations of Public History*. Iowa City: University of Iowa Press, 2013.

Conley, Phillip Mallory. "Life in a West Virginia Coal Field." Charleston, WV: American Constitutional Association, 1923.

———, ed. *West Virginia Encyclopedia*. Charleston: West Virginia Publishing, 1929.

Copple, Barbara. *Harlan County USA*. DVD. Harlan, KY: Cabin Creek, 1976.

Crowell, Suzanne. *The Appalachian People's History Book*. Louisville, KY: Mountain Education Associates, 1970.

DeMasi, Susan Rubenstein. *Henry Alsberg: The Driving Force of the New Deal Federal Writers' Project*. Jefferson, NC: McFarland, 2016.

Diggins, John Patrick. *Up from Communism: Conservative Odysseys in American Intellectual History*. New York: Columbia University Press, 1975.

Duke, David C. *Writers and Miners*. Lexington: University Press of Kentucky, 2009.

Eastman, Max. *Reflections on the Failure of Socialism*. New York: Devin-Adair, 1955.

Eller, Ronald D. *Miners, Millhands, and Mountaineers*. Knoxville: University of Tennessee Press, 1982.

———. "Toward a New History of the Appalachian South." *Appalachian Journal* 5, no. 1 (Autumn 1977): 74–81.

Feldman, Glenn. *Politics, Society, and the Klan in Alabama*. Tuscaloosa: University of Alabama Press, 1999.

Ferris, Marcie Cohen. "'The Deepest Reality of Life': Southern Sociology, the WPA, and Food in the New South." *Southern Cultures* 18, no. 2 (Summer 2012): 6–31.

Firstenberger, William A. *In Rare Form: A Pictorial History of Baseball Evangelist Billy Sunday*. Iowa City: University of Iowa Press, 2005.

Fitzpatrick, Ellen. *History's Memory: Writing America's Past, 1880–1980*. Cambridge, MA: Harvard University Press, 2004.

Fry, Joseph A. "Rayon, Riot, and Repression: The Covington Sit-Down Strike of 1937." *Virginia Magazine of History and Biography* 84, no. 1 (January 1976): 3–18.

Gardner, Sarah. *Reviewing the South: The Literary Marketplace and the Southern Renaissance, 1920–1941*. New York: Cambridge University Press, 2017.

Gentzkow, Matthew, Edward L. Glaeser, and Claudia Goldin. "The Rise of the Fourth Estate." National Bureau of Economic Research, Working Paper no. 10791 (September 2004).

Gilmore, Glenda Elizabeth. *Defying Dixie: The Radical Roots of Civil Rights, 1919–1950*. New York: W. W. Norton, 2008.

Griswold, Wendy. *American Guides: The Federal Writers' Project and the Casting of American Culture*. Chicago: University of Chicago Press, 2016.

Hale, John Peter. *Trans-Allegheny Pioneers*. Charleston, WV: Kanawha Valley Publishing, 1931.

Hamelle, W. H. *A Standard History of White County, Indiana*. Chicago: Lewis, 1915.

Harlan Miners Speak: Report on Terrorism in the Kentucky Coal Fields. Prepared by Members of the National Committee for the Defense of Political Prisoners; Theodore Dreiser, Lester Cohen, Melvin P. Levy, et al. Lexington: University Press of Kentucky, 2015.

Harris, James W., Jr., comp. *State Papers and Public Addresses: H. G. Kump, Nineteenth Governor of West Virginia, March 4, 1933–January 18, 1937*. Charleston, WV: n. p., 1937.

Hennen, John. *The Americanization of West Virginia*. Lexington: University Press of Kentucky, 1996.

Herndon, Angelo. *Let Me Live*. New York: Random House, 1937.

Hevener, John W. *Which Side Are You On?: The Harlan County Coal Miners, 1931–39*. Chicago: University of Illinois Press, 2002 [1978].

Hirsch, Jerrold. *Portrait of America: A Cultural History of the Federal Writers' Project*. Chapel Hill: University of North Carolina Press, 2003.

Hofstadter, Richard. *Anti-Intellectualism in American Life*. New York: Vintage, 1966.

———. *The Progressive Historians*. New York: Alfred A. Knopf, 1968.

Howard, Josh. "The Edith Lett Papers: The Federal Writers' Project, West Virginia, and the Everyman Writer." *West Virginia History: A Journal of Regional Studies* 10, no. 2 (2016): 111–32.

Howard, Walter T. *Forgotten Radicals: Communists in the Pennsylvania Anthracite, 1919–1950*. Lanham, MD: University Press of America, 2005.

Hughes, William E., comp. *State Papers and Public Addresses of Homer A. Holt*. Charleston, WV: n. p., 1942.

Hume, Brit. *Death and the Mines: Rebellion and Murder in the United Mine Workers*. New York: Grossman, 1971.

Hunter, Robert F. "Virginia and the New Deal." In *The New Deal: Vol. 2*, edited by John Braeman, Robert H. Bremner, and David Brody. Columbus: Ohio State University Press, 1975.

Imscher, Christoph. *Max Eastman: A Life*. New Haven, CT: Yale University Press, 1917.

Isenberg, Nancy. *White Trash: The 400-Year Untold History of Class in America*. New York: Viking, 2016.

Kammen, Michael, ed. *"What Is the Good of History?": Selected Letters of Carl L. Becker, 1900–1945*. Ithaca, NY: Cornell University Press, 1973.

Kelley, Robin D. G. *Hammer and Hoe*. Chapel Hill: University of North Carolina Press, 1990.

Koch, Stephen. *The Breaking Point: Hemingway, Dos Passos, and the Murder of José Robles*. New York: Counterpoint, 2006.

Lambert, Oscar D. *Pioneer Leaders of Western Virginia*. Parkersburg, WV: School Printing, 1935.

Lawrence, Anne. *On Dark and Bloody Ground: An Oral History of the UMWA in Central Appalachia, 1920–1935*. National Endowment for the Humanities Youthgrant Report. Charleston, WV: Miner's Voice, 1973.

Le Blanc, Paul. *Marx, Lenin and the Revolutionary Experience: Studies of Communism and Radicalism in the Age of Globalization*. New York: Routledge, 2006.

Lee, Janet. *Comrades and Partners: The Shared Lives of Grace Hutchins and Anna Rochester*. New York: Rowman and Littlefield, 2000.

Leep, Mark. "The First Seeds of Virginia's Sterilization Act of 1924: Joseph T. Mastin and the State Board of Charities and Corrections." *Methodist History* 57, no. 3 (2019): 143–52.

Legnini, Jessica. "Radicals, Reunion, and Repatriation: Harlan County and the Constraints of History." *Register of the Kentucky Historical Society* 107, no. 4 (2009): 471–512.

Leidholdt, Alexander S. *Editor for Justice: The Life of Louis I. Jaffe*. Baton Rouge: Louisiana State University Press, 2002.

———. "'Never Thot This Could Happen in the South!': The Anti-Lynching Advocacy of Appalachian Newspaper Editor Bruce Crawford." *Appalachian Journal* 38, no. 2–3 (Winter–Spring 2011): 198–232.

Levy, Melvin. *The Last Pioneers*. New York: Alfred H. King, 1934.

———. *Wedding*. New York: The Unicorn Press, 1927.

Lewis, Virgil. *History and Government of West Virginia*. Chicago: Werner School Book, 1896.

Lingeman, Richard. *Theodore Dreiser: An American Journey, 1908–1945*. New York: G. P. Putnam's Sons, 1990.

Maher, Neil. *Nature's New Deal: The Civilian Conservation Corps and the Roots of the American Environmental Movement*. Oxford: Oxford University Press.

Mangione, Jerre. *The Dream and the Deal*. Syracuse, NY: Syracuse University Press, 1996 [1972].

Mapping American Social Movements Project. Civil Rights and Labor History Consortium, University of Washington. https://depts.washington.edu/moves/index.shtml.

Marow, Leo. "George Bellows and Religious Art." In *George Bellows Revisited*, edited by M. Wolf. Newcastle upon Tyne, UK: Cambridge Scholars Publishing, 2016.

Martin-Purdue, Nancy. "Talk about Trouble: The Virginia Writers' Project, 1938–1941." *Virginia Cavalcade* 46, no. 5 (1997): 226–39.

McCormick, Charles Howard. *This Nest of Vipers*. Urbana: University of Illinois Press, 1989.

McHenry, Justin J. "Silent, No More: The 1974 Kanawha County Textbook Controversy and the Rise of Conservatism in America." MA thesis, West Virginia University, 2006.

McLoughlin, William G. *Billy Sunday Was His Real Name*. Chicago: University of Chicago Press, 1955.

Miller, Jacklyn J. S. "Cultivating Capital." PhD diss., University of Kansas, 2016.

Miller, James A. *Remembering Scottsboro*. Princeton, NJ: Princeton University Press, 2009.

Mooney, Fred. *Struggle in the Coal Fields*. Morgantown: West Virginia University Library, 1967.

Moore, John Hammond. "The Angelo Herndon Case, 1932–1937." *Phylon* 32, no. 1 (1971): 60–71.

Moore, Leonard. *Citizen Klansman*. Chapel Hill: University of North Carolina Press, 1997.

Myer, Dillon S. *Uprooted Americans*. Tucson: University of Arizona Press, 1971.

Myers, J. Howard., ed. *West Virginia Blue Book*. Charleston: West Virginia Senate Clerk's Office, 1945–1946.

Myers, Mark. "Coal Mechanization and Migration from McDowell County, West Virginia, 1932–1970." MA thesis, East Tennessee State University, 2001.

Newbeck, Phyl. *Virginia Hasn't Always Been for Lovers*. Carbondale: Southern Illinois University Press, 2004.

Nugent, Tom. *Death at Buffalo Creek*. New York: W. W. Norton, 1973.

N. W. Ayer and Son's American Newspaper Annual and Directory, 1915–1940.

Ohl, John Kennedy. *Hugh S. Johnson and the New Deal*. DeKalb: Northern Illinois University Press, 1985.

O'Neill, William L. *The Last Romantic: A Life of Max Eastman*. New York: Oxford University Press, 1978.

Oppenheimer, Daniel. *Exit Right: The People Who Left the Left and Reshaped the American Century*. New York: Simon and Schuster, 2016.

Patterson, James T. *New Deal and the States: Federalism in Transition*. Princeton, NJ: Princeton University Press, 1969.

Pizer, Donald, ed. *Theodore Dreiser Recalled*. Clemson, SC: Clemson University Press, 2018.

Plein, Stewart. "Portraits of Appalachia: The Identification of Stereotype in Publishers'

Bookbindings, 1850–1915." *Journal of Appalachian Studies*15, nos. 1–2 (Fall 2009): 99–115.

Portelli, Alessandro. *They Say in Harlan County*. New York: Oxford University Press, 2011.

Prichard, Arthur C. "'In West Virginia I Had More Freedom': Bruce Crawford's Story." *Goldenseal* 10, no. 1 (Spring 1984): 34–37.

Rice, Otis K, and Stephen Wayne Brown. *West Virginia: A History*. Lexington: University Press of Kentucky, 1985.

Ritterhouse, Jennifer. *Discovering the South: One Man's Travels through a Changing America in the 1930s*. Chapel Hill: University of North Carolina Press, 2017.

Rochester, Anna. *Labor and Coal*. New York: International Publishers, 1931.

Rosen, Corey, and Staughton Lynd. "How Bad a Deal Is Weirton Steel?" *Labor Research Review* 1, no. 7 (1985): 108–14.

Rottenberg, Dan. *In the Kingdom of Coal*. New York: Routledge, 2003.

Rukeyser, Muriel. *The Book of the Dead*. Morgantown: West Virginia University Press, 2018.

Rusch, Frederic E., and Donald Pizer, eds. *Theodore Dreiser: Interviews*. Urbana: University of Illinois Press, 2004.

Schaikewitz, Steve, and Gregory Lisby. "Harry F. Byrd and Louis I. Jaffe, Allies in a Just Cause: Virginia's Anti-Lynch Law of 1928." *Virginia Social Science Journal* 43 (Spring 2008): 21–37.

Shapiro, Henry. *Appalachia on Our Mind*. Chapel Hill: University of North Carolina Press, 1978.

Shepherd, Samuel C., Jr. *Avenues of Faith: Shaping the Urban Religious Culture of Richmond, Virginia, 1900–1929*. Tuscaloosa: University of Alabama Press, 2001.

Sherman, Mandel, and Thomas Robert Henry. *Hollow Folk*. New York: Thomas Y. Crowell, 1933.

Shifflett, Crandall A. *Coal Towns*. Knoxville: University of Tennessee Press, 1991.

Shriver, Harry. "Opinion No. 442: Union Carbide Corporation, Project No. 1856." *Federal Power Commission Reports*, vol. 32 (July 1, 1964–December 31, 1964): 770–803.

Silverman, Melvin P., Joan N. Gordon, and Irving Wender. "Food from Coal-Derived Materials by Microbial Synthesis." *Nature* 211 (1966): 735–36.

Sirgiovanni, George. *An Undercurrent of Suspicion: Anti-Communism in America during World War II*. New Brunswick, NJ: Transaction Publishers, 1990.

Smith, J. Douglas. *Managing White Supremacy*. Chapel Hill: University of North Carolina Press, 2002.

Smith, Robert Sidney. *Mill on the Dan: A History of Dan River Mills, 1882–1950*. Durham, NC: Duke University Press, 1960.

Spindler Scott, Elizabeth. "An Experiment in Southern Letters." MA thesis, University of Richmond, 1984.

Stanton, Mary. *Red, Black, White*. Athens: University of Georgia Press, 2019.

State Papers and Public Addresses of Matthew M. Neely. Charleston, WV: n. p., 1948.

Stoll, Steven. *Ramp Hollow: The Ordeal of Appalachia*. New York: Hill and Wang, 2017.

Summers, Festus, and Elizabeth Cornetti, eds. *Documentary History of West Virginia*. Morgantown: West Virginia University Library, 1966.

Thomas, Jerry Bruce. *An Appalachian New Deal: West Virginia in the Great Depression*. Lexington: University Press of Kentucky, 1998.

———. "'The Nearly Perfect State': Governor Homer Adams Holt, the WPA Writers' Project, and the Making of West Virginia: A Guide to the Mountain State." *West Virginia History* 52 (1993): 91–108.

Titler, George Joy. *Hell in Harlan*. Beckley, WV: BJW Printers, 1972.

Tucker, Bruce. "Harry Caudill and the Problem of the Past." *Journal of Appalachian Studies* 9, no. 1 (2003): 114–46.

Uhlmann, Jennifer Ruthanne. "The Communist Civil Rights Movement: Legal Activism in the United States, 1919–1946." PhD diss., UCLA.

Walker, Adelaide. "Pioneer's Return." *American Mercury* 47, no. 186 (June 1939): 142–47.

Walker, Charles R. *Bread and Fire*. Boston: Houghton Mifflin, 1927.

———. *Our Gods Are Not Born*. Freeport, NY: Books for Libraries Press, 1970.

Walker, Charles R., and Adelaide Walker. *Modern Technology and Civilization: An Introduction to Human Problems in the Machine Age*. New York: McGraw, 1962.

———. *Technology, Industry, and Man*. New York: McGraw-Hill, 1968.

Watkins, A. Hale, ed. *West Virginia Blue Book*. Charleston: West Virginia Senate Clerk's Office, 1941–1942.

Watkins, Fred B., ed. *West Virginia Blue Book*. Charleston: West Virginia Senate Clerk's Office, 1943–1944.

Weller, Jack. *Yesterday's People*. Lexington: University Press of Kentucky, 1963.

Wiley, Harvey. "The Education of a Backwoods Hoosier." *Indiana Magazine of History* 24, no. 2 (June 1928): 78–95.

Whisnant, David. *All That Is Native and Fine*. Chapel Hill: University of North Carolina Press, 2009.

Williams, John Alexander. *West Virginia*. New York: W. W. Norton, 1984 [1976].

Wixson, Douglas. *Worker-Writer in America*. Urbana: University of Illinois Press, 1994.

INDEX

Printed in the USA
CPSIA information can be obtained
at www.ICGtesting.com
LVHW011555230824
789095LV00004B/351